ROYAL HISTORICAL SOCIETY
STUDIES IN HISTORY
SERIES

No. 43

BRITAIN AND PALESTINE DURING THE SECOND WORLD WAR

BRITAIN AND PALESTINE DURING THE SECOND WORLD WAR

Ronald W. Zweig

Published by
The Boydell Press
for The Royal Historical Society
1986

First published 1986

Published by
The Boydell Press
an imprint of Boydell & Brewer Ltd
PO Box 9 Woodbridge Suffolk IP12 3DF
and 51 Washington Street Dover New Hampshire 03820 USA
for
The Royal Historical Society
University College London WC1

The Society records its gratitude to the following whose generosity made possible the initiation of this series: The British Academy; The Pilgrim Trust; The Twenty-Seven Foundation; The United States Embassy Bicentennial Funds; The Wolfson Trust; several private donors.

ISBN 0 86193 200 5

Printed in Great Britain by Short Run Press Ltd, Exeter

TO MY PARENTS

Recent volumes published in this series include

CONTENTS

ABBREVIATIONS

A.A.	Australian Archives
A.H.C.	Arab Higher Committee
C.-in-C.	Commander in Chief
C.C.S.	Contraband Control Service
C.I.D.	Criminal Investigation Department
C.O.	Colonial Office
C.Z.A.	Central Zionist Archives
F.O.	Foreign Office
G.O.C.	General Office Commanding
H.Cr.	High Commissioner
I.S.A.	Israel State Archives
J.A.	Jewish Agency
J.D.C.	American Jewish Joint Distribution Committee
M.E.I.C.	Middle East Intelligence Centre
O.A.G.	Officer Administering Government
P.I.C.M.E.	Political Intelligence Centre, Middle East
P.R.O.	Public Record Office
S.I.M.E.	Security Intelligence
S.O.E.	Special Operations Executive
W.O.	War Office

PREFACE

The research on which this book is based began as an investigation into one aspect of British diplomatic history during wartime, with the inevitable focus on the workings of the Foreign Office, the Cabinet and those other corridors of power in Whitehall where 'high policy' was made. Initially I had scant regard for the workings of the Colonial Office and the evolving trends of colonial policy in general. Palestine was separated from the mainstream of British imperial experience by the complex and ambiguous relationship between Britain, the Zionist movement and the Jewish world. Nevertheless, it quickly became apparent that in order to understand the course of Britain's Palestine policy after the adoption of the White Paper of May 1939 it would be necessary to consider not only the changing interplay of strategic, diplomatic and political interests which determine policy at the Cabinet level but also to look at the practical problems of a colonial administration charged with implementing that policy 'on the ground'. The policy towards Palestine which had been adopted in May 1939 after much deliberation and controversy was in the long run only one of the determinants of Britain's subsequent actions there. In the evolving crisis of war and genocide the Colonial Office and the Mandatory Government of Palestine could only react to events on a day to day basis. Policy guide-lines conceived in London were implemented only when possible, and with varying degrees of enthusiasm. By the end of the Second World War the circumstances in which the policy of 1939 had been conceived had so radically changed that London was eventually forced to abandon any hope of orderly decolonisation in Palestine. As so often in the history of the empire, events at the periphery could not be controlled by policy-makers in London, and my research became as much a venture in colonial as in diplomatic history.

I acquired many debts of gratitude during the preparation of this book. Professor F.H. Hinsley supervised the doctoral research on which the book is based, and I am particularly grateful for both his scholarly guidance and his many personal kindnesses. My indebtedness to the late Professor J. Gallagher in Cambridge, as well as to Professor Y. Bauer in Jerusalem and Professor G. Cohen in Tel Aviv is apparent in the text. I learnt much from each of them. I am indebted to Martin Gilbert and Professor M.J. Cohen who read the manuscript at an early stage and offered much practical advice, and also to Dr. Dalia Ofer, with whom I have been able to exchange ideas. Sir John Martin, Sir Keith Hancock, Mr. Joseph Linton and Professor A. Hourani generously shared their recollections of the period and of the personalities mentioned in the book.

For their assistance I am indebted to the staffs of the various libraries and archives in which I worked: the Public Record Office; Cambridge University Library; Rhodes House, Oxford; the Bodleian Library, Oxford; the Israel State Archives, Jerusalem; the Central Zionist Archives, Jerusalem; the Middle East Centre, St. Anthony's College, Oxford; the Foreign Office Library, London; the Jewish National and Hebrew University Library, Jerusalem; the Australian Archives, Canberra; Churchill College, Cambridge; and the library of the Oxford Centre for Postgraduate Hebrew Studies. The Rt. Hon. Julian Amery, M.P. generously allowed me to read the papers of Leo Amery; the Earl of Halifax similarly allowed me access to the papers of his father, the 1st Earl of Halifax.

St. John's College, Cambridge provided both financial support and the physical setting necessary to complete my research. An appointment as Junior Fellow in Modern History at the Oxford Centre for Postgraduate Hebrew Studies afforded me the opportunity of using the Centre's valuable research resources as well as enjoying its physical facilities while I wrote the book. I am grateful to the Director and Trustees of the Centre for their encouragement and support.

Crown-copyright records in the Public Record Office appear by permission of the Controller of H.M. Stationery Office. The editors of *HaZionut* kindly granted permission to reprint material first published in that journal. Mrs. C. Linehan bravely accepted the task of seeing the manuscript through the press.

Ronald W. Zweig
July, 1984

INTRODUCTION

It had become apparent during the Arab revolt in Palestine of 1936-9 that Britain's dual task of encouraging the growth of the Jewish National Home there while at the same time protecting the rights of Palestine's Arab inhabitants, as set out in the League of Nations Mandate, could no longer be implemented. The British Mandatory authorities had lost effective control of ninety per cent of the country and it had taken 16,000 troops and the imposition of martial law to reestablish any kind of law and order. In February 1939 the British Government convened a conference in London in an attempt to negotiate a settlement of the Palestine problem. Representatives of the Zionists, the Palestinian Arabs and the independent Arab states (Egypt, Iraq and Saudi Arabia) met separately with His Majesty's Government to discuss a series of proposals which, it was hoped, would satisfy Arab demands while at the same time offering some degree of protection for Jewish rights in Palestine. Perhaps inevitably, the conference failed — the Jewish delegates walked out, the Palestinian Arab delegation rejected the British proposals, and the Arab states, both at the conference and at subsequent secret negotiations, refused to endorse them. Consequently the British Government announced that it considered itself free to present its own recommendations, which were set out in a White Paper two months after the conference broke up.

The White Paper on Palestine of 17 May 1939 (Cmd. 6019) was one of many attempts to resolve the Arab-Jewish conflict in Palestine that followed the Balfour Declaration of 1917. Unlike previous attempts, however, it marked a major turning point in British Middle East policy. By declaring that the Jewish National Home had already been established in Palestine and that therefore the promises of the Balfour Declaration had been fulfilled, the British Government was able to pursue a policy which separated the Jewish problem from the problem of Palestine. By focusing on this latter problem alone, Britain adopted in the White Paper a policy which favoured the interests of the Arab majority of the population rather than those of the Jewish minority, in the hope of ending the Arab revolt in Palestine and ensuring the support of the Arab states should Italy side with Germany in a war that would challenge Britain's interests in the Middle East.

In the White Paper, the British Government attempted to meet as far as possible the three major demands of the Arabs: on Jewish immigration into Palestine, on the constitutional future of the

Mandate and on the sale of land to Jews.

The White Paper empowered the High Commissioner in Palestine, Sir Harold MacMichael, to limit the sale of land to Jews. The regulations aimed to solve the problem of a growing class of landless peasants and to provide for the rural settlement of future generations of the Arab population. Of all the provisions of the White Paper, the land regulations were the most clearly defined, the most liberally administered and were in any case so widely circumvented that after the initial controversy which followed the promulgation of the necessary legislation in February 1940, they were no longer the subject of much debate.[1]

Conversely, the White Paper provisions on the restriction of Jewish immigration into Palestine and the constitutional development of the Mandate were the subject of great controversy and raised major problems of implementation.

In 1920, when British control over Palestine was confirmed at the San Remo Conference, there were approximately 85,000 Jews in Palestine, twelve per cent out of a total population of 700,000. Between 1920 and 1934 the net Jewish immigration was 165,000. But in 1935, following Hitler's rise to power and the deteriorating position of European Jewry, Jewish immigration was almost 62,000 in one year alone, and the Arab population — which was itself growing rapidly — now represented only seventy per cent of the total population (from ninety per cent at the time of the Balfour Declaration). This sudden upsurge in Jewish immigration was one of the major causes of the Arab Revolt which commenced in 1936. The White Paper limited Jewish immigration to a total of 75,000 spread over five years, which would have brought the Jewish population from thirty per cent to one third of the total population. All Jewish immigration was then to be banned except in the unlikely event of the Arabs allowing it to continue.

Both the immigration provisions of the White Paper and those concerning constitutional development frustrated Zionist aspirations

---

[1] The introduction of the regulations restricting land sales coincided with a severe shortage of funds available to Jewish institutions in Palestine, a factor which facilitated the administration of the regulations. In the first twelve months following their introduction the sale of land by Arabs to Jews dropped to 22 per cent of the annual average for the period 1921-35 i.e. when normal conditions prevailed in the countryside prior to the outbreak of the Arab revolt. (MacMichael to Moyne, Despatch, 28 March 1941, CO 733/435/75072/9 (1941)).

for an eventual Jewish majority in Palestine, and the White Paper was rejected by the Zionists. This in itself would have ensured a major political struggle between Britain and the Zionist movement. However, Britain's insistence on implementing the immigration restrictions of the White Paper even after it had effectively abandoned the constitutional provisions of its new policy, and the rigidity with which these restrictions were enforced despite the deteriorating circumstances of European Jewry during the War, did more than anything else to radicalise the Jews in Palestine and elsewhere, uniting them behind the Zionist movement in support of the demand for a Jewish state.

In the constitutional provisions of the new policy, the British Government advocated the creation of an independent bi-national Palestinian state with a large Arab majority, which was to be brought into being in three stages over a ten year period. As soon as 'peace and order' were restored in Palestine, the Mandatory Authorities were to prepare the local population for eventual self-government by placing Palestinians — Arab and Jewish — in charge of departments of the administration. At the end of five years a constitutional conference would be held to consider the nature of the Palestinian state that was to emerge, and to decide on the steps then necessary to establish it and terminate the Mandate. After a further five years and if Britain considered circumstances permitted, an independent Palestinian state would be declared.

The right of the Jews to participate in the final constitutional conference was guaranteed by paragraph 10(6) of the White Paper, and this paragraph was, to the British, a central feature of the new Palestine policy. The authors of the White Paper assumed that the Jewish community in Palestine (the Yishuv) would be able to obtain the constitutional protection of its minority rights in the new Palestinian state in return for its agreement to the creation of a state with a large Arab majority. The Yishuv, Whitehall postulated, might even obtain Arab agreement to continuing limited Jewish immigration after the first five years had passed.

However, any attempt to ensure that the Jewish population of Palestine would have a role (and, it was feared, a power of veto) in the steps leading up to independence was fundamentally unacceptable to the major Palestinian Arab political parties (represented on the Arab Higher Committee), and ensured their rejection of the White Paper.[2]

[2] Cf. para. 2 of Palestine Arab Higher Committee's Statement in Answer to the White Paper, 30 May 1939 (CO 733/408//75872/30 Part 1); submission of Jamal Husseini to the Permanent Mandates Commission (P.M.C.), 12 June 1939 (CO 733/410// 75872/91); and protocol of meeting with Arab Delegates, 6 March 1939, FO 371/23227 E1746.

However, as Britain's central objective was to obtain the support of the Arab states for its new policy, and as they were prepared to accept paragraph 10(6), Britain dismissed the objections of the Palestinians and paragraph 10(6) was retained in the White Paper.

The final important constitutional provision was set out in paragraph 10(8): 'His Majesty's Government will do everything in their power to create conditions which will enable the independent Palestine State ' to come into being within ten years'. The original British proposal qualified this by adding that 'should circumstances require the postponement of the establishment of an independent State' then the British Government, acting alone, had the right to decide on such a postponement. The Arab states, in diplomatic exchanges which followed the failure of the St. James Conference, insisted that they should be a party to any postponement. However, Britain considered that its independence of action in such a decision was vital and resolved to commit itself only to consult the Arab states in the event of any delay in the creation of an independent Palestine.

That a difference of opinion existed between London and the Arab states became apparent only during the negotiations after the Conference. But the Secretary of State for the Colonies, Malcolm MacDonald, convinced the Cabinet Committee on Palestine (which supervised the negotiations) that '. . . if we took a firm line and insisted on the maintenance of the formula as agreed in London, we should carry our point'.[3] Consequently it was decided to retain the original formulation and publish the White Paper in the hope that the Arab states would at least give their tacit support to the new policy once it was released.[4]

All matters relating to Palestine were the subject of controversy in England, and the release of the White Paper, which was intended to be the Chamberlain Government's last word on Palestine policy, did nothing to end the debate. When it was placed before the House of Commons, the Government's overall majority of 248 was reduced to eighty-nine. Two Cabinet ministers (Hore Belisha and Walter Elliot) and 110 backbenchers abstained, and more than twenty Tories defied a three line whip to vote against it (including Churchill, Amery, Bracken, Cazalet, Richard Law, Locker Lampson and Harold Macmillan). Churchill led the attack on the White Paper, which he

[3]P(38), 10th Meeting, FO 371/23234 E2995.

[4]Oliphant to Lampson, 4 May 1939, FO 371/23234 E3241. Also minutes and memorandum, 19-20 April 1939, FO 371/23233 E2930. For a detailed account of the St. James Conference and the subsequent negotiations, cf. M.J. Cohen, 'Appeasement in the Middle East: the British White Paper on Palestine, May 1939', *The Historical Journal,* Vol. 16(3):571-96(1973).

described as 'another Munich' and a 'surrender to Arab violence'.[5] Both Labour and Liberal parties declared that they would not consider themselves bound by the policy in any future government that they might form.

In the League of Nations the White Paper was given an even more hostile reception. As Palestine was a Mandate of the League, all major policy developments had to be confirmed by the League Council, acting on the recommendation of its Permanent Mandates Commission. The Commission met in Geneva in June 1939 and by a vote of four to three rejected the White Paper as inconsistent with the terms of the Mandate.[6] The Council was to have met in September, and planned to consider the White Paper itself, but with the outbreak of war it never reconvened, and, as the Colonial Office recorded with some relief, the opinion of the Permanent Mandates Commission remained 'academic' and of no practical importance.[7]

Neither the condemnation of the White Paper by the Permanent Mandates Commission, the hostility accorded to it in the House of Commons, nor its rejection by both Arabs and Jews, deterred those departments in Whitehall responsible for Palestine affairs. Arguing that any policy which had been rejected by all sides to a dispute was equally fair to all, the Colonial Office summed up its view: 'The objections of the extremist Arabs and of the Jews to the White Paper policy are so fundamental that in neither case will [these] objections be dispelled by tinkering with that document. We must now go straight ahead with a firm front and let both sides know we have said our last word.'[8] At the root of this resolve was a large area of agreement on Palestine policy between the Eastern Department of the Foreign Office and the Middle East Department of the Colonial Office. Both agreed that the Mandate was no longer workable, that some radical new initiative was necessary, and that given the strategic importance of the Moslem world to Britain in a period of increasing international tension the only initiative possible was one which made concessions to the Arabs at the expense of the Zionists.

---

[5] House of Commons Debates, 5s/346/Cols 2168-75, 23 May 1939.

[6] Observations of 22nd and 23rd meeting of Permanent Mandates Commission, 21 and 22 June 1939, on FO 371/23248 E5267.

[7] Thomas minute, 2 September 1939, CO 733/414//75962/5 (1939). The relief was no doubt partly due to the fact that the Foreign Office considered the Jewish Agency's memorandum to the P.M.C. against the White Paper 'extremely difficult to answer' (Baggallay minute, 16 June 1939, FO 371/23250 E4090).

[8] Downie minute, 11 July 1939, CO 733/408//75873/18 (1939).

1

IMPLEMENTING THE CONSTITUTIONAL PROVISIONS

Once the British Government had resolved to release the White Paper, despite its failure to win support for the new policy from any of the parties to the dispute, the Colonial Office was faced with the task of setting out in detail the steps to be taken to implement it. Of the constitutional provisions of the new policy only paragraph 10(4), the Heads of Departments scheme, required early action and it was here that the Middle East Department of the Colonial Office focused its attention.

The Heads of Department scheme was an administrative solution to the problem of power-sharing in a colonial political system which lacked even the most elementary form of representative legislature of the sort that was already common in most of Britain's other colonies. There were sixteen departments of the Palestine Government to be taken into account, together with the positions of Chief Justice and Attorney-General. It was immediately decided that some posts were too sensitive to be handed over to local politicians (Attorney-General, Chief Justice, and Heads of the Police and Prisons, and Migration and Statistics Departments.) Other departments were too unimportant or too technical (Antiquities, Audit, etc.), leaving eleven departments for which local Heads could be appointed. The Colonial Office suggested that of the eleven departments, those concerned with the social services should be dealt with first. As appointments needed to be made in proportion to the size of the respective communities, it was suggested that a start be made by appointing one Moslem, one Christian Arab and one Jew to the Departments of Health, Education and Welfare.

The most sensitive question to be resolved was that of the responsibilities of those appointed, and their authority vis à vis the British officials who would work under them. This question had only been considered very briefly in the course of negotiations over the White Paper, and in the subsequent Colonial Office deliberations it was decided that the matter should be left to the discretion of the High Commissioner. Similarly it was resolved that the High Commissioner should make the appointments, subject only to approval by the Secretary of State, although a provision was included for consultation with the Jewish Agency and representative Arab politicians.[1]

[1]Downie minute, 9 May 1939, CO 733/410//75872/85(39).

The Colonial Office's decisions were put to the High Commissioner in a lengthy despatch on 13 May 1939. Despite its length the despatch was not an effective guide to the problems that the scheme would inevitably face. A large part of the Colonial Office's deliberations had been devoted to the question of whether or not the Palestinian Heads of Department should be required to take an oath of allegiance, while the more substantial issues were left for the High Commissioner himself to decide.[2] In a separate letter to MacMichael, MacDonald explained that the Heads of Department were to be accorded a status somewhere between that of salaried government officials and 'ministers in embryo'. As usual MacMichael was charged with resolving any difficulties that this might cause.[3]

MacMichael had been critical of the Heads of Department scheme throughout the negotiations which had preceded the White Paper, calling it 'unreal and illusionary'.[4] Arguing that his first concern was the practicality of the new policy and not whether the Arab states would endorse it, he felt that no transfer of power, however limited, should be attempted until some degree of communal reconciliation between Jews and Arabs in Palestine had been achieved, and until moderate forces opposed to the Mufti and his policy of violence had emerged in local Palestinian Arab politics. Formally at least MacMichael had to concede to superior authority, and he privately assured the Colonial Secretary that despite his reservations he would endeavour to make the Heads of Department scheme work.[5] Nevertheless, in his reply to the Colonial Office's despatch, he stated:

> It is impossible for me at this stage to nominate individuals owing to the fact that the Jews are adopting a line of complete non-acceptance of the basic principles of His Majesty's Government's Statement of Policy and representative Arabs are, with the exception of the Defence (Nashahibi) Party, almost a minus quality. So soon as the position is rectified in either respect I propose to submit names for your consideration.[6]

It had been made clear in the White Paper, at Arab insistence, that the non-cooperation of the Jewish community in Palestine would not be

---

[2] Secretary of State to HCr, Despatch, 13 May 1939, *ibid.*

[3] MacDonald to MacMichael, Private and Personal, 15 May 1939, *ibid.*

[4] HCr to CO No. 275, 8 March 1939, FO 371/23228 E1823.

[5] MacMichael to MacDonald, Private and Personal, 22 May 1939, CO 733/410// 75872/85(39).

[6] HCr to Secretary of State, Despatch, 16 June 1939, *ibid.*

allowed to delay the implementation of paragraph 10(4). However, as the lack of Arab candidates whom the High Commissioner considered suitable for the new positions was not likely to be remedied in the immediate future, MacMichael himself was effectively delaying the implementation of paragraph 10(4) indefinitely.

Despite the haste with which the Middle East Department had compiled its first despatch outlining the steps to be taken towards implementing 10(4), MacMichael's unenthusiastic reply deflated the Colonial Office's sense of urgency. The relevant file accumulated minutes in a leisurely fashion, reaching the Secretary of State over five weeks after the High Commissioner's reply had been received, and MacDonald himself put it aside for another fortnight. When he finally did comment, he made it clear that he shared the High Commissioner's reservations and recognised the difficulties which MacMichael had set out. As MacDonald minuted: 'What is wanted in Palestine almost more than anything else is a really good moderate Arab leader, who will rival the Mufti in ability and influence.' The Secretary of State's reservations further discouraged departmental interest in the Heads of Department scheme, and when MacMichael came to London in August 1939 the Colonial Office found that 'no opportunity occurred of discussing this matter with the High Commissioner'.[8] The outbreak of war in September provided a more substantial excuse for further delay, and during October MacMichael was officially informed that the Colonial Office was doubtful whether there was anything to be gained from pursuing the matter at that time.[9]

Earlier, in June 1939 MacMichael had raised a problem which had not yet been seriously considered in London: which of the parties within the Arab community of Palestine could provide effective leadership in the orderly progress towards independence? The only Arab party which had accepted the White Paper policy was the Defence Party.[10] But, as MacMichael pointed out, that party was 'in the throes of an internal crisis and viewed askance by the generality of Arabs. Its leader is a "past number", its erstwhile Secretary, Fakhri Nashashibi, has gone too far in the fields of politics and morality alike even for the strongest stomachs. . . . .'[11] The only Palestinian

[7]MacDonald minute, 18 August 1939, *ibid*.

[8]Luke minute, 29 August 1939, *ibid*.

[9]Shuckburgh to MacMichael, semi-official letter, 9 October 1939, *ibid*.

[10]HCr to CO No. 641, 30 May 1939, CO 733/406//75872/12(39).

[11]HCr to Secretary of State, Despatch, 31 December 1939, CO 733/410// 75872/85(39).

Arab politicians who commanded popular support were the Mufti (Haj Amin al-Husayni) and those associated with him in the Arab Higher Committee. They, however, were exiled from Palestine, were hostile to the Mandate and had rejected the White Paper.

The question of policy towards the Mufti and the other exiled politicians associated with the Arab revolt was the subject of much debate in London, a debate which reflected the conflicting objectives of the White Paper policy itself. In so far as the White Paper was an attempt not only to restore law and order but also to find a just solution of the Palestine problem, and the constitutional provisions a real path toward independence, then the Government of Palestine considered that its task was to encourage the emergence of moderate Arab politicians and to isolate the Mufti. British military authorities in Palestine, who were responsible for restoring law and order, strongly supported this attitude. As Military Intelligence explained in its estimate of the likely impact of the White Paper:

> If the Government stands firm to its announced policy, refuses concessions, and withholds any amnesty except to those who are prepared to accept its proposals completely, it is likely that in a short time the Arab Higher Committee will break up and that the more moderate members will seek a separate peace. . . . If the Government remains firm to its policy it is probable that the local population will swing more or less rapidly to the side of law and order.[12]

This was in fact the strategy consistently pursued by the High Commissioner and supported by the Colonial Office. However, the White Paper was also a gesture towards the Arab states, designed to win their support in the forthcoming international crisis, and the Foreign Office wanted to meet as many of the demands of those states as possible, including the granting of an amnesty and some form of settlement with the Arab Higher Committee.

The question of the Mufti's personal future had been considered during the formulation of the new policy. The High Commissioner and the General Officer Commanding in Palestine (Lt.-General R.H. Haining) wanted him permanently banned from Palestine,[13] but the Foreign Office considered that a permanent ban was both unrealistic and provocative.[14] The Colonial Office had originally supported a

[12]Intelligence Report, G.S.I., Palestine Forces H.Q., 15 May 1939, FO 371/23237 E4103.

[13]Cf. minutes, FO 371/23234 E3269.

[14]Baxter minute, 19 April 1939, FO 371/23233 E2930.

temporary ban which would have allowed the Mufti's return once he had come to terms with the more moderate factions in Palestinian Arab politics.[15] However MacMichael argued that the slightest possibility of the Mufti's return would intimidate Arab politicians and prevent the emergence of a moderate leadership. The debate continued during May with the British ambassadors in Cairo and Baghdad supporting the Foreign Office in deprecating any long term ban, while the High Commissioner and the G.O.C. insisted on permanent exile. In the end MacMichael succeeded in imposing his views and the Foreign Office agreed to a compromise formula whereby the Mufti was excluded indefinitely at the same time as the White Paper was released.[16]

Two weeks after the release of the new policy the first signs of a split in the Arab Higher Committee appeared. Lampson, the British ambassador in Cairo, informed the Foreign Office that he had been approached (via the Iraqi chargé d'affaires in Cairo) by Yacoub al-Ghusayn,[17] a member of the Committee, with an offer to try and persuade the Mufti to accept the White Paper. Should the Mufti refuse to do so, al-Ghusayn said that together with other members of the Committee he intended to break with the Mufti. In order to do so al-Ghusayn asked for 'something in the nature of an apparent concession to show the Arabs' in the form of 'certain interpretations' of the constitutional provisions of the White Paper. Al-Ghusayn presented Lampson with a detailed list of the desired 'interpretations', most of which concerned the allocation of posts under the Heads of Department scheme to people approved by the Arab Higher Committee.[18]

Al-Ghusayn was not considered to be an important enough politician to merit attention, but in mid-June Awni 'Abd al-Hadi[19] and Ahmed Hilmi Pasha,[20] more senior members of the Arab Higher

[15]Cf. MacDonald's comments to Cabinet Committee on Palestine, P(38)10 Cab 27/652.

[16]Minutes, FO 371/23234 E3270.

[17]Al-Ghusayn, a teacher from Ramle, formed the Arab Youth Congress during the 1930s. Although it was represented on the A.H.C. this party was not a significant force in Palestinian Arab politics (A. Abu-Ghazaleh, *Arab Cultural Nationalism in Palestine* (Beirut, 1973), p. 44).

[18]Lampson to FO No. 164(Saving), 3 June 1939, FO 371/23237 E4077.

[19]A founder of the Palestine Istiqlal (Independence) Party, Awni 'Abd al-Hadi was exiled from Palestine during the Arab revolt. He was a member of the Palestinian Arab delegation to the St. James Conference and was considered by H.M.G. as 'one of the best educated Palestinian Arabs and one of the most able Arab leaders'. (Personalities Report prepared by the Foreign Office of participants in the St. James Conference, FO 371/23227 E1758).

[20]Member of the Istiqlal Party and the A.H.C. Deported to the Seychelles in 1937.

Committee, also suggested (via intermediaries) that they would be prepared to accept the White Paper if a 'face saving device' could be found.[21] Consequently, a representative of the Palestine Government was sent to Cairo in July for three days of talks with 'Abd al-Hadi, during which he made clear that he and other members of the Arab Higher Committee felt that the rebellion had achieved its aims and should be called off. 'Abd al-Hadi also claimed that the Arab states would be prepared to endorse the White Paper if enough members of the Committee asked them to do so (an opinion which the Foreign Office shared.)[22] The only serious points of difference which prevented acceptance of the White Paper, he argued, were the constitutional provisions concerning the time span within which the Legislative Council would be established and ministers appointed. In subsequent talks with the British embassy in Cairo, 'Abd al-Hadi called for a statement by the British Government 'interpreting' these points in the White Paper in the Arabs' favour.[23] In a parallel approach to the embassy, George Antonius, author of The Arab Awakening, also called for a further statement by Britain making it clear that it intended to implement the White Paper fully, a proposal which the embassy itself strongly supported.[24]

The possibility of a statement which would make the White Paper more acceptable to Arab opinion was debated in London on 3 August 1939. In talks with the Foreign Office, the Colonial Office noted the critical reception the White Paper had received outside the Middle East and insisted that no such statement could be made until Britain had managed to reverse the condemnation of the White Paper in the Permanent Mandates Commission, by means of an appeal to the Council of the League of Nations. As the Foreign Office endorsed this argument, the question of a statement which might have induced the Arab states and some of the members of the Arab Higher Committee to accept the White Paper was put aside, and the talks with 'Abd al-Hadi were not resumed.[25]

The 'interpretation' of the White Paper which had been demanded in these approaches through the Cairo embassy was in effect an assurance that where the new policy left open various alternative

[21]Lampson to FO No. 375, 15 June 1939, FO 371/23237 E4357.
[22]Report by Kingsley-Heath, Assistant Head of Palestine Police, FO 371/23239 E5631.
[23]Sterndale-Bennett to FO No. 215(Saving), 29 July 1939, FO 371/23239 E5422.
[24]Ibid.
[25]Lampson to FO No. 204(Saving), 21 July 1939, FO 371/23238 E5276.

courses of action in Palestine, a particular course favourable to the Arabs would be followed. But the Foreign Office, keen as it was to win Arab support for the policy, accepted the Colonial Office view that such a concession to Arab opinion was not possible until after the White Paper had been accepted by the League. The question of concessions after the League's expected endorsement was left open. In the interim the only concession that the British Government could make was an offer of amnesty for those Palestinians in exile or interned in Palestine as a result of their actions during the revolt. As an Arab endorsement of the White Paper could not be obtained at that stage, the Foreign Office argued, an amnesty should be offered in exchange for an appeal by the Arab states for an end to the disturbances in Palestine.[26]

The army, however, was against an amnesty, arguing that it would only harm the military campaign against the disturbances. As the G.O.C. Lt.-Gen. Haining reported in a despatch covering the period November 1938 to 1939 March 31, the willingness of the Government to negotiate with Arabs, and the presence of the Mufti's representatives at the St. James Conference made the Arab population considerably less willing to cooperate with H.M. Forces in Palestine.[27] Furthermore, following the release of the White Paper in May and its subsequent rejection by the Arab Higher Committee, rebel activity intensified.

During August and September the internal security situation deteriorated again, a fact which Haining's successor as G.O.C., Lt.-General M.G. Barker, attributed 'primarily to intensive efforts by the Mufti to revive rebellion'.[28] MacMichael cabled the Colonial Office suggesting that the French authorities in Syria and Lebanon (where most of those associated with the Mufti were in exile) be asked to arrest the Mufti, twenty Palestinian nationalist politicians and eleven rebel gang leaders immediately on the outbreak of war.[29] However the Foreign Office would do no more than ask the French authorities to increase their surveillance of the Mufti.[30]

Shortly after the start of the war the Foreign Office renewed its attempts to persuade the Arab states, if they could not endorse the White Paper, at least to call a truce over Palestine for the duration of

[26] Eyres minute, 10 July 1939, FO 371/23238 E4794.
[27] Haining to WO, Despatch, 24 April 1939, CO 733/404//75528/74(39).
[28] GOC to WO, HP 1271, 6 September 1939, WO 169/148.
[29] HCr to CO No. 1042, 26 August 1939, FO 371/23239 E6141.
[30] FO to Havard No. 35, 1 September 1939, FO 371/23239 E6186.

the hostilities and to advise the Mufti to end the rebellion.[31] While this idea was being discussed within the Foreign Office, a cable arrived from the British representative in Beirut stating that the Mufti himself was considering such a truce.[32] While this appeared to be a vindication of Foreign Office strategy, the War Office sided with the Colonial Office in calling for decisive action against the Mufti.[33]

During September it became clear that French surveillance of the Mufti was not particularly effective. However the British representatives in Beirut and Damascus informed the Foreign Office that the Mufti had by now 'sunk into oblivion'[34] – assessments which contradicted the views of their counterparts in Baghdad and Cairo, who had a few weeks earlier been quoted by the Foreign Office when it advised against taking any action against the Mufti. Rather than agreeing with the War and Colonial Offices that the Mufti could now be arrested without risking repercussions, the Foreign Office interpreted the views of Havard (in Beirut) and Mackereth (in Damascus) to mean that it was no longer necessary even to protest to the French authorities in Syria against the laxity of the Mufti's surveillance.[35]

The Mufti's apparent obscurity was balanced by the increased activity of his closest associates (including Jamal al-Husayni),[36] who should also have been under house arrest in Syria but were in fact free to travel to Baghdad for talks with the Iraqi Government. On 3 October Sir Basil Newton, the British Ambassador in Baghdad, informed London that the Iraqi Government had offered to make an appeal to the Mufti to end the disturbances.[37] Newton argued that such an appeal would weaken German propaganda in the Middle East and remove the Palestine question from Iraqi domestic politics for the duration of the war. Both of these were considerable advantages which had to be weighed against the risk of reviving the Mufti's prestige, and at an interdepartmental conference on 10 October the

---

[31] Draft cable to Lampson and Newton, FO 371/23239 E6382.

[32] Havard to FO No. 41, 8 September 1939, *ibid.*

[33] Army Council to Under-Secretary of State, Foreign Office, 10 September 1939, FO 371/23239 E6404.

[34] Mackereth to FO No. 60, 16 September 1939, FO 371/23240 E6539, and Havard to FO No. 46, 20 September 1939, FO 371/23240 E6587.

[35] Eyres and Baggallay minutes, September 1939, FO 371/23240 E6642.

[36] Jamal Al-Husayni was a delegate to the St. James Conference, a member of the A.H.C., leader of the Palestine Arab Party, and a distant cousin of the Mufti. Foreign Office reports described Husayni as '. . . unswervingly loyal to Haj Amin [the Mufti], bitterly anti-Jewish and uncompromisingly opposed to the continuation of the Mandate' (FO 371/23227 E1758).

[37] Newton to FO No 369, 3 October 1939, FO 371/23240 E6784.

Foreign Office prevailed upon the War and Colonial Offices to accept the offer of the Arab states to approach the Mufti independently and advise a truce.[38]

The possibility of an amicable solution to the thorny problem that the Mufti presented to British Palestine policy was shortlived. Before the Government's reply to the Iraqi initiative could be sent, the Mufti and his closest associates escaped to Baghdad, apparently invited by the Iraqi Government.[39] Once in Iraq the Mufti was effectively outside British control and he proceeded to rebuild his political influence. The Foreign Office's hopes that he could be isolated and forced into oblivion, or that he might accept an independent appeal by the Arab states to end the disturbances in Palestine, came to naught and British prestige in the Middle East received a setback.

In the course of the development of policy towards the Mufti, the question of a general amnesty for the large number of Palestinians who had either fled Palestine or were exiled during the disturbances, remained unresolved. Shortly after the outbreak of war the Egyptian Government called for a general amnesty, the release of all detainees and the return of all the exiles to Palestine. The Egyptian Prime Minister, Ali Maher, made it clear that an appeal by the Arab states to the Arabs of Palestine for cooperation with Britain was linked to the favourable outcome of the amnesty question in general.[40] The Colonial Office had previously opposed such an amnesty but now agreed to put the question to the High Commissioner. In its telegram the Colonial Office pointed out that as no further concessions in the form of 'interpretations' of the White Paper had been made, a liberalisation of the security measures in Palestine was desirable and would help obtain a favourable statement from the Arab states.[41] MacMichael concurred, and now decided to go even further than asked by London in restoring general liberties.

In December 1939 the Palestine Government made a public declaration stating that all those against whom no formal exclusion orders had been issued could now return to Palestine, although there would be no immunity from prosecution for those who had committed crimes of violence.[42] Of the twelve Palestinians who had been

[38] Minutes of 10 October meeting held at Colonial Office, *ibid*.

[39] Newton to FO No. 403, 23 October 1939, FO 371/23240 E7156.

[40] Ali Maher to Lampson, 24 September 1939, CO 733/408//75872/28.

[41] CO to HCr No. 845, 20 September 1939, *ibid*. The Colonial Office was under pressure from the War Office to relieve H.M. Forces in Palestine of their civil functions, including abolition of the military courts established one year earlier.

[42] CO to HCr No. 955, 24 November 1939, FO 371/23242 E7777.

formally excluded during the disturbances, MacMichael was prepared to accept eight of them back on condition that they petitioned the Palestine Government for permission to return and agreed to engage only in legal political activity.[43] These eight included those members of the Arab Higher Committee who were not considered to be part of the Mufti's party. The remaining four, whom the Palestinian Government would not allow to return under any circumstances, were the Mufti, Jamal al-Husayni and two rebel gang leaders.[44] In the months that followed seven of the eight excluded personalities petitioned the High Commissioner and were unobtrusively allowed to return. Only one, Awni 'Abd al-Hadi, refused to make such a petition, and the Colonial Office considered that its policy of splitting the Arab Higher Committee and isolating the Mufti had succeeded.[45]

During 1940 the Arab governments continued to make representations on behalf of those exiles who would face trial if they returned, and in favour of further relaxation of the emergency measures in general. They particularly objected to the execution of those convicted of crimes committed during the revolt, especially of those exiles who had returned in the belief that they would be pardoned. In February 1940 alone twelve Arabs were executed, a fact which German propaganda commented on at length.[46] The Foreign Office was sympathetic to these representations as it sought to meet Arab opinion by 'doing something for the exiles'.[47] However, while the Colonial Office was prepared to press the High Commissioner, it was not prepared to override him on this question and rejected Foreign Office appeals for a general amnesty.[48] Despite continued representations from the Arab states during the first half of 1940 the stalemate between the desire on the part of the Foreign Office to appease the Arab states by further concessions on the amnesty issue and the Palestine Government's unwillingness to endanger the relative stability in Palestine continued until the issue was revived in a general review of British Middle East policy prompted by a serious deterioration of Britain's international position in May 1940.

[43]Dr. Husayn al-Khalidi, Fu'ad Saba, Ahmad Hilmi 'Abd al-Baqi, Alfred Rok, Rashid Al-Hajj Ibrahim, Yacoub al-Ghusayn, Awni 'Abd al-Hadi, and 'Abd al-Latif Salah.

[44]Izzat Darwaza and Muhammad Izhak Darwish al-Husayni.

[45]Downie minute, 7 February 1940, CO 733/428//75986/2 (Part 1)(1940).

[46]*Ibid., passim.*

[47]Baggallay minute, 23 January 1940, FO 371/24565 E180.

[48]Downie to Baggallay, 19 February 1940, CO 733/428//75986/2 (Part 1)(1940).

Regardless of differences over the pace and extent of liberalisation, by December 1939 concrete steps had been taken to lift the emergency measures, and not surprisingly the Middle East Department concluded that if it was possible to relax martial law and release detainees it should also be possible to proceed with the implementation of the Heads of Department scheme.[49] Once again, however, the High Commissioner objected, repeating his argument of six months earlier that moderate Palestinian Arab circles were still in disarray and not yet ready to be an effective vehicle for the British Government's plans for Palestine's constitutional development.[50] In response to his reiterated objections and to a telegram in January 1940 from Ibn Saud urging progress on 10(4), the Colonial Secretary asked the Middle East Department to meet the Foreign Office and decide once and for all whether His Majesty's Government intended to proceed with the constitutional provisions of the White Paper during the war.[51]

Both the Foreign and the Colonial Offices debated the question at length during February 1940, and both came to the conclusion that with the improved internal security situation in Palestine, the return (or impending return) of many of the more moderate Palestine Arab leaders and the apparent isolation of the Mufti, the time had come to do something positive about the appointment of Heads of Department.[52] Having finally resolved to act, Whitehall now only needed to convince the Cabinet that the time was right.

The first major debate at Cabinet level on Palestine policy since the release of the White Paper in May 1939 took place in December 1939. As part of the Zionist campaign to encourage the British Government to suspend the White Paper during the War, Lord Lothian, British ambassador in Washington, had been approached by American Zionists and asked to make a statement on the status of the White Paper policy. The Eastern Department in the Foreign Office wanted to counter the Zionist lobbying against the White Paper, which had continued throughout 1939, by making an unequivocal reply. Consequently they drafted a reply to Lothian stating that His Majesty's Government considered the White Paper to be 'the most just solution of the Palestine problem', that it would not abandon its policy just because neither Arabs or Jews supported it, and that 'neither Arabs nor Jews could influence the Government's resolve by

---

[49]CO to HCr No. 984, 6 December 1939, CO 733/415//75986/1(1939).

[50]HCr to Secretary of State, 31 December 1939, CO 733/410//75872/85(1939).

[51]MacDonald minute, 25 January 1940, *ibid*.

[52]Minutes, February 1940, *ibid*.

promises of support during the war'.[53] The Eastern Department wanted this reply to be sent to Washington quickly, but the Secretary of State for Foreign Affairs, Lord Halifax, intervened and instructed that the Colonial Office should be consulted first and the matter then brought before the Cabinet.[54]

Chamberlain did not consider a full Cabinet debate necessary, and suggested instead that the draft reply to Lothian be circulated as a Cabinet paper. If no objections were raised within three days then the draft could be cabled to Washington.[55] This was done, and as no objections had been recorded within the three days the cable was despatched on 24 December. Churchill, who had led the campaign against the White Paper in the Commons when it was introduced in May 1939, was now First Lord of the Admiralty and a member of the War Cabinet. Although he was therefore no longer able to take a public stand against the policy, he had, soon after coming into office, informed the Jewish Agency in London that he would revive the question of Palestine policy at Cabinet level, and would even resign if the War Cabinet did anything contrary to the Mandate.[56] He failed to see the reply to Lothian when it was first circulated, but one day after it had been despatched to Washington he responded by circulating a draft reply of his own which suggested that Lothian should state that although the White Paper could not be withdrawn neither was it the last word on the problem. A final settlement of the Palestine problem was one of the questions which would find its place in a general settlement at the end of the war; meanwhile nothing would be done in implementing the White Paper policy which might prejudice the final form which such a settlement might take (ie. progress on the con-stitutional provisions). The one thing Lothian ought not to say, Churchill argued, 'was that with the world in flux and the life of every European nation and the British Empire hanging in the balance, the sole fixed immutable, inexorable fact was that Jewish immigration into Palestine would come to an end after five years in accordance with the White Paper'.[57]

[53] Baggallay draft and minutes, 9 December 1939, FO 371/23242 E7874.

[54] Halifax minute, 10 December 1939, ibid. Colonial Office deliberations on this issue are on a closed file – CO 733/411//75872/102(1939).

[55] Chamberlain minute, 19 December 1939, FO 371/23242 E8032. The draft reply was circulated on 20 December 1939 as WP(G)(39)161 (Cab 67/3).

[56] M. Gilbert, Churchill and Zionism (lecture, London, 1973), p. 21. Churchill had told Chaim Weizmann that he not only opposed the White Paper but that after the war he wanted to see a Jewish state in Palestine of three to four million Jews (ibid).

[57] WP(G)(39)163, 25 December 1939, Cab 67/3.

While these papers were being circulated the legislation on the control of land sales was being finalised, and MacDonald convinced the Cabinet that discussion on the papers should be deferred until they could be considered together with the new land laws.[58] In the interim the Foreign Office reply to Lothian was suspended and a brief reply omitting all references to the future of the White Paper was sent in its place.[59] It was three weeks before any discussions were resumed and the Foreign Office used the interval to prepare and circulate a detailed critique of Churchill's paper and to outline more fully the reasons why the White Paper should be re-endorsed. The Cabinet Paper prepared by the Eastern Department argued that nothing the Government did in Palestine would influence the position of American Jews, or Jews anywhere for that matter, since they were virtually a captive ally and it was not necessary to make concessions to win their support. Even if Jewish opinion was alienated, its influence was overestimated and was in fact in no way decisive in America. On the other hand, the Foreign Office paper argued, Arab opinion was vital, and any retreat from the White Paper would produce an Arab reaction which 'might even be catastrophic'.[60]

In mid-January Chamberlain informed the Cabinet that he would try to find a compromise formula in talks with Halifax, MacDonald and Churchill.[61] Churchill and MacDonald had had a five hour meeting to discuss Palestine policy on 28 December, and it is very probable that they had already reached a compromise.[62] On the very day that Chamberlain informed the Cabinet that he would attempt to find a compromise, MacDonald wrote to him suggesting that Churchill would not actively oppose the Regulations if no public statement of the Government's commitment to the White Paper was made.[63] Consequently Chamberlain prepared a reply to Lothian (replacing the original Foreign Office draft) telling him not to make any public statement on the British Government's attitude to the White Paper, but authorising him to inform interested parties that while the land regulations would be introduced, the British Government would prefer 'to postpone for the duration of the war any action

[58] WM 123(39)7, 27 December 1939, Cab 65/2.

[59] WP(G)(40)1, 1 January 1940, Cab 67/4.

[60] WP(G)(40)4, 16 January 1940, Cab 67/4.

[61] WM 15(40)3, 16 January 1940, Cab 65/5.

[62] N. Rose (ed), *Baffy: The Diaries of Baffy Dugdale* (London, 1973), p. 157, entry for 28 December 1939.

[63] MacDonald to Chamberlain, 16 January 1940, Prem 1/420. (The letter is dated 16 January 1939, but the contents clearly show that the correct date is 1940.)

in Palestine which might tend to revive political controversy'.[64] In return, when the Regulations were discussed in Cabinet, Churchill placed his objections to them on record – he even circulated a paper condemning them[65] – but stated that he would not press his opposition any further. Instead he thanked his colleagues for having met him on the wider issues of the reply to Lothian.[65]

In Palestine the Zionists viewed the introduction of the land transfer regulations as an indication that the Government did intend to press ahead with the White Paper despite the war, and therefore as a major defeat. Churchill believed the opposite to be true. Although immigration was being curbed and land sales to Jews were now restricted, the opposition of the High Commissioner together with the indecision of the Colonial Office in the implementation of the constitutional provisions of that policy coincided with Churchill's opposition to the White Paper as a whole. This facilitated a *modus vivendi* at Cabinet level as suggested in Churchill's first Cabinet Paper, whereby nothing would be done in implementing the White Paper which would prejudice a reconsideration of Palestine policy after the war.[67] The *modus vivendi* within the Cabinet was possible only because of the practical difficulties the Government was facing at the time in appointing Heads of Department. The Foreign and Colonial Offices still intended to proceed with the White Paper, and the Foreign Office secured Chamberlain's confirmation of this during the discussions in January. At Halifax's suggestion, Chamberlain inserted in his draft of the reply to Lothian a clear qualification to the effect that the Government had agreed only to avoid public controversy and had made no decisions which would prejudice the eventual implementation of the White Paper as a whole.[68] But in the light of the compromise reached in the Cabinet it was now clear to the departments concerned that the time was not yet ripe for progress towards constitutional development or for the implementation of the Heads of Department scheme.

[64]WP(G)(40)38, 4 February 1940, Cab 67/4.

[65]WP(G)(40)61, 24 February 1940, Cab 67/5.

[66]WM 39(40)12, 12 February 1940, Cab 65/5.

[67]For an alternative account of the Colonial Office's position in the Cabinet debate, cf. G. Cohen, *HaCabinet HaBriti Ve'she'elat Eretz Yisrael, April-Yuli 1943* (The British Cabinet and the Palestine Question, April-July 1943) (Jerusalem, 1977).

[68]Halifax to Chamberlain, 30 January 1940, FO 371/24564 E665.

2

CHURCHILL AND THE WHITE PAPER

In May 1940 Whitehall turned once again to the question of amnesty, both as a possible gesture towards Arab opinion[1] and as a response to the War Office's desire to release British forces in Palestine from their internal security commitments.[2] Some of the Arab states' most persistent demands were met when the High Commissioner was informed, despite his protests, that the military courts must abandon their power to impose the death penalty, that no executions resulting from the decisions of civil courts be conducted without prior consultation with London, and that the exiles scattered throughout the Middle East (except for the Mufti and his closest aides) be encouraged to return to Palestine.[3]

On the outbreak of war in September 1939 there were eleven infantry battalions, two cavalry regiments and auxiliary detachments stationed in Palestine, all but three battalions (which formed part of the Middle East Reserve) acting as garrison forces.[4] Due in large part to their experience in putting down the Arab revolt, these forces represented some of the best-trained troops available to Britain in the early months of the war. In October 1939 Churchill had suggested to the Cabinet that the regular battalions be withdrawn and deployed elsewhere, and that Arabs and Jews be recruited for internal security needs. This went directly against Colonial and War Office policy which was to disarm the local population rather than utilise it for the defence of Palestine or for internal security purposes. The disarming of the Arab population was already under way as part of the campaign to end the Arab revolt. Following the successful suppression of most of the internal disorder, and (more significantly) the adoption of the White Paper in the face of Zionist opposition, it was decided to disarm the Yishuv as well 'against the possibility of Jewish armed unrest'.[5] The Colonial Office believed that the garrison forces could be released for participation in the war effort and internal security maintained by the reconstitution of the Palestine Police force, basing

[1] Lampson to FO Nos. 222 & 242, April 1940, CO 733/428//75986/2(Part 2); Luke minutes of 9 May 1940 (*ibid.*); and representations by the Egyptian Ambassador to the Foreign Office, FO 371/24566 E1952.

[2] WO-CO correspondence, March-May 1940, CO 733/428//75986/1(1940).

[3] CO to HCr No. 439, 2 June 1940, CO 733/428//75986/2 (Part 2).

[4] These figures are given in WP(G)(40)16, 20 January 1940, Cab 67/4.

[5] Moult minute, 22 May 1940, CO 733/416//75015(1940).

it in fortified police forts (Tegart Forts) which were to be built throughout the countryside. The Tegart Forts were to be completed by August-September 1940, and Chamberlain's Cabinet had resolved to delay consideration of the redeployment of the garrison until then, while at the same time authorising the disarming of the Jews. Churchill's proposals to do the opposite as a means of releasing the troops for immediate use elsewhere was firmly rejected.[6]

When Churchill became Prime Minister on 10 May 1940, and when the Labour and Liberal parties joined the War Cabinet (with Leo Amery as Secretary of State for India), the opposition to the White Paper at Cabinet level was greatly strengthened. Shortly after the change in government, Churchill revived his proposal for the redeployment of the Palestine garrison, emphasising to the Chiefs of Staff the urgent need for these troops for the defence of the U.K.[7] The Chiefs of Staff rejected the proposal, not because of the effect it would have on Palestine's internal security but because of the effect it would have on Britain's overall strength in the Middle East.[8] But Churchill persisted, describing the withdrawal to the U.K. of the Palestine garrison as one of the decisions 'which seem indispensable in view of the impending danger to Great Britain'[9] and instructing the Chiefs of Staff to reconsider their position.[10] When he had first put the proposal to Chamberlain's Cabinet in 1939 Churchill talked of arming both Arabs and Jews to replace the garrison, but this time he was franker, making it clear that when the troops were withdrawn only the Jews were to be armed in their own defence.[11] Similar instructions were sent to the Colonial Office.

The Colonial Office called an urgent interdepartmental meeting the day Churchill's instructions reached them. There 'Lord Lloyd [MacDonald's successor as Secretary of State for the Colonies] and all the Colonial Office' made it clear that they were 'bitterly opposed to the idea of arming the Jews', a view shared by the War and Foreign Offices.[12] Recognising that Churchill's main interest was the redeploy-

[6]WM 39(40)13, Cab 65/5.

[7]Churchill to Chiefs of Staff, 18 May, CoS(40)(364), Cab 80/11.

[8]CoS(40)365, 18 May 1940, *ibid*.

[9]Churchill Memo to Ismay, 23 May 1940, Prem 4/51/9 Part 2.

[10]Churchill to CoS, 23 May 1940, CoS(40)379, Cab 80/11.

[11]Churchill to Lloyd, 23 May 1940, Prem 4/51/9 Part 2.

[12]The relevant CO file on this question (75990(40)) is missing from the CO 733 series in the P.R.O.. The account here is based on parallel FO files. Bagallay minute, 24 May 1940, FO 371/24569 E2062. In volume two of *The Second World War* Churchill

ment of the garrison, and that the arming of the Jews was a secondary consideration, Lloyd sought a compromise. In late May he wrote to Churchill that a consensus of opinion amongst the authorities responsible for Palestine affairs was against the withdrawal of the garrison except under certain conditions – that the semi-equipped British units and the Australian units stationed in Palestine be available for internal security purposes; that 'there is no deviation from the White Paper policy which might inflame Arab feeling' and that 'no provocation is offered to Arab sentiment by [the] creation of a Jewish armed force for internal security purposes'.[13] Concerning this latter point Lloyd attempted to mollify Churchill by explaining at length the steps which had already been taken during the Arab revolt to allow isolated Jewish settlements to defend themselves. With remarkable disingenuity, however, Lloyd failed to add that the policy of arming the Jewish settlements had been reversed and that steps were currently being taken to disarm the Yishuv.[14]

While the redeployment of the Palestine garrison was being considered, various Jewish groups revived the question of British support for a Jewish army, made up of Jews from around the world who would fight under British leadership against the Germans. This proposal was considered by the departments concerned to be even more dangerous than the arming of the Palestinian Jewish population for self-defence, for a Jewish army, fighting under its own flag, would further the recognition of the Jewish people as a nation, give the Jews a claim to participate in discussions about peace terms at the end of the war and would doubtless lead to a Jewish demand for the creation of a Jewish state in Palestine as a reward for Jewish military assistance.[15]

recounted: 'I wished to arm the Jews at Tel Aviv, who with proper weapons would have made a good fight against all comers. Here I encountered every kind of resistance' (p.373).

[13] Lloyd to Churchill, 28 May 1940, Prem 3/348.

[14] However six weeks after Lloyd's omitting to mention this to Churchill the policy of *actively* disarming the Jewish settlements and the illegal Jewish military organisations was suspended. At a G.O.C. Conference on 9 July 1940, Lt-General Giffard stated: 'With regard to hidden Jewish arms, he wanted at the moment to let sleeping dogs lie, and searches for these would not be carried out. Nevertheless, Jews found illegally carrying arms would be dealt with' (WO 169/147). In September the Palestine Forces H.Q. set out policy in operational instructions: 'If reliable information regarding hidden arms is received, a search should be carried out with particular care to avoid any unnecessary untoward incident. In default of definite information, no systematic or wholesale search should be made' (CR/PAL/16009/G, 2 September 1940, *ibid*).

[15] Lloyd to Churchill, 22 May 1940, Prem 4/51/9 Part 2. For a full discussion of the Jewish Army question, cf. Y. Gelber, *Hahitnadvut ve'Mekoma be'Mediniut HaZionit ve'HaYishuvit 1939-1942* (Jerusalem, 1979).

Although in practice separate questions, the Jewish army proposals and the problem of arranging for the internal security of Palestine while withdrawing the British garrison, were discussed at the same time, and were clearly linked. In both cases the opinion of all the authorities dealing with Palestine was that any concession to Jewish opinion on the Jewish army question or to Churchill in his insistence on arming the Jews for internal security purposes would not only affect stability in Palestine but would also present a challenge to Britain's ability to carry out its accepted policy in that territory in the future.

The question of the withdrawal of the Palestine garrison came before the Cabinet the day after Lloyd had informed Churchill of the conditions which the Colonial Office, the High Commissioner and the G.O.C. in Palestine felt must be accepted before they could agree to any redeployment of these troops outside Palestine. Lloyd attempted to obtain a guarantee from the Cabinet that at least the Australian troops in Palestine would be made available for internal security activities if necessary.[16] However no such guarantee could be given, and consequently no conclusion was reached in Cabinet on withdrawing the garrison. Nevertheless, despite the fact that no decision had been taken, Churchill proceeded to instruct Lloyd (and all the other ministers concerned) to bring eight of the regular infantry battalions home, leaving the question of the protection of the Jewish settlements open.[17]

In the course of the controversy over the garrison, Churchill's suggestion that the Jews be armed for internal security duties was easily deflected as it was entirely secondary to the Prime Minister's main concern, namely that the highly experienced troops available in Palestine be brought back to the U.K. By the end of the first week of June, with the successful withdrawal of British and French troops from Dunkirk, there was nothing that the Palestine garrison could have contributed to the defence of the U.K., and Churchill finally dropped the idea. All that remained of the controversy was a general concern at the way in which Churchill had attempted to by-pass both the Cabinet and the Chiefs of Staff on the matter, and also that he had been willing to put forward suggestions (such as the arming of the Yishuv) which were so completely out of sympathy with the accepted, official policy on Palestine.

[16] WM 146(40)9, 29 May 1940, Cab 65/7.
[17] Churchill to Lloyd, 29 May 1940, Prem 3/348.

In this atmosphere of uncertainty concerning the future of Palestine policy under the new government, Sir Basil Newton informed London on 27 May that the Iraqi Minister of Foreign Affairs Nuri es-Said had presented a list of demands to the British Embassy in Baghdad, the central one of which concerned Palestine.[8] Nuri requested that:

> as a complement to measures which are being taken by the Iraqi Government themselves to defeat enemy trickery, His Majesty's Government, and if possible the French Government as well [concerning Syria] should issue a clear and unambiguous pronouncement guaranteeing immediately, or at least at the end of the war, the execution of promises already given for organisation of self-government in these two countries [Syria and Palestine]. Such an announcement. . .would not only facilitate the Iraqi Government's task of combating Fifth Column activities in Iraq but would also without doubt have a beneficial influence over the whole Middle East.[19]

The 'promises already given for the organisation of self-government' referred to the constitutional provisions of the White Paper, which the Cabinet had already decided to suspend for the duration of the war. Nuri's démarche now revived the question.

The Foreign Office had already resolved to do what it could to strengthen the position of Nuri, and the Government of which he was a member, within Iraqi domestic politics, and had considered his earlier requests for concessions on the amnesty and other Palestine-related issues in this light.[20] Following Churchill's initiative on the withdrawal of the Palestine garrison and the arming of the Yishuv, both the Eastern Department in the Foreign Office and the Middle East Department of the Colonial Office, together with their respective Secretaries of State, Lords Halifax and Lloyd, had come to share the Iraqi Foreign Minister's doubts and they too wanted some form of commitment by Churchill's Government to the Palestine policy of its predecessor. The Foreign Office still doubted whether any further declaration on Palestine which the British Government 'could honestly and sincerely make' would 'really satisfy Arab aspirations' or guarantee Arab support, and they believed, as Newton in Baghdad did, that the only way of ensuring the latter was to convince the Arabs that Britain was going to win the war.[21] Some sort of diplomatic reply

[18]Newton to FO No. 190, 26 May 1940, FO 371/24566 E2063.

[19]*Ibid.*

[20]FO 371/24568 E1970/G.

[21]Bagallay minute, 3 June 1940, FO 371/23566 E2077.

to Nuri's démarche had to be sent, and since the change in political leadership in London the Foreign Office (and the Colonial Office) felt that no reply, no matter how diplomatically vague, could be prepared until the Government's position on the White Paper had been clarified.[22]

On 6 June 1940 Lloyd and Halifax, together with the Heads of the Eastern and Middle East Departments, met at the Foreign Office to frame a Cabinet paper explaining the need for a favourable reply to Nuri's demands and the overriding need to retain the White Paper intact.[23] Although officials in both ministries had only recently argued against making further 'concessions and assurances', they now changed their minds. As Sir John Shuckburgh, Assistant Under-Secretary in the Colonial Office, later explained to the Permanent Under-Secretary of the Colonial Office, '. . .some statement of the kind must be made to Nuri Pasha, unless it is the intention of H.M.G. to reconsider the White Paper at the end of the war. And that as you know is just what we want to avert'.[24]

After this meeting, in an attempt to determine which concessions might be made, the Colonial Office asked the High Commissioner whether he was still strongly opposed to the appointment of Heads of Department, and if he was, whether he would be opposed to a promise of the eventual implementation of the constitutional provisions of the White Paper after the war.[25] In his reply MacMichael again rejected the immediate appointment of Heads of Department, arguing this time not the dearth of suitable Arab politicians (as he had in 1939) but rather the extent of the likely Jewish reaction. However he agreed that some sort of declaration on the *eventual* implementation of all the provisions of the White Paper was 'difficult to decline'.[26]

The Cabinet paper arguing for a positive reply to Nuri was prepared by the Foreign Office after consultation with the Colonial Office. Although the issue was brought to the Cabinet with the intention of obtaining an overall endorsement of the White Paper, the need for an urgent reply to Nuri was pushed to the forefront. Thus a preface by Halifax stating that the matter had to be brought before the Cabinet 'in view of the changes which have since occurred in the Government' was left out of the final draft, and 'recent developments

[22]*Ibid.*
[23]Shuckburgh minute, 8 June 1940, CO 733/426//75872/85(1940).
[24]*Ibid.*
[25]CO to HCr No. 459, 6 June 1940, *ibid.*
[26]HCr to CO No. 517, 7 June 1940, *ibid.*

in the Middle East' were given as the reason instead. Addressing the main issue, the Cabinet paper continued:

> We are in effect asked, and we shall continue to be asked, whether the present Government means to carry it out or not, and we must answer either 'Yes' or 'No'. To say 'No' would probably be fatal, and would not only cause grave reactions throughout the Moslem world, but also reopen the chapter of disorder in the Middle East which in large measure was closed by the White Paper policy.

The paper recommended a statement be made to the effect that after the war the government would proceed with the constitutional development of Palestine as laid down in the White Paper.[27]

At the same time as this Foreign Office paper was being circulated to the Cabinet, a similar paper was being prepared for the Chiefs of Staff by the Air Ministry (which, as the Ministry responsible for the Air Intelligence Centre in Habbaniya, Iraq, was recognised as having a special expertise in Iraqi affairs). Arguing that Iraq's adherence to the Allied cause was 'in considerable danger', the paper claimed that 'Palestine is the principle source of trouble' and that therefore 'a wide public reaffirmation of our determination to stick to the White Paper after the war might do good'.[28]

The Foreign Office paper was discussed by the new Cabinet on 15 June, the first occasion on which it considered the fate of the White Paper as a whole, and therefore the first opportunity for the Labour and Liberal members of the Cabinet to express an opinion on the Government's Palestine policy. Although Attlee spoke against a positive reply to Nuri's demarche, the general trend of the debate was

[27]WP(G)(40)149 'The Arab States and Palestine', 12 June 1940, Cab 67/6. The draft of this paper is on FO 371/24566 E2077. It is interesting to compare this alarmist view of the consequences of failing to reaffirm the White Paper publicly with another statement of FO opinion on Britain's relations with the Arab world made in the same month but to a committee of officials, not the Cabinet; and concerning matters not directly related to Palestine. When the Middle East (Official) Committee debated the question of the future of the French Mandate in Syria on 26 June (following the fall of France), the Foreign Office argued *against* meeting Arab demands that the French Mandate be declared null and void and that Syria be declared independent. Amongst the reasons given by the Foreign Office for declining to make concessions to Arab opinion was the following: 'Moreover, from a more general point of view, it is permissible to point out that the military value of even the most whole-hearted Arab support would be very small, and that at present it is the Arabs who need British and French protection even more than Great Britain and France need Arab assistance' (FO Memorandum to Middle East (Official) Committee, ME(0)(40)21, Cab 21/1439).

[28]CoS(40)446, 11 June 1940, 'Internal Security in Iraq', Cab 80/12. The Chiefs of Staff had earlier instructed the Chief of the Air Staff to bring these views to Churchill's attention (CoS(40)166th meeting, 3 June 1940, Cab 79/4).

in favour of making a positive reaffirmation of the Government's intention to implement all the provisions of the White Paper after the war.[29] However, Churchill intervened, arguing that he saw no reason for an immediate reply to Nuri's request, and recommended that a final decision be delayed for three or four days. Thus he avoided a defeat in the Cabinet.[30]

While the Colonial and Foreign Offices considered their response to Churchill's delaying tactics, Anglo-Iraqi relations deteriorated because of Iraq's refusal to break off diplomatic relations with Italy (despite the Anglo-Iraqi Treaty of Alliance) following Italy's entry into the war. Newton cabled from Baghdad advising that no further concessions be made to Iraq at present.[31] The Foreign Office therefore drafted a reply to Nuri which stated that 'owing to reverses suffered by the French armies' the Government was too busy to make any new statements. Only if pressed was the ambassador allowed to add that the White Paper remained in force.[32] This reply would most probably have satisfied Churchill, and the matter might well have rested there, with the opportunity of forcing Churchill to endorse the White Paper under pressure of events in Iraq passing by default. However Lord Lloyd, together with the Head of the Eastern Department of the Foreign Office, Lacy Baggallay, resolved to confront Churchill directly with a forthright statement of the case for the White Paper policy.[33] Foreign Office officials consequently prepared a new draft paper (which was approved by the Secretary of State for the Colonies) bluntly stating that:

> Palestine is a mill-stone around our necks at the worst crisis of
> our history. It hangs there because of our efforts to help the
> Zionists. If they cannot realise this, they must realise that our
> position in Palestine stands or falls with our position in the
> Middle East generally and that the Jews will be the worst
> sufferers if we have to abandon the Middle East. It seems to me
> that the reiteration of our intention to stand by our policy is a
> small price for the Zionists to pay for the terrible risks we are
> now running as a result of establishing the national home.[34]

---

[29] WM 167(40)13, 15 June 1940, Cab 65/7.

[30] Churchill regularly used the tactic of delaying a decision when it seemed that he would be defeated by a vote in the Cabinet.

[31] Newton to FO No. 296, 26 June 1940 (cited in Bagallay minute, 1 July 1940, FO 371/24563 E2220).

[32] Draft in Bagallay to Downie, 21 June 1940, *ibid*.

[33] Bagallay minute, 24 June 1940, *ibid*.

[34] Draft on *ibid*.

This statement on the role of the Palestine problem in Anglo-Arab relations grossly over-simplified the range and source of the problems that bedevilled those relations, and the Foreign Office, when it was not defending the White Paper, recognised this. But the Eastern Department (together with the Colonial Office) wanted to impress on the Cabinet and the Prime Minister the dangers of abandoning the Palestine policy of the last twelve months. Thus the new draft paper was endorsed by the responsible Assistant Under-Secretary of State, Horace Seymour, and the Permanent Under-Secretary of the Foreign Office, Sir Alexander Cadogan,[35] only to be stopped by the Foreign Secretary himself.

Despite Lord Lloyd's support and the impressive official backing for the new draft paper, Halifax declined to pass it on to Churchill. Presumably wishing to avoid direct confrontation over the White Paper, Halifax sent the Prime Minister an alternative draft reply to Nuri which attempted to meet Churchill's reservations by being even vaguer on future policy than the original Foreign Office draft which had been discussed in Cabinet. According to this latest version, Nuri was to be told:

> The policy of His Majesty's Government for Palestine was clearly laid down in May 1939, and has not been changed. . . [although nothing could be done during the war, H.M.G.] hope and expect that when the war is ended conditions in Palestine will permit the various stages of constitutional development to follow one another in orderly succession on the lines laid down.[36]

Halifax suggested two possible courses of action – either Churchill personally approve this compromise and equivocal formulation, in which case the Foreign Office could pass it on to Baghdad automatically, or else it could first be brought to the Cabinet for approval. Churchill chose to bring it to the Cabinet, and consequently Halifax's letter to him was circulated as the second Cabinet paper on the reply to Nuri and was debated there on 3 July.[37] Newton's advice of a week earlier, that no futher concessions should be made to the Iraqis at that moment, influenced the Cabinet debate, and Halifax's suggested reply to Nuri was changed once again. Reflecting the Cabinet's unwillingness to declare that the White Paper was *the* Palestine policy of the British Government, it adopted instead the formula that 'their policy for Palestine as laid down in May 1939... remains unchanged'. The Cabinet resolved that only if specifically pressed on the point

[35]Minutes on *ibid*.

[36]Halifax to Churchill, 26 June 1940, on CO 733/426//75872/85(1940).

[37]WM 192(40)9, Cab 65/8.

were British representatives in the Middle East authorised to say that after the war, if conditions in Palestine permitted, 'the various stages of constitutional development' would 'follow one another in orderly succession, on the lines already laid down'.[38]

Such a statement was very far from what both the Foreign and Colonial Offices had hoped to achieve when they had resolved, a month earlier, to bring to the War Cabinet Nuri Said's request for a reaffirmation of British policy on Palestine. Instead of obtaining the Churchill Government's definitive commitment to the policy of its predecessor, it was now quite clear that Churchill not only disliked the policy but that he intended eventually to change it. Until that was possible the relevant authorities were authorised to implement the land and immigration provisions of the White Paper (which were already in force). However in accordance with the *modus vivendi* which had governed deliberations on Palestine policy since Churchill first challenged the White Paper from within the War Cabinet in January-February 1940, and which was confirmed now, they were not to do anything which would prejudice a reconsideration of Palestine policy at the end of the war. Even the words 'White Paper policy' were to be replaced, as far as possible, with 'policy of May, 1939'.[39]

The conflict with the Chiefs of Staff over the withdrawal of the Palestine garrison to the U.K. was not primarily a conflict over the effects of such a move on Palestine internally, although Churchill's suggestion that the Yishuv be armed alarmed official and military circles in London and the Middle East. At issue was the strategic question of the priority of the Middle East theatre over the defence of the U.K. and requirements in Western Europe. When the debate over the garrison is seen together with Churchill's disregard for the Foreign Office view on the dire consequences of failing to re-endorse the White Paper in the reply to Nuri, it would appear that during May and June 1940 Churchill did not give Middle Eastern affairs a high priority at this early stage of the war. During this period both Amery and Lloyd constantly complained that the Middle East was being neglected,[40] and in his diary entry for 30 June, Amery records that in

[38]*Ibid.*

[39]FO to Newton No.300, 10 July 1940, FO 371/24563 E2220.

[40]The creation of the Middle East (Ministerial) Committee in July 1940 was intended to provide both Amery and Lloyd with an opportunity to influence policy on the conduct of war in that theatre. (Churchill to Sir E. Bridges (Secretary to the War Cabinet) 10 July 1940, Prem 4/32/6). However, it met infrequently, 'was never popular with Whitehall' (A. Eden, *The Reckoning* (London 1972), p. 126), was not informed of forthcoming military actions or shown sensitive cables. (Churchill Memo

talks with Churchill he 'found him very little interested in either India or the Middle East'.[41] However, after the successful evacuation of Dunkirk by early June, Italy's entry into the war, the subsequent outbreak of hostilities in the Middle East in early July, and the loss of the French forces in Syria in late July, the Middle East theatre received a higher priority in Churchill's thinking, and by mid-July he 'had taken a grip on the Middle East situation'.[42] Nevertheless, his disregard for the Foreign Office analysis of events in the Middle East remained, and was demonstrated a number of times during the war when the affairs of Palestine and of the Arab world were discussed.

The failure of the attempt to extract a commitment to the White Paper from Churchill's Government coincided with a period of serious weakness in Britain's military position in the Middle East.[43] In so far as Britain had a consistent foreign policy towards the Arab world, since the outbreak of war (and until the defeat of Rommel in late 1942) that policy was first and foremost to maintain British bases in the Middle East and to minimise the threat to those bases posed by internal Arab unrest. This meant accomodating those Arab demands that could be reasonably accomodated, and in this context the White Paper had become the cornerstone of British policy in the Arab world. While the White Paper did not satisfy all the Arabs' demands, reference was continually made to it as a token of how far Britain had gone, in the face of opposition (Zionist, in this case), to satisfy them. The Cabinet's ban on unnecessary reference to White Paper policy, and its refusal to make a forthright commitment to it, meant that the Foreign Office had lost an important instrument of its Middle East diplomacy. In its internal discussions on how best to improve Britain's perilous position in the Middle East, the Foreign Office now decided that any political gesture to Arab opinion would be useless. Only a major concession, 'going far beyond the terms of the White Paper' could have had any real effect,[44] but not even Chamberlain's

C3/1, 3 January 1941, Cab 21/1182). When Eden visited Cairo in October 1940 the M.E.(M) Committee was not shown the cables Eden sent back until Amery and Lloyd jointly protested to Churchill. (Amery and Lloyd to Churchill, 24 October 1940, *ibid*.) Amery frequently wrote in his diary of the futility of the Committee's meetings. The Middle East (Ministerial) Committee never approached the sort of influence which the Middle East (Official) Committee enjoyed. In July 1941 it was finally disbanded.

[41] Amery Diaries, 30 June 1940.

[42] P. Cosgrave, *Churchill at War*, Vol.1 (London, 1974), p. 332.

[43] On 26 August 1940 the Cabinet approved the evacuation of Service families from the Middle East (WM 234(40), Cab 65/8).

[44] Bagallay minutes 17 July 1940, FO 371/24549 E2283. Seymour, R.A. Butler, Cadogan and Halifax endorsed Bagallay's argument.

Government had considered totally abandoning the Jewish National Home, and Churchill clearly would not either.

In mid-1940 only Lord Lloyd felt that something could still be achieved by further talks with the Arabs over Palestine. Lloyd was generally considered to favour the Arab cause in Palestine,[45] and there is evidence that he felt that he could come to terms with the Mufti or at least with other leading members of the Arab Higher Committee.[46] In June and July 1940, while the Cabinet debated its own commitment to the White Paper and its willingness to make a public reaffirmation of it, Lloyd encouraged a private initiative designed to make contact with members of the Higher Committee in Baghdad in order to establish their terms for an accommodation with the British Government. In May Colonel S. Newcombe, an Arabist who had been associated with Lawrence during the First World War, offered his services to the Colonial Office to try to persuade members of the Higher Committee whom he knew personally to accept Britain's Palestine policy.[47] Initially the Colonial Office wanted to reject the offer, but nothing was done before the change of government. After

[45] One can only speculate on Churchill's motives in appointing Lloyd to the Colonial Office for their sympathies on Palestine were diametrically opposed. Most probably the appointment was meant to reassure both the Conservative Party and the Arab world that there would be no immediate radical initiatives on Palestine policy. (A Labour member of Churchill's first War Cabinet, Arthur Greenwood, later recounted to a member of the Jewish Agency in London that 'In 1940, when the Prime Minister had asked them [anti-Zionist members of Cabinet] to join the government, they had asked about Palestine'. (Protocols of the Jewish Agency Executive, London, 4 October 1943, C.Z.A. Z4 302-27)). Although Lloyd was widely considered to be pro-Arab he had made a favourable impression on Zionist leaders. Both Ben Gurion and Weizmann, after meeting Lloyd on 15 May 1940, a few days after his appointment, considered the new Secretary of State to be straightforward and not unsympathetic. Weizmann then wrote that Lloyd was a 'friend of the Arabs and not an enemy of the Jews' (G. Cohen, *Churchill ve'She-elat Eretz Yisrael* (Jerusalem, 1976), p. 31, n.39). More significantly, there is evidence that Lloyd shared Churchill's interest in a solution to the Palestine problem in the context of an Arab federation (see below).

[46] Lloyd was certainly more favourably disposed towards the Mufti than most people who had dealings with Palestine. After meeting him in 1937 Lloyd wrote: 'The Mufti and I are now very old acquaintances, and though both his nature and circumstances have conspired to drive him into extremism I still do not think him so intractable and evil as do his many critics here. He has once or twice at different times listened to reason at my hands and faithfully carried out his pledges to me. . .' (C.F. Adam, *The Life of Lord Lloyd* (London, 1948), p. 275). Furthermore in 1938 he had already attempted to find a solution to the Palestine problem through the 'honest brokerage' of Nuri Said, when he attempted to bring Nuri, Weizmann and Ben Gurion together in October of that year during the discussions on partition (N. Rose, *Gentile Zionists* (London, 1973), p. 170).

[47] All the major Colonial Office files on the Newcombe Mission remain closed, and the account presented here is based on scattered references in official files dealing with other matters, the memoirs of Newcombe's interlocutors in Baghdad, and secondary sources. Lampson described Newcombe in his diaries as 'perhaps not unnaturally very pro-Arab and intensely anti-Zionist over Palestine. I should say rather a good fellow'.

Lloyd became Secretary of State Newcombe was sent to the Middle East (under the auspices of the British Council, of which Lloyd had been chairman prior to becoming Colonial Secretary) with an official task related to British Council schools in Baghdad but with the confidential, and ostensibly limited, task of influencing through personal contacts and bribery, the Iraqi media and important personalities towards a less anti-British stance.[48] However, it appears that Newcombe had also been personally briefed by Lord Lloyd – he was to contact Jamal al-Husayni and Musa Alami,[49] both members of the Arab Higher Committee, and discover on what terms the A.H.C. would be prepared to abandon its anti-British campaign in Iraq and accept the White Paper on Palestine.[50]

If Newcombe did in fact have this third task, and subsequent events suggest that he did, the High Commissioner in Palestine was not informed of it. MacMichael briefed Newcombe when he visited Jerusalem en route to Baghdad, and impressed upon him the Palestine Government's policy of rebuilding Palestinian Arab politics gradually and of tying constitutional development to the growth of moderate Arab political circles.[51] At the same time, the Cabinet in London had resolved on 3 July (in the debate on the reply to Nuri's démarche of May), to restrict all references to the White Paper, and the Colonial

(Lampson Diaries (mss), 14 June 1940, p. 147(verso), Middle East Centre, St. Anthony's, Oxford.) For Newcombe's original offer of aid to the Colonial Office, cf. Newcombe to MacDonald, 8 May 1940, CO 733/428//75986/2(40).

[48] CO to HCr No. 508, 22 June 1940, FO 371/24549 E2152.

[49] Musa Alami, 1897-1984, scion of one of Palestine's leading Arab clans, graduate of Cambridge, close friend of Lord Lloyd's Private Secretary C. Eastwood, employed by the Palestine Government until 1937 when he was dismissed for his political activities and expelled from Palestine. Member of the Palestine Arab delegation to the St.James Conference in 1939. Permitted to return to Palestine in early 1940 as a result of MacDonald's personal intervention (minutes in CO 733/428//75986/2 Part 1 (1940)). Left Palestine for Iraq at the time of Newcombe's visit there, returning only in August 1941. According to Security Intelligence, Middle East (S.I.M.E.) he broke with the Mufti after the latter's flight to Persia in May 1941 (S.I.M.E. Summary to M.E.I.C. Summary No. 606, 13 September 1941).

[50] In an account of the talks with Newcombe which he gave in 1943 or 1944 to the Office of the Minister of State in Cairo, Alami stated that: 'Colonel S.F. Newcombe was sent to Iraq by Lord Lloyd with instructions to get in touch with the Palestinians and other Arab leaders there with a view to arriving at a solution of the Palestine question and the Arab attitude with regard to the White Paper' (FO 921/151). Twenty-five years later Alami gave his biographer a slightly different version of the talks: '[Newcombe] had come charged with a mission from Lord Lloyd. . .Newcombe's instructions, which he produced when called on . . .Nuri Said and was asked for his credentials, were to contact two named Palestinian Arabs, Musa Alami and Jamal Husseini, and to explore with them the possibility of modifying the White Paper policy so that the Higher Arab Committee could be brought to accept it' (G. Furlonge, *Palestine is My Country* (London, 1968), p. 127).

[51] HCr to CO No. 580, 23 June 1940, FO 371/24549 E2152.

Office now instructed Newcombe (already in the Middle East) to make only the vaguest references to that policy in his forthcoming talks in Baghdad.[52] However originally conceived, Newcombe's mission was now changed and strictly limited to quietly impressing upon any members of the Arab Higher Committee whom he was to meet that the British Government would proceed with the White Paper's constitutional provision when circumstances permitted. Even this much represented the hopes of the Foreign and Colonial Offices and not, as was now clear in London, the consensus of Cabinet opinion.

Newcombe arrived in Baghdad on 18 July[53] and began talks with Musa Alami and Jamal al-Husayni, with Nuri Said and the Saudi Minister Sheikh Yusuf Yasin as observers. Despite the repeated instructions (after the Cabinet decision of 3 July) that he avoid any promise of concessions to the Arabs, Newcombe very considerably exceeded his official brief. Together with Nuri and Jamal al-Husayni he drew up a plan whereby Iraq would enter the war on the side of the Allies, and the Arab Higher Committee would accept the White Paper, on condition that a total amnesty be declared and 'a start to self-governing institutions' be made 'as soon as possible'.[54] (Subsequent accounts strongly suggest that Newcombe agreed to the *immediate* implementation of the 'constitutional clauses' and not just implementation 'as soon as possible'.[55]) Whether this was to apply to paragraph

[52]CO to HCr No. 560, 4 July 1940, *ibid.*

[53]Cohen dates Newcombe's talks in Iraq prior to Nuri's demarche of 25 May, (Cohen, *HaCabinet HaBriti*, p. 14, no.16) which obscures the significance of the Newcombe Mission. The Mission took place *after* the Cabinet had decided on its reply to Nuri and in contradiction to the nature of that reply. The terms which Newcombe negotiated in July incorporated demands which far exceeded those made by Nuri in May.

[54]Newton to FO (for Lloyd) No. 409, 2 August 1940, FO 371/24549 E2152. Newcombe only hinted in this telegram at the Iraqi offer of military cooperation and subsequent FO files on the Newcombe mission (FO 371/24549 E2413/2029/65), like CO files, remain closed. However some indication of their probable content is given in M. Khadduri, *Independent Iraq from 1932 to 1958* (London, 1960): 'The Iraqi Government decided, in August, that in return for such settlement it would make a formal declaration of war on the Axis powers and place one-half of its forces (two divisions) at the disposal of the Middle East Command for service outside Iraq. Nuri told the present writer [Khadduri] that he left for Cairo to communicate this decision to General Wavell, and the whole arrangement was referred to London, but there was no reply from the British Government' (p.171). Newcombe also informed London that settlement with the Mufti would ensure Iraqi participation in the war (Lampson to FO (Newcombe for Lloyd) No. 962, 23 August 1940, CO 733/426//75872/85).

[55]In Alami's account to the Minister of State's Office in Cairo he stated that there was to be 'one alteration' of the White Paper – 'that the constitutional clauses should be implemented immediately instead of at the end of the first five year period' (FO 921/151).

34

10(4) or to all the constitutional provisions of the White Paper remains unclear. As the amnesty was to include the Mufti and Jamal al-Husayni, it would seem that the Husayni faction (contrary to the Government's policy) was to be allowed to play a dominant role in the 'self-governing institutions'. When Newcombe left Baghdad, both Nuri and the Arab Higher Committee felt that the major concessions which they had demanded in 1939 were about to be made.

When Newcombe cabled a very brief outline of his talks to London on 2 August[56] they were dismissed as being nothing more than 'the maximum Arab demands which we have heard a hundred times before'.[57] Although full details of Newcombe's negotiations were not yet known to the Foreign Office, it was clear that he had disobeyed the instructions issued after the Cabinet decision of 3 July, and the Eastern Department expressed the hope that Newcombe would be sent somewhere 'where he could do less harm'[58] and that the episode be forgotten. However, Sir Basil Newton (who, all sources agree, was kept closely informed by Newcombe of the progress of the talks) immediately afterwards sent a lengthy cable in support of a plea by Lampson from Cairo in July for the immediate implementation of the constitutional provisions of the White Paper, and in general support of the terms agreed to by Newcombe in his talks. As the ambassador endorsed the concessions that Newcombe had advocated, the Foreign Office now became concerned that unauthorised promises had been made during the Newcombe talks which would only raise Arab expectations, and at an inter-departmental conference (between the Foreign Office, Colonial Office and Air Ministry) it was resolved that Newcombe be banned from returning to Iraq.[59]

Shortly after Newcombe's visit, Nuri mooted the possibility of an Arab conference to discuss Syria and Palestine, and made it clear that the Arabs would feel free to consult Italy and Germany if necessary.[60] Nuri was exploiting Britain's weakness in the Middle East at that stage of the war, and in talks with Lampson in Cairo he also demanded that Palestinian ministers, rather than Heads of Department be appointed immediately.[61] When Lampson protested that this went beyond the terms of the White Paper, Nuri replied that 'circumstances

[56]Newton to FO (Newcombe for Lloyd) No. 409, 2 August 1940.
[57]Eyres minute, 5 August 1940, FO 371/24549 E2152.
[58]Ibid.
[59]Bagallay minute, 9 August 1940, ibid.
[60]Newton to FO No. 381, 25 July 1940, CO 733/426//75872/85(40).
[61]Lampson to FO No. 940, 19 August 1940, CO 733/426//75872/85.

had changed since the White Paper and we were practically alone in the world'.[62] From Saudi Arabia, the British ambassador Stonehewer-Bird reported that Ibn Saud was attempting to extract concessions by different means, advising Britain that it should avoid an Arab approach to the Axis powers by deciding now on the future fate of the Arabs.[63]

These cables from the Middle East reached London as the Foreign Office was formulating its response to the recommendations of Newton and Newcombe for major concessions. Although the reactions of the Colonial and Foreign Offices to the full details of Newcombe's talks (when they became known) are on closed files,[64] it must have appeared in London that H.M. representatives in Cairo and Baghdad (together with Newcombe) were spending more time advocating maximum Arab demands on Palestine to the British Government than they were devoting to the task of explaining British policy to the governments to which they were accredited.

Newcombe's negotiations in Baghdad, the recommendations of Lampson and Newton, Nuri Said's new demands going beyond the White Paper and Ibn Saud's demand that Britain make an immediate decision on the Arabs, revived in Whitehall the debate on Middle East policy that had taken place a month earlier. But now, in the autumn of 1940, the Colonial and Foreign Offices were doubly constrained in determining Britain's response. The decisions taken a year earlier against capitulating to the Husseini faction of the A.H.C., adopting instead the High Commissioner's gradualist approach of creating a new political reality in Palestine by nurturing the fragile circles of Arab moderates, had acquired by 1940 an aura of established policy which could not easily be overturned. This fact would have made any concessions to the Higher Committee which went beyond the White Paper extremely difficult, even disregarding Churchill's probable opposition to such a step. This too was made clear in the reply to Newton.[65] The remaining possibility was to make a cautious start on implementing the constitutional provisions of the White Paper by appointing a few Heads of Department. But the

[62]*Ibid.*

[63]Stonehewer-Bird to FO No. 189, 16 August 1940, *ibid.*

[64]The minutes relating to the drafting of a reply to Newton and Nuri Said are on E2413/G, which remains closed (cf. Seymour minute, 21 August 1940, FO 371/24549 E2283). However the minutes recorded when Newton's telegrams Nos. 408 & 409 arrived in the FO are open (E2283) as is the text of the FO reply to Baghdad.

[65]FO to Newton No. 418, 20 August 1940, FO 371/24549 E2283.

36

Cabinet had ruled on 3 July against such a step and Newton was told (as he had been five weeks earlier) that this ruling could not be modified.[66]

These instructions from London, repeated to all British diplomatic posts in the Middle East, finally resolved the question of a settlement with the extremist remnants of the Arab Higher Committee. After August 1940 there was no further consideration of dealing with the Higher Committee, and after the Mufti's flight to Italy and then Germany in 1941 the question was no longer relevant. The instructions, moreover, marked the limits of the Foreign Office's success in finding a path between Churchill's opposition to the White Paper and Arab (or at least Iraqi) demands for concessions, in a period when Britain's strength and prestige in the Middle East were greatly weakened. As the Foreign Office implied in its communications with Newton, the very most that could be done at that stage of the war was to keep the White Paper policy alive as a formal government commitment.

While such questions of high policy were being deliberated in London, the Palestine Government continued to pursue its policy encouraging cooperative Arab politicians. In a despatch in June 1940, MacMichael reported that the exiles whom the Government had permitted to return had stimulated local political activity and that prominent Arabs opposed to the Husayni faction had held 'many discussions here and there regarding the possibility of forming a new party, either independent of the Defence Party or by its whole or partial absorption'.[67] The High Commissioner's advisor on Arab affairs, A.L. Kirkbride, met various Arab personalities[68] in mid-June, and concluded that although it had been resolved not to form a new political party at that stage, there was the nucleus of a movement which would be prepared to cooperate with the British government.[69]

The entire despatch and the developments it described were ignored by the Middle East Department for over a month. Only in the course of responding to representations from Newton, Newcombe, Lampson and Nuri during August did the Colonial Office recognise that there might, in these talks in Palestine, be scope for some sort of gesture to allay the pressure of Arab (and British diplomatic) opinion.

[66]*Ibid.*

[67]MacMichael to Lloyd, 27 June 1940, Despatch, CO 733/426//75872/85(40).

[68]Sulayman Tawqan, the Mayor of Nablus; Shukri Bey Taji, a wealthy landowner; and Sheikh 'Abd al-Qadir Al-Muzaffar.

[69]Kirkbridge to Chief Secretary 19 June 1940, Enclosure to Despatch of 27 June 1940, CO 733/426//75872/85(40).

In mid-August Lloyd wrote personally to MacMichael pointing out
that he sympathised with the request of these politicians for 'some
gesture on the part of the Government', and suggested to the High
Commissioner that informal recognition might be offered to an 'Arab
Advisory Committee . . . a body to be consulted in practice on
matters. . . affecting the Arab community in Palestine. . . This
arrangement would be in no sense a substitute for the constitutional
changes contemplated in the White Paper, but a provisional measure
to meet the practical needs of the situation until it is possible to put the
constitutional changes into effect.'[70]

In a cable unconnected with this suggestion from the Secretary of
State, MacMichael independently and coincidentally suggested the
creation of a mixed Arab-Jewish Advisory Council as a step towards
constitutional development and in place of the Heads of Department
scheme.[71] When he received Lloyd's suggestion of an informal Arab
Advisory Committee as a provisional measure until the Heads of
Department scheme could be implemented, MacMichael attempted
to combine it with his own suggestions by proposing that an informal
council or committee might eventually be given constitutional status
(i.e. a permanent role intended to circumvent the Heads of Department
scheme).[72]

In its reply to Palestine, the Colonial Office authorised MacMichael
to proceed with the appointment of an Advisory Council, by whichever
means he chose, but only as a purely provisional measure until peace
and order had been restored in Palestine.[73] The Colonial Office made
it clear that it did not intend such a Council to be a substitute for any of
the commitments of the White Paper, and in fact Lloyd's personal
commitment to the eventual implementation of the constitutional
provisions was apparent in the wording of the despatch. By relating
the words 'peace and order' to the internal security of Palestine the
Colonial Office had abandoned the delaying tactic employed under
the previous Secretary of State Malcolm MacDonald, when 'peace
and order' was taken to mean the end of the war. Clearly Lord Lloyd,
regardless of Churchill's victory in the Cabinet in July, intended to
revive the Heads of Department scheme as soon as circumstances in
Palestine allowed.

[70]Lloyd to MacMichael, 14 August 1940, Secret and Personal, CO 733/426//
75872/85(40).
[71]HCr to CO No. 809, 24 August 1940, *ibid.*
[72]*Ibid.*
[73]CO to HCr No. 857, 20 September 1940, *ibid.*

Acting on these instructions, MacMichael discussed the idea of an Arab Advisory Council with Sulayman Tawqan (mayor of Nablus), suggesting a large number of economic and welfare issues affecting Arab interests as matters which the Palestine Government hoped to be able to raise with it.[74] At the same time he attempted to forestall any local pressure for the implementation of paragraph 10(4) by conveying to Tawqan the Cabinet's reply to Nuri of 3 July. Despite its ambiguity, Tawqan took this communication to mean that the British Government did intend to proceed with the constitutional provisions of the White Paper after the war and agreed that an Advisory Council might be established in the meantime.[75] Further talks were arranged, but they could not take place until November, after the Fast of Ramadan. Modest as these developments were, they represented the first real progress in the High Commissioner's efforts to foster moderate Arab politics in Palestine. That the Colonial Office (who saw them solely as interim measures prior to the implementation of the Heads of Department scheme) had different objectives did not for the moment matter, and by October 1940 the question of the implementation of the constitutional provisions of the White Paper became inactive on the files of the Foreign and Colonial Offices.

Matters in London, rather than the Middle East, soon brought the question back on to the political agenda. In October 1940 the Cabinet endorsed in principle the concept of a Jewish Fighting Force, and an announcement to the effect was to be made shortly after the American Presidential elections of 5 November. In order to lessen the likely consequences of such an announcement in the Arab world, the Permanent Under Secretary at the Colonial Office, Sir A. Cosmo Parkinson, suggested that steps be taken to appoint Heads of Department at the same time as steps were taken to create a Jewish Fighting Force.[76] Linking the two proposals would not only temper hostile Arab reaction to the Jewish Fighting Force, but might also help overcome hostile Cabinet reaction to the Heads of Department scheme. Lloyd immediately endorsed the suggestion, informing the Middle East Department that he would propose to the Cabinet that the Palestinian Heads of Department be appointed at once, and he began to marshall support amongst members of the Cabinet.[77] No

---

[74] MacMichael to Lloyd, Despatch, 11 October 1940, *ibid.*

[75] *Ibid.*

[76] Parkinson minute, 5 November 1940, CO 732/86//79238(40), and minutes of 6 November, CO 733/426//75872/85(40).

[77] 'I believe Lord Halifax – Mr. Eden – Lord Beaverbrook would agree – I am in close touch with Lord Halifax – on the matter' (Lloyd minute, 5 November 1940, CO 732/86//79238(40). Throughout these events the initiative for linking the two proposals

mention was made of the fact that he had, only six weeks earlier, instructed the High Commissioner in Palestine to proceed with the establishment of Arab Advisory Councils as an alternative, interim measure.

MacMichael was informed that the Colonial Office's interest in the Heads of Department scheme had suddenly been revived by a telegram which, while hinting at the Secretary of State's personal interest in the question, strongly suggested that the Colonial Office would no longer accept MacMichael's own procrastination.[78] In fact, the Middle East Department proceeded to draft a Cabinet Paper calling for the immediate appointment of Heads of Department even before the High Commissioner's reply was received.[79] When MacMichael's reply did arrive the various objections he raised against implementing the scheme at that time were overruled.[80]

Both the Colonial and the Foreign Office (which had suggested that the draft paper be submitted to the Cabinet as a joint memorandum) were very conscious of the opposition that the proposal would meet in the Cabinet, and the draft underwent seven revisions before both Departments were satisfied, on 25 November, that it was ready for circulation.[81] It argued that, as the British Government would shortly announce that it had accepted the Jewish offer to raise military units in America and elsewhere, the time had come to implement the Heads of Department scheme.[82] Linking the scheme to the Jewish Army proposals in fact only influenced the Colonial and Foreign Offices' timing, and their hopes that the scheme would now be acceptable to the Cabinet. Their principal concern was not Arab reaction to the

came from the Colonial Office. The Foreign Office received copies of all relevant correspondence but was not consulted until the Colonial Office had actually drawn up a draft Cabinet paper. The idea of linking the proposals was first mentioned in Foreign Office files on 9 November (FO 371/24567 E2925).

[78] Lloyd to MacMichael, Private and Personal, 9 November 1940, CO 733/426// 75872/85(40).

[79] MacMichael's reply was in effect a surrender to higher authority. HCr to CO, Most Secret and Personal, 12 November 1940, *ibid*.

[80] Minutes by Shuckburgh and Parkinson, 13 November 1940, *ibid*. In a subsequent telegram MacMichael argued that he did not think that there was a good case for linking the announcements on a Jewish Fighting Force and progress on the Heads of Department Scheme: 'I do not think that the Arabs in the least mind how many Jews are recruited under this head, and there is no need to counter-balance it on their account' (MacMichael to Lloyd, Private and Personal, 29 November 1940). This telegram is on a closed file (76021(1940)) but the above extract was quoted in a minute by Downie on 13 February 1941, CO 968/39//13117/15C Part 1 (41)).

[81] Cf. minutes for 13-14 November 1940, FO 371/24565 E2894, and Downie minute, 25 November, CO 733/426//75872/85(40).

[82] Seventh (Revise) Draft(Final), CO 733/444//75872/85(41).

Jewish Army scheme but that the lack of progress on constitutional development would acquire the status of established policy both in Palestine and within the Cabinet, to the detriment of the White Paper as a whole. When war broke out in 1939 the Jewish Agency had proposed a 'truce' over the White Paper (which the Foreign Office had firmly turned down), similar to the *modus vivendi* Churchill obtained in the Cabinet a few months later. In their Cabinet paper the Colonial and Foreign Offices attempted to establish that they did not accept the Jewish assumption that a 'truce' did tacitly exist. The Jewish Agency was a more acceptable target in a Cabinet paper than the Prime Minister, and although departmental minutes make no mention of the fact, it is clear that if the proposal to link the Jewish Army scheme to the start of the implementation of the constitutional provisions of the White Paper had been accepted, the significant target would not have been the illusions of the Jewish Agency but rather the understanding Churchill had reached earlier in 1940 on the non-implementation of those provisions during the war.

However, just when Lloyd and Halifax were ready to present their joint paper for Cabinet circulation, the Colonial Office's administration of the White Paper restrictions on immigration came under serious attack within the Cabinet as a result of the sinking of the S.S. *Patria*. As the announcement on the creation of a Jewish Fighting Force was being held back on other grounds, and as the atmosphere in the Cabinet had turned suddenly hostile to the Colonial Office, they decided to delay circulating the paper.[83]

Lloyd died suddenly in early February 1941, and the loss of his personal interest removed much of the impetus within the Colonial Office for constitutional progress in Palestine. A few days after his death the question of announcing the Jewish Army scheme came up again, and this time the War Office suggested that it be linked to the immediate appointment of Heads of Department.[84] Without Lloyd the Middle East Department split over the issue. Shuckburgh reminded Lord Moyne, Lloyd's successor, that the Zionists had sympathisers in 'the highest quarters', while H.S. Downie strongly supported immediate progress on the constitutional provisions of the White Paper.[85] Moyne put the question to MacMichael in Palestine.[86]

---

[83] An additional consideration in favour of delay was the decision to withhold the immigration quota for October 1940-March 1941, which was announced in December 1940 (Shuckburgh and Downie minutes, 13-14 February 1941, CO 968/39//13117/ 15C Pt.1).

[84] Haining to Shuckburgh, 10 February 1941, *ibid*.

[85] Downie and Shuckburgh minutes, 13-14 February 1941, *ibid*.

[86] CO to HCr No. 232, 17 February 1941, *ibid*.

At first the High Commissioner maintained his opposition to the appointment of Heads of Department. However, a few days later, when he learned that the proposed Jewish Fighting Force would not be excluded from serving in the Middle East theatre, (an exclusion he strongly recommended) he suddenly reversed his stand and called for the immediate appointment of Heads of Department regardless of the hostile Jewish reaction that such a move would inevitably generate in Palestine.[87] MacMichael recognised that the Yishuv's opposition to the White Paper, when combined with the presence of armed Jewish units in or near Palestine, would create a serious problem for Britain after the war. He therefore concluded that Jewish opposition had better be faced at once and that steps should be taken which would irreversibly commit the British government to the creation of a government in Palestine which reflected the existence of an Arab majority.

Ironically, now that the High Commissioner had finally come to accept the Heads of Department scheme, the Colonial, Foreign and War Offices succeeded in convincing Churchill to again delay making any announcement about the Jewish Army, and the prospect which so alarmed MacMichael was averted. The Colonial Office consequently decided against raising the question of implementing paragraph 10(4) 'until [a] favourable opportunity for reconsideration presents itself'[88] – that is, presumably, when the Jewish Army question came before the Cabinet again, six months later. However, when this did happen, in October 1941, the Cabinet decided to abandon the whole scheme in favour of the far less controversial expansion of recruiting possibilities for Palestinian Jews in the British Army in the Middle East.[89] Once this decision had been taken there was no longer any need to counterbalance a concession to the Jews with a start on the constitutional provisions of the White Paper.

While all this was happening in London, MacMichael proceeded with his attempt to form an Arab Advisory Council. After his talks with Sulayman Tawqan in October 1940, the latter reported back that he had had little success in mobilising support amongst Arab notables, most of whom (correctly) felt that the new body would have no power and feared that their cooperation would arouse the hostility of the Mufti's supporters.[90] Nevertheless, MacMichael wanted to

[87]HCr to CO No. 221, 19 February 1941, and No. 245, 24 February 1941, *ibid*.

[88]CO to HCr No . 567, 17 April 1941, CO 733/444//75872/85(41).

[89]WM 102(41)6, 13 October 1941, Cab 65/19.

[90]HCr to CO, Most Secret and Personal, 16 January 1941, CO 733/444//75872/85(41).

continue his efforts and asked for authority to convene 'occasional meetings of selected Arabs of mixed political complexions to discuss some non-political questions' with the government.[91] As both he and Sulayman Tawqan had failed to attract the support of non-Defence Party politicians, MacMichael wished to keep these talks as informal as possible. The Colonial Office endorsed his plans[92] and during 1941 two such meetings were held between invited Arab notables and MacMichael (together with members of the Executive Council, District Commissioners and [British] Heads of Departments). The meetings were indeed non-political, discussing soil erosion and food production, and were well attended.[93] However, this experiment in cooperation between the Palestine government and leading Palestinian Arab notables achieved little towards the High Commissioner's goal of establishing an Arab Advisory Council. MacMichael's reluctance and inability to offer any meaningful positions of power combined with, and no doubt in part caused, a general reluctance on the part of any serious Arab politician, beyond the discredited Defence Party, to participate, and the meetings were not resumed.[94] Thus by the end of the first three years of the White Paper there had been no real progress towards either implementing the constitutional provisions of that policy or establishing Advisory Councils as an alternative.

The military events of 1942 did not allow for significant political initiatives in Palestine, and when Downie was transferred from his post as Head of the Middle East Department in mid-1941, paragraph 10(4) lost its last active champion within the Colonial Office. The Colonial Office resolved in early 1942 to keep its commitment to the Heads of Department scheme formally alive and to instruct MacMichael to abandon his efforts to create an Advisory Council. However, when the High Commissioner visited London in April 1942 for formal talks with the Colonial Office on Palestine's future, neither the Heads of Department scheme, nor any other of the constitutional provisions of the White Paper were even discussed.[95]

In defending his reservations on the question of constitutional development, MacMichael had always argued that the Arab population of Palestine, as opposed to their politicians and those of the

[91]*Ibid.*

[92]CO to HCr, Most Secret and Personal, 30 January 1941, *ibid.*

[93]Minutes of these meetings in March and June 1941 are on CO 733/444//75872/114(41).

[94]There are no subsequent 75872/114 files for 1942 and 1943.

[95]Minutes, CO 733/4488//76155(42).

neighbouring states, was concerned more than anything else with the immigration restrictions of the White Paper. Lack of progress on the constitutional provisions of the White Paper made it all the more necessary for the British Government to 'demonstrate the honesty of its intentions in practice' (as a joint Foreign Office – Colonial Office memorandum put it) by enforcing the other major provisions of that policy – land regulations and immigration restrictions.

3

IMMIGRATION POLICY 1939-41

The administration of immigration policy in Palestine was inordinately complex. During the years prior to the White Paper, a body of administrative procedure had grown up which centred on the calculation of 'economic absorptive capacity,' that is, the extent to which Palestine could absorb Jewish immigrants in any one period without causing disruption to the general economy. This formulation had been established by Churchill as Secretary of State for the Colonies in 1922, and was the sole restricting factor on Jewish immigration until 1937. In effect, it only limited the immigration of those who would become job-seekers. 'Capitalists,' religious officials, students, dependants, and pensioners were issued with immigration certificates after meeting certain minimal requirements. As a result of a rapid upsurge in Jewish immigration in 1935 and the growing violence of Arab reaction to it, political restrictions were added to the 'economic absorptive' limit. On the recommendation of the Royal (Peel) Commission of 1937, a 'political high level' of 12,000 per year for all categories of Jewish immigrants was imposed, subject to the economic situation. For the first time the High Commissioner acquired the authority to determine the overall number of immigrants and to determine the maximum number of persons to be admitted within any particular category. These new regulations were designed as a temporary measure, and were superseded by the immigration provisions of the White Paper of May 1939.

Under the new policy, an end to Jewish immigration was written into the regulations. During the first five years of the White Paper (starting, for the purposes of immigration policy, from 1 April 1939) a total of 75,000 Jewish immigrants were to be allowed in — which, allowing for the different rates of natural increase, would have brought the Jewish population to approximately one-third of the total population of Palestine. They were to enter at a maximum rate of 10,000 per year, subject to the Higher Commissioner's estimate of the country's 'economic absorptive capacity'. In addition, 'as a contribution towards the solution of the Jewish refugee problem', 25,000 refugees were to be admitted when the High Commissioner was 'satisfied that adequate provision for their maintenance is ensured'. At the end of the five year period Jewish immigration into the National Home was to end 'unless the Arabs of Palestine are prepared to acquiesce in it'. Any illegal Jewish immigration would be deducted from the overall total of

75,000.[1]

This formulation of policy was a radical departure in the history of the Mandate, and resulted in a prolonged period of administrative chaos both in the departments of the Palestine Government concerned with immigration and in the British Passport Control Offices in Europe. Nevertheless the Colonial Office and the Palestine government pursued two clear objectives — all Jewish immigration into Palestine would come to an end within five years unless the Arabs agreed otherwise, and the flood of Jewish refugees attempting to escape Europe had to be kept out of Palestine. When, during the course of the war, it became clear that most Jewish refugees were potential illegal immigrants to Palestine, the emphasis of immigration policy shifted from keeping them out of Palestine to preventing them leaving Europe.

The problem of European (mainly Jewish) refugees, which had been an international concern since the Nazi rise to power in 1933, entered a new phase following the German Anschluss of Austria and occupation of Czechoslovakia. The number of Jews now seeking to emigrate increased dramatically just as those countries which had previously accepted refugees announced they were no longer able to absorb many more.[2] To compound the problem, the Polish and Rumanian governments exerted constant pressure on the international organisations concerned with refugees, and on the British government, to facilitate the emigration of at least part of their respective Jewish populations.[3] During 1938-9 the British government attempted to identify potential areas of immigration in the Colonial Empire outside Palestine which might provide some relief both to the general refugee problem and to the mounting pressure on the immigration restrictions into Palestine. The most promising of the non-Palestine territorial solutions was British Guiana, and in February 1939 an Anglo-American commission went to the colony to examine the possibilities of large-scale European settlement there. Their report, which reached the Foreign Office in late April 1939, was 'decidedly more favourable' than the Foreign Office had expected.[4] Although it recommended only a small experimental start to settlement, with 3,000-5,000 refugees for the first two years, the Refugee Section of the General Department[5] of the Foreign Office concluded that larger numbers

[1] Quotation from paragraph 14 of White Paper on Palestine, Cmd 6019.

[2] A.J. Sherman, *Island Refuge* (London, 1973), chap. 8, *passim*.

[3] FO 371/22539 W16393 and W16119. Quoted in Sherman, p. 229.

[4] FO 371/24089 W6980, minute by Reilly, 1 May 1939.

[5] In 1942 the Refugee Section became a separate Department within the Foreign Office.

could eventually be absorbed and recommended that 'the whole thing should be treated as a question of imperial development'[6] — that is, not just charitable relief. An interdepartmental meeting considered the report on 3 May and it was agreed that 'everything possible should be done to press on as quickly as could be with the proposals made in the Report,' although the Colonial Office insisted that 'the possibility of any funds being provided by His Majesty's Government. . . was completely ruled out'.[7] Instead the scheme was to be financed by the various Jewish relief organisations in the U.K. and America.

However, preliminary discussions with these organisations showed that they had no funds left to finance even the experimental settlement, let alone the entire scheme. Despite the lack of non-public funds, and despite the Foreign Office wish to make 'a really striking contribution to the refugee problem',[8] and therefore to entertain the idea of British financial assistance, the Colonial Office felt that such aid would not be possible and their view was accepted by the Cabinet Committee on Refugees[9] and by the Cabinet itself.[10]

This difference of opinion between the Foreign and Colonial Offices was just one manifestation of the fundamentally different attitudes of the two Departments towards the Jewish refugee problem, its origins and Britain's obligations. During the war their differences led to open conflict, a fact which considerably affected the development of policy. All government departments concerned, however, agreed that a positive official response to the British Guiana scheme would be good tactics — that is, it would temper the expected hostile reaction to the White Paper on Palestine which was due to be released during May.[11] Such a response, stopping short of actual assistance (beyond an offer to help finance the construction of a network of roads in the colony) was prepared urgently, and on 12 May Chamberlain's Government released a White Paper endorsing the recommendations of the Anglo-America commission in favour of the settlement of refugees in British Guiana.[12] Press reaction, however, was not enthusiastic and the scheme was lost in the

[6]FO 371/24089 W6980.

[7]FO 371/24089 W7499.

[8]FO 371/24089 W7439, minute by Reilly, 8 May 1939.

[9]C.R.P. (39) 4th Meeting, 9 May 1939, FO 371/24090 W7564.

[10]Cab 23/99, 26(39)5, 3 May 1939.

[11]C.R.P. (39) 4th meeting.

[12]*Report of the British Guiana Refugee Commission to the Advisory Committee on Political Refugees Appointed by the President of the United States,* Cmd 6014, 12 May 1939.

controversy that followed the release of the White Paper on Palestine five days later. The Jewish relief organisations did not have the funds for it, committed as they were to the maintenance of refugees in Great Britain, while the Zionists were unsympathetic to any diversion of effort from Jewish settlement in Palestine. The scheme was formally dropped following the outbreak of war.[13] In fact, the spread of German control in Europe in 1938-9 and the increasing pace of Nazi anti-Semitic activity caused the refugee problem to grow beyond the proportions of any likely official, governmental solution. As war approached, 'unofficial' solutions on the part of the refugees themselves became widespread. In the majority of cases this meant illegal immigration into Palestine.[14]

It was generally accepted by the British government that by 1939 some 40,000 Jews and 10,000 Arabs had entered Palestine illegally.[15] An initial attempt at organised illegal Jewish immigration began with one ship in 1934, and was resumed more seriously in 1938.[16] Most of the larger ships involved in the traffic were already operating before the White Paper was issued, and in April 1939 the High Commissioner, Sir Harold MacMichael, informed the Colonial Office that 'there are about half a dozen ships hovering off the coast of Palestine waiting to land their passengers'.[17] During the first six months of 1939 approximately 9,000 refugees landed in Palestine illegally.[18] The spectre of a flood of Jewish refugees defeating all the attempts of the Palestine

[13]Emerson to MacDonald, 18 September 1939, FO 371/24095 W13953.

[14]There was also considerable illegal Jewish immigration into Latin America. (Y. Bauer, *My Brother's Keeper. A History of the American Joint Distribution Committee. 1929-1939* (New York, 1974), pp. 286-9).

[15]MacMichael to CO No. 276, 8 March, CO 733/409/75872/55(39).

[16]Y. Bauer, *From Diplomacy to Resistance. A History of Jewish Palestine 1939-1945* (Philadelphia, 1970), p. 61. Details of illegal immigration in 1938 are on FO 371/23246 E794.

[17]HCr to CO, No. 453 in FO 371/24089 W6979. According to lists prepared by the Palestine C.I.D., six boats and one schooner attempted to land their passengers in April. Most were intercepted in the process and driven away by force. The S.S. *Aghios Zoni* succeeded in landing *circa* 600 refugees, of whom 427 evaded arrest. In all, 1,024 illegal immigrants were recorded as landing in April and were deducted from the quotas (C.I.D. Report in CO 733/430//76021/24(40)). In what was certainly a highly exaggerated estimate, the Navy on 8 May 1939 informed the Admiralty that 63 vessels were suspected of being involved in the traffic, each carrying between a dozen and 750 passengers (H.M.S. *Hero,* Haifa to Admiralty, 8 May, U2/4354, CO 733/395//-75113/2/1(39)).

[18]It was very difficult to maintain reliable records and official statistics underestimated illegal immigration by one-third in early 1939. Illegals deducted from the quotas included not only those that were arrested but also those 'whose landings were inferred from reliable evidence'. The Colonial Office was never certain of the exact total of illegals landed, nor of how many had been deducted from the quotas. It was therefore never certain how many of the 75,000 certificates remained unused.

Government to keep them out loomed large just when the British Government was trying to come to terms with the Arab world by offering to restrict and then end Jewish immigration.

The refugees came from 'Greater' Germany, the Balkans and Poland, generally on ships via the Danube, through the Bosphorus and into the Mediterranean. Where possible, they were intercepted and returned to sea — a policy pursued with partial success till April 1939 and unsuccessfully until late 1940 — or simply prevented under fire from landing in Palestine, thereby forcing the ships back into the Mediterranean.[19] In Palestine itself the authorities deported to Europe any individual illegal immigrant who managed to land, whose country of origin could be established and whose government was prepared to accept him back. But as most of the refugees had either been stripped of their nationality on leaving Germany or simply threw their passports away at the sight of a British destroyer, deportation did little to stem the tide.

In April, while Britain was still negotiating the final form of the constitutional provisions of the White Paper, the High Commissioner received permission to announce (prior to the official release of the new policy) that the number of illegal immigrants would be assessed and deducted from the quotas for legal immigrants within the 75,000 overall limit.[20] MacMichael had wanted to suspend all legal immigration during May — a request following logically from the principle of deduction, as the rate of illegal entry during April had exceeded the planned quota for May.[21] The Colonial Office debated the issue at length and the Secretary of State for the Colonies, Malcolm MacDonald, who was concerned with the likely reception of the White Paper,

---

[19] In April the S.S. *Aghios Nicholaos* with 691 persons on board, the S.S. *Assimi* with 473 and the S.S. *Astir* with 694 passengers, were forcibly driven back from the coast of Palestine. The *Assimi*, however, managed to land half its passengers first (J.D.C. Report, 1 June 1939, in FO 371/24092 W10038). In the case of the *Aghios Nicholaos* one refugee was killed and others wounded when the police opened fire on it on 31 March 1939. The Palestine government originally attempted to suppress this information but under the pressure of Parliamentary questions, by Locker Lampson and Josiah Wedgwood, the High Commissioner provided details on 9 May (HCr to CO No. 527 in CO 733/394//75113/2 PQ). As a result of this incident the relevant sections of the Palestine Immigration Ordinance which permitted firing into refugee ships were secretly suspended (Luke minute, *ibid.*). This was not, however, the last time there were casualties as a result of police interception of the ships.

[20] HCr to CO No. 453, 23 April 1939, CO 733/394/75113/2 PQ, and HCr to CO No. 266, CO 733/393//75113. Deductions were made for '(a) number of illegal travellers actually recorded; (b) number of illegal entrants taken into custody; (c) number of illegal immigrants inferred from reliable evidence' (HCr to CO No. 618, 24 May 1939, *ibid)*.

[21] HCr to CO No. 515, 8 May 1939, *ibid.*

eventually resolved that a quota for May 1939 would be issued.[22] This, however, was the last time the Colonial Office was forced to consider the political expediency of appeasing Jewish opinion. Once the White Paper was published, policy on immigration was dictated by its administrative requirements, in pursuit of the desire to placate Arab opinion at least on immigration questions — especially as it could not be satisfied on other issues concerning Palestine.

As a general practice, quotas for legal immigrants were issued for six-monthly periods. However, while the publication of the White Paper was pending, the Palestine Government had released monthly quotas, for April, and, on MacDonald's instructions, for May. After the publication of the White Paper on 17 May, the overall quota for 1 April to 30 September had still to be announced. MacMichael proposed a total of 10,220 certificates, 5,000 of which were for ordinary Jewish immigrants and 4,500 for Jewish refugees.[23] Under the terms of the Mandate, economic absorptive capacity was to be established in consultation with the Jewish Agency, although since 1937 the High Commissioner had had the last word on the size of the quota. Under the terms of the White Paper, the Palestine Government was also obliged to consult representative Arab opinion on the country's ability to absorb Jewish immigrants. This MacMichael had refused to do for the first quota issued under the White Paper, arguing that since 1937 the only 'representative Arab body' — the Arab Higher Committee — had been outlawed by the Palestine Government. Subsequently, that particular provision was forgotten.

While the provisions of the White Paper were being translated into workable administrative regulations for legal immigration, the policy towards illegal immigration — prevention of landing, deportation where possible and release of those who could not be deported — was in need of urgent revision. On 2 May, a division of Navy destroyers was added to the patrol boats of Palestine police engaged in intercepting the refugee boats.[24] However, the policy of turning the boats back did not stop the flow of refugees. Neither did it free the British Government of involvement in their fate. One week after the release of the White Paper, H.M. ambassador to Greece (under whose flag many of the refugee boats sailed) informed the Foreign Office that a serious situation had arisen with regard to the boatloads of refugees most recently turned back from Palestine. Some were in

[22]CO to HCr No. 326, 12 May 1939, *ibid*.

[23]HCr to CO No. 619, 24 May 1939, *ibid.* The balance of 720 certificates were for non-Jews.

[24]CO 733/395//75113/2/1.

50

Greek ports, others, on Greek boats, were sailing aimlessly in the Eastern Mediterranean. The Greek Government, he said, would not allow the refugees into Greece, nor did it have the weight to force the governments concerned to readmit them to their countries of origin. Conditions on the boats were 'reminiscent of the slave trade' and the ambassador warned of the growing interest of the British press in the story.[25] In May 1939 some six to eight boats had either been turned back from Palestine or were heading there. Each carried between 600 and 800 refugees.[26]

As a result of this telegram, and the growing pace of illegal immigration generally, the Colonial Office and the Foreign Office met urgently on 26 May to devise an alternative strategy. They decided to attempt to stop illegal immigration by bringing pressure on the (mainly Balkan) governments concerned to prevent the embarkation of the refugees, and to force them to accept back those that reached Palestine. Those that could not be returned to their countries of origin or embarkation might be interned in Cyprus until they could be sent 'elsewhere' (presumably British Guiana). At this stage most of the Jews passing through the Balkans were of German, Austrian or Czech origin, and in order to encourage the various countries of embarkation to take them back, the Foreign Office proposed offering temporary financial support to those refugees after their return to the port of embarkation.[27] Although this proposal was quickly dropped, the Government launched a major diplomatic campaign designed to stop the flow of refugees through the Balkans towards Palestine. Thus the Rumanian, Greek, Yugoslav, Hungarian and Polish Governments were asked to make entry into their respective countries of 'persons in transit' (i.e. Jewish refugees) dependent on proof of permission to enter a third country, or at least to prevent the embarkation in their ports of any person not possessing a visa for a third country.[28] The Bulgarian Government was similarly approached in early July[29] as were other governments in the months that followed.

As the bulk of the traffic either moved through or originated in Rumania, the Foreign Office was concerned when the Rumanians replied that while they were willing to help with traffic originating in Rumania, under international law they could not interfere with traffic

[25]Sir S. Waterlow to FO No. 224, 23 May 1939, FO 371/24090 W8689.

[26]'Summary of Information Available', 26 May 1939, *ibid*.

[27]Minutes of meeting, 27 May 1939, FO 371/24090 W8689.

[28]FO to Sir R. Hoare (Bucharest) No. 248, 27 May 1939. Repeated to Athens, Belgrade, Budapest and Warsaw. FO 371/24090 W8689.

[29]Rendel (Sofia) to FO No. 66 (Saving), 8 July 1939. FO 371/24092 W10557.

on the Danube that originated further up river,[30] an excuse which the Foreign Office felt was 'plausible, but. . . reveals an absence of any wish to collaborate with HMG to stop this traffic'.[31] In fact, after 1939 a growing proportion of the passengers on the refugee boats were Rumanian nationals,[32] and, as the British consul in Galatz said ' . . . the Rumanian authorities are guilty, not merely of permitting but of encouraging and joining the trade'.[33] This was true of the Balkan states in general. They were not keen to interrupt the flow of Jews out of their own territories, and often intercepted refugee boats in order to load more Jewish refugees onto them. The Colonial Official responsible for Palestine immigration affairs, J.S. Bennett described the problem facing Britain accurately: 'There is scarcely a Government in Europe that has not *something* to gain by winking at the organisation within its territory of illegal immigration into Palestine.'[34] Not surprisingly, the diplomatic campaign had little immediate effect on the influx of illegal immigrants in mid-1939. MacMichael reported an increase in illegal landings in Palestine and warned that Arab reaction would be hostile and perhaps violent. His remedy was to revive his earlier recommendation to suspend all legal immigration under the White Paper 'unless and until the illegal traffic stops'.[35]

Rejecting the total suspension of legal immigration as a likely spur to the illegal traffic, the Colonial Office approved the suspension of quotas for the forthcoming half-yearly quota period only (September 1939 to March 1940) and stated that the situation would be reviewed again at the end of that period. But as an immediate deterrent to illegal immigration, the Colonial Office also decided that henceforth all illegal immigrants would be interned in a camp to be set up in some British colonial territory, 'preferably a small island where their control would be easier'.[36] This was designed to replace the policy of releasing in Palestine all those illegal entrants who had been arrested but could not be deported. As originally conceived, internment was not meant to be punitive, however it quickly became apparent that no site outside Palestine would be available and that consequently any internment camp would have to be in Palestine itself.[37] But as the

[30]Hoare to FO No. 144, 31 May 1939. FO 371/24091 W8850.
[31]Randall minute, 14 June 1939, *ibid*.
[32]FO Memorandum, FO 371/24091 W9953.
[33]H.M. consul, Galatz to Hoare, Bucharest, 17 June 1939, *ibid*.
[34]Bennett minute, 22 June 1939, CO 733/396//75113/38(39).
[35]HCr to CO No. 796, 5 July 1939, FO 371/24092 W10753.
[36]CO to HCr No. 498, 8 July 1939, CO 733/395/75113//3/2/5(39).
[37]CO 733/395//75113/2/5(39) *passim*.

52

refugees 'might consider a Palestine concentration camp preferable to a German one' it was decided that 'conditions in the concentration camps, while humane, must not be comfortable, and they cannot be treated as ordinary refugee camps'.[38]

When the decision on internment camps was referred back to the Secretary of State, MacDonald refused to authorise punitive camps. All that he was prepared to allow was the establishment of a temporary camp at Athlit in Palestine to hold 1,700 illegal entrants, leaving its nature unspecified.[39] The High Commissioner, however, was strongly opposed to establishing any camp at all in Palestine, pointing out that the one authorised at Athlit would not have any deterrent value, and that with over 5,000 already at sea, provision would in any case have to be made for an eventual 10-20,000 illegal immigrants. He strongly advocated that those immigrants who could not be deported back to their country of origin or embarkation should be diverted to camps outside Palestine before they reached its shores, and he persisted in his approach despite the difficulties the Government was having in finding a likely site for such a camp.[40] Such differences within the Colonial Office and between it and the High Commissioner remained unresolved during 1939. The outbreak of war and subsequently the freezing of the Danube caused a drop in the illegal traffic and allowed the Colonial Office to suspend the matter of internment camps for the time being.

By the end of July diplomatic representations had been made to twelve Balkan, Latin American and Mediterranean governments whose territories, ships, documentation or nationals were involved in the illegal traffic. Countries of transit were asked to refuse transit visas, countries whose consuls (generally Latin American) granted nominal visas which allowed their holders to leave Europe were asked to stop doing so, countries under whose flags the ships engaged in the traffic sailed were asked to deregister them, and countries whose ports were used were asked to create administrative difficulties for the ships concerned.[41] Most of the pressure was, in fact, placed on Rumania, and British financial assistance to that country was made conditional

[38]Minutes of Inter-departmental Committee on Palestine Illegal Immigration, 10 July 1939. FO 371/24092 W10993.

[39]CO to HCr No. 524, 14 July 1939, CO 733/395//75113/2/1(39). His Parliamentary Under-Secretary of State, Lord Dufferin and Ava, was prepared to be bolder. He recommended the death penalty for anyone involved in organising the traffic (Dufferin minute, 13 October 1939, *ibid*).

[40]HCr to CO No. 908, 28 July 1939 and No. 878, 19 July 1939, *ibid*.

[41]Memorandum by J. Carvell, Refugee Section, 15 February 1940. FO 371/25293 W2500.

on Rumanian cooperation.[42] This was now forthcoming. Consequently when the High Commissioner announced on 28 July the capture of the S.S. *Colorado* with 363 illegals aboard,[43] the Colonial Office felt it was now possible to implement the new, tougher policy and instructed that the refugees be held until they could be deported back to their countries of origin.[44] Such resolve could not be matched by action. Their country of origin could not be determined as the Rumanian authorities had themselves confiscated the refugees' documents before they left Rumania, and as there were no facilities yet available for internment, there was no alternative but to follow previous procedure and release the refugees in Palestine.[45] The High Commissioner then gave a further reason why the refugees could not be deported: any attempt to do so, he informed London, would provoke large scale and violent disorder in the Yishuv.[46]

The Colonial Office suspected that MacMichael was attempting to force the Government's hand on the question of detention camps in Palestine, and insisted that the deportations be carried out with the use of whatever force was necessary. Otherwise, they argued, 'it would appear that any serious attempt to deal with this abuse must be abandoned'.[47] MacMichael again replied that such a policy would provoke 'armed rioting and outrages. . . and the use of force in suppressing them may give rise to a considerable number of casualties'.[48] On 20 August MacMichael, in London on leave, attended a joint meeting of the Foreign and Colonial Offices and succeeded in impressing his view on the officials concerned. They became alarmed at the possibility that 'riots, casualties and pathetic scenes over deportations' would turn British public opinion against the whole White Paper policy.[49] The High Commissioner was consequently ordered to proceed according to previous policy and to release the *Colorado*'s passengers[50] and those of three further refugee boats which arrived during September.[51]

[42]FO to Le Rougetel No. 379, 28 July 1939, FO 371/24092 W11085.

[43]HCr to CO No. 908, 28 July 1939, CO 733/395//75113/2/1(39).

[44]CO to HCr No. 576, 31 July 1939, *ibid.*

[45]HCr to CO No. 945, 4 August 1939, *ibid.*

[46]HCr to CO No. 976, 10 August 1939, *ibid.*

[47]CO to HCr No. 607, 11 August 1939, *ibid.*

[48]HCr to CO No. 998, 16 August 1939, *ibid.*

[49]Minutes of meeting, 20 August, FO 371/24093 W11580.

[50]*Ibid.*

[51]The *Tiger Hill* with 1402, the *Neomi Julia* with 1123, and the *Rudnitchar* with 368 passengers. The *Tiger Hill,* after having been fired on by a police launch and sustaining

The division of destroyers (which, since early May, had been employed on the task of intercepting and turning back the refugee boats) was withdrawn on 7 August. The Government, both in London and in Palestine, had therefore reached a complete impasse in its campaign against illegal immigration. Illegal immigrants whose boats succeeded in reaching Palestinian territorial waters could only be landed, deducted from the overall quota of 75,000 and released. Bennett again summed up Britain's dilemma: 'The root of the trouble is that, once these people are on board their ships, they have literally nothing to lose but their lives, which they know we will not and cannot take. Their blackmail, if pursued to the full, cannot fail.'[52] Within six weeks of the release of the White Paper, the Colonial Office began to lose faith in its ability to enforce its provisions on immigration. As Sir A. Cosmo Parkinson (Permanent Under Secretary at the Colonial Office) said: 'I am doubtful whether, with all the forces which are arrayed against us, we shall succeed in the struggle against illegal Jewish immigration into Palestine.'[53]

Following the suspension of legal immigration in mid-July, MacDonald suggested to the High Commissioner the terms of an agreement with the Jewish Agency — if the Agency withdrew support from illegal immigration then legal immigration could be resumed and a supplementary quota (drawing from the 25,000 refugee certificates available under the White Paper) might be issued to help cope with the sudden flood of refugees.[54] MacMichael strongly opposed any 'deal' with the Agency, arguing that it would cause a total loss of face with the Arabs and would confirm the Jews in their 'tactics'.[55] His reply, which was heartily endorsed by the Middle East Department of the Colonial Office, confirmed the Government's attitude to any suggestion of cooperation with the Jewish Agency on the question of illegal immigration, at least till the reassessment that occurred in early 1942 after the sinking of the *Struma*.

It was, furthermore, consistent with his general policy of undermining the authority and role of the Jewish Agency in Palestine. MacDonald's suggestion on the other hand, was prompted by the belief that the Agency was itself involved in the organisation of the

casualties, including two killed, abandoned its plans for a secret landing and beached itself on Tel Aviv's main public beach. In the ensuing melee 1200 of its passengers were arrested, to be released later, and a further 200 escaped (HCr to CO No. 1099, 3 September 1939, CO 733/395/75113//2/3(39)).

[52]Bennett minute of 15 September, *ibid*.

[53]Sir A.A. Cosmo Parkinson minute, 25 June 1939, CO 733/396//75113/38(39).

[54]CO to HCr No. 529, 17 July 1939, CO 733/395//75113/2/1(39).

[55]HCr to CO No. 867, 18 July 1939, *ibid*.

illegal traffic, or at the very least it could, if it wanted, have suppressed it. The entire question of the origins of the refugee problem and the organisation of illegal immigration was complicated by a contradiction between what the Britain Government knew (from diplomatic, intelligence and police sources), and what it wished to believe.

The first serious report on the organisational side of the problem was prepared by the Palestine C.I.D. on the day the White Paper was published, and reached London in mid-June 1939.[56] It described in detail how refugees in Germany were organised and embarked on the boats which attempted illegal landings in Palestine. The organisers were generally affiliated to one or other Jewish Palestinian organisation, although private operators working for profit were responsible for a significant proportion of the traffic as well.[57] Neither the Revisionists nor Aguda Yisrael, whose involvement in the traffic the report singled out, belonged to the World Zionist Organisation or were represented in the Jewish Agency, which was dominated by the parties of the Left. As the report stated, the Left, through the Jewish Agency, had control of immigration by the legal schedule method, consequently they 'have not yet brought their full resources into play in the illegal field'.[58] The C.I.D. was aware that the Histadrut[59] was in some way involved, but added that 'very little information regarding their organisation has so far been obtained'.[60] In fact, although the Left was also active in illegal immigration, none of the reports from Palestine could establish any official link between the left-controlled Jewish Agency and the illegal traffic, much to the chagrin of the Colonial Office.

The official Zionist movement was in fact split on the question of illegal immigration. Left-wing Zionists, who dominated the major institutions of the Yishuv, saw illegal immigration as both a humanitarian and a Zionist task, increasing the Jewish population of Palestine and circumventing the White Paper. But others within the Zionist movement, including some participants of the 21st Zionist Congress held in Geneva in August 1939,[61] some members of the Jewish

[56] C.I.D. Report, Jerusalem, 17 May 1939. CO 733/396//75113/29(39).

[57] *Ibid.*

[58] *Ibid.*

[59] The General Federation of Jewish Labour, controlled by Mapai and part of the official 'establishment' of the Yishuv.

[60] C.I.D. Report, Jerusalem, 17 May 1939.

[61] Cf. Baffy Dugdale account of debate of 20 August in Rose, *Baffy*, pp. 144-5. Cf. also speeches by Nachum Goldmann and Rabbi Abba Hillel Silver, *Protocols of 21st Congress,* C.Z.A.

56

Agency Executive in Jerusalem,[62] and most of the Jewish Agency Executive in London,[63] were suspicious and during the period 1939-40 opposed to the whole concept of illegal immigration. Such immigration prevented any selection of the immigrants and introduced people who might not be suited to the task of building the Jewish National Home; it absorbed resources which were needed for other tasks at a time of large scale unemployment in Palestine,[64] and exacerbated relations with the British at a time when Zionist strategy was to win the reversal of the White Paper by providing valuable assistance in the forthcoming war effort.

This situation was known to the Foreign Office, the Colonial Office and the Palestine Government, although only the Refugee Section (of the Foreign Office) took it into account when formulating policy.[65] MacMichael knew that the Jewish Agency could not have stopped illegal immigration even if it had wanted to,[66] but the Colonial Office, throughout the war, chose to believe the opposite. Sir John Shuckburgh (Assistant Under-Secretary of State and longest serving Palestine expert of the Colonial Office), Downie and Bennett, considered the failure of the Jewish Agency and of the Zionist movement as a whole to prevent illegal immigration to be evidence that it was not a refugee movement but 'an organised political invasion of Palestine which exploited the facts of the refugee problem'.[67] Although they recognized that part of the refugee traffic was organised by profiteering ship-owners, the bulk of the traffic was, they believed (despite the reports reaching them from British sources overseas, from the High Commissioner and from the Refugee Section

[62]Because of opposition to the traffic from members of the Jerusalem Executive, discussion of illegal immigration was kept within Mapai (Labour Party) forums, where attitudes was far more sympathetic.

[63]The Executive of the Agency in London was frankly hostile to the traffic during 1939-40. As an example of their views, cf. discussion of 30 May 1939, Z4/302/23, C.Z.A.

[64]Cf. discussion of Executive of Jewish Agency, Jerusalem, 1939-40, S25, C.Z.A.

[65]MacMichael understood Jewish ambivalence on the question, and described it well in a narrative despatch to London: '. . . Jewish orthodox opinion at the moment may be said to be torn between conflicting emotions — pity for the desperate state of the new arrivals and embarrassment as to their disposal, accompanied by a deeply-felt wish that they had never arrived to complicate an already difficult situation' (MacMichael to MacDonald, Narrative Despatch No. 4, 9 July - 20 August 1939, CO 935/22). That the Foreign Office understood the difficulties the traffic posed for the Agency is shown by Randall's minute of 7 June 1939, FO 371/24090 W8564.

[66]Mac Michael to MacDonald, Despatch of 31 December, CO 733/410//75871/85 (39)).

[67]Colonial Office — Foreign Office Memorandum, December 1939 - January 1940, CO 733/396//75113/38(40).

of the Foreign Office) a 'deliberate and organised attempt on the part of the Jews to defeat the Policy which the House of Commons has recently approved',[68] a 'political conspiracy. . . prompted by the Zionists. . . to fill Palestine with Jews and secure domination over the country'.[69] Such an approach on the part of the Colonial Office precluded any thought of a 'deal' with the Jewish Agency, as proposed by MacDonald in July 1939, and by the Agency itself in late 1940.

Despite the diplomatic campaign and the suspension of legal immigration, the flow of illegals did not let up in August and September, with 5,125 illegals recorded by the C.I.D. as arriving during those months.[70] Furthermore, as the cases of the three ships which arrived in September showed the new policy of interning the illegals had not proved feasible and their passengers had been released. During the first six month quota under the White Paper (April to September) 11,412 illegals had actually been recorded,[71] and no doubt more had landed unrecorded, compared to the 10,200 legal certificates available for the same period. The issue had become a highly visible one, both in Parliament, where the Colonial Office was frequently subjected to critical comment sympathetic to the refugees, and throughout the Middle East, where Britain's failure to stop the refugees was seen to cast doubt on its general intentions on the White Paper.

As the position of European Jewry deteriorated during 1939, the size of the potential refugee problem grew. This was especially true after the Germans and Russians invaded Poland which had a Jewish population more than five times the size of those of Germany, Austria and Czechoslovakia combined. This fact, together with the difficulties faced before then in controlling the flow of refugees, made it increasingly necessary to construct an administrative barrier between the mass of European Jews who might wish to escape Europe and come to Palestine, and the 75,000 immigration certificates which the Government had promised the Arabs would be the limit of future Jewish immigration. The outbreak of war provided an opportunity for erecting such a barrier.

The opportunity to define British policy on the refugee problem in general during wartime came on 25 September when the Cabinet Committee on the Refugee Problem met to consider the instructions

[68]MacDonald to Lazarus, 6 September 1939, CO 733/407//75872/15(39).
[69]Downie memorandum, CO 111/772//60412(40).
[70]C.I.D. (monthly report), CO 733/430//76021/24.
[71]Ibid.

to be given to Lord Winterton, the British representative on the Inter-Governmental Committee for Refugees. The meeting, chaired by MacDonald and attended by representatives of all the major ministries, resolved:

> that as a matter of principle it would be impossibe for H.M.G. to assist in any way the exodus of the nationals of a country with which it was at war, and that H.M.G. could not differentiate between refugees and other German nationals. This would apply to territories under German control as well as to Germany proper.[72]

Two policy decisions derived from this decision on principle. The first concerned the future of the Inter-Governmental Committee, established at the Evian Conference in 1938 to work for a solution of the Jewish refugee problem. At a meeting on 3 October,[73] it was decided that if the Inter-Governmental Committee intended to continue to negotiate with the German government for the emigration of German Jews (which the German Government was keen to achieve),[74] the British representative would withdraw from the Committee. The second concerned the administrative barrier necessary to prevent the White Paper being submerged in a flood of Jewish refugees. It was resolved that in future only Jews outside enemy and enemy-occupied territory would be eligible for the 75,000 certificates for legal immigrants and refugees.

This decision was justified by reference to security and blockade considerations but the main reason for it was the need to reduce as far as possible the number of Jews who could be considered potential, legal immigrants into Palestine.[75] Thus when Russia occupied the Baltic States in mid-1940 — areas which, together with Russian-occupied Poland, included the largest concentrations of Jews in Europe — the Colonial Office approached the Foreign Office with the request that Russia, although in fact a neutral state, might be

---

[72]C.R.P. (39) 6th meeting. Minutes, CO 733/396//75113/47(39).

[73]Minutes, *ibid.*

[74]Cf. p. 3 of minutes, *ibid.*

[75]The Colonial Office subsequently offered a number of additional explanations for the ban. One was that they did not want the Germans to circumvent the economic blockade and 'relieve themselves of so many useless mouths' (Bennett minute, 28 September 1939, CO 733/396//75113/47(39)); another, and more fundamental to Colonial Office thinking was the fear that '... the Jewish Agency may cooperate with the German Government on organising the 'expulsion' of Jews from Poland. . . ' (Bennett minute, 4 December 1939, CO 733/396//75113/46(39). The High Commissioner was actually warned of this 'danger' (CO to HCr No. 981, 4 December 1939, *ibid*). Neither the Foreign Office, with its clearer understanding of German-Jewish relations, nor the Palestine Government, with its knowledge of the Jewish Agency's ambivalence towards illegal immigration, entertained such a possibility.

considered an enemy country for the purposes of Jewish immigration policy.[76] After the imposition of the ban in September, foreign governments were informed that in the event of immigration being resumed after March 1940 (i.e., the next quota period), no Jews who were in enemy or enemy-occupied territory would be eligible, and they were therefore 'advised to institute strict watch of their frontiers against such persons'.[77] A few exceptions to the ruling were allowed but they had no impact on the general course of events, and until it was liberalised in 1942 the ruling played a major role in the campaign to restrict Jewish immigration into Palestine.[78] All immigration from German-controlled Europe was now illegal by definition, and the diplomatic campaign against illegal immigration between 1940 and 1942 concentrated on trying to prevent Jews escaping those areas.[79]

[76]CO to FO, 8 June 1940, CO 733/420//75113/54(40).

[77]CO to HCr No. 733, 30 September 1939, CO 733/396//75113/47(39).

[78]Following further representations by the Jewish Agency on the question of immigrants trapped in Germany at the outbreak of the war, the Colonial Office agreed to allow certificate holders to receive visas outside Germany, and for 169 children between the ages of 12 and 16 (out of a total of 309 children)to whom certificates had been allocated but not yet distributed by 3 September, to proceed to Palestine (CO 733/396//75113/46(39)). A further exception was made in April 1940 when 270 Halutzim from Denmark were also allowed to proceed to Palestine.

[79]Full details of the British campaign to prevent Jews escaping Nazi occupied Europe are not yet open to research, as the most important files concerned are either closed beyond the normal thirty year period (e.g. CO 733/429//76021, Parts 1 & 2 (1940)) or show evidence of having had many documents removed (e.g. CO 733/419//75113 (40) and CO 733/436//75113 (1941-3)). The lengths to which the campaign was sometimes carried is illustrated by the case of illegal immigration via Yugoslavia. Palestine Censorship intercepted correspondence which suggested that the German authorities issued special passports to Jews without the usual 'J' ('Juden') marking so that the Italian and Yugoslav authorities would issue transit visas to them (CO to FO, 4 December 1939, CO 733/396//75113/38(39)). Presumably this ploy was necessary to circumvent the closure of borders to Jews from Germany as a result of British pressure. In order to get around this German move, the British ambassador to Belgrade, Sir Ronald Campbell, was instructed to make 'urgent requests' to the Yugoslav authorities to ensure that when issuing transit visas to Jews the Yugoslavs should take ' . . . particular care that the passports are labelled with the necessary letter "J" and that in every respect they are provided with all the necessary visas and other formalities allowing the bearer to proceed to and disembark in Palestine'. (From reply of the Yugoslav Ministry of Foreign Affairs to Campbell, 19 February 1939, FO 371/25240 W3207). As, by February, no Jews coming from Germany could have had such visas (although some may have had legal immigration certificates), the effect was to close the borders to Jews entirely. It is not, however, clear whether the import of the reference to the 'J' marking was that the Yugoslavs had been asked by the British Government to stamp the 'J' in themselves where the Germans had not done so, or simply to take the absence of a 'J' from passports held by Jews as evidence that the holder was an intending illegal immigrant to Palestine. There is no further documentation on the matter in the FO files, and the CO files on illegal immigration through Yugoslavia (CO 733/429//76021/4(40)) are closed for fifty years — the only CO files relating to a Balkan country to be so treated. Yugoslavia was a country of transit for illegal immigrants from Austria whose departure had been arranged with the cooperation of the Nazi authorities (cf. note 101 below).

During October 1939, the shortage of shipping caused by the outbreak of war made itself felt and illegal traffic dropped to its lowest level for a year.[80] But in mid-October reports were being received that preparations for more sailings were being made in Bulgaria, whose government was not proving responsive to British pressure to prevent illegal immigration.[81] On 27 October information reached London that the S.S. *Rudnitchar,* a boat well known in the illegal traffic, was preparing to sail for Palestine carrying over 450 refugees, with the cooperation of the Bulgarian Government.[82] The Bulgarians had actually loaded some forty of the passengers onto the boat. On 29 October the ship left Varna, and on 2 November the Colonial Office approached the Admiralty with a request that the Navy again involve itself in the campaign against illegal immigration, starting with the interception of the *Rudnitchar.* The Colonial Office wanted the Navy to reestablish a Naval patrol and prevent the landing of the passengers or their transfer to smaller craft outside territorial waters (a practice which allowed the larger vessel to escape). Once intercepted, the Colonial Office asked that the *Rudnitchar* be forcibly returned to Bulgaria.[83]

The Admiralty did not want to take this task upon itself, suggesting instead that the Naval Contraband Control Service be employed to force the ships into Haifa for 'contraband inspection'. Once there, the illegal immigrants, captain, crew and boat, could be arrested for contravening Palestine immigration law.[84] While this correspondence was being conducted, the *Rudnitchar* landed its passengers (on 14 November) and escaped, although 457 of the refugees were arrested.

Then, late in November 1939 the British embassy in Bucharest warned that there were at least 1,300 German Jewish refugees waiting to embark at Sulina, in Rumania, for Palestine. This group was seen as the start of a German-engineered wartime flood of refugees, and the British ambassador warned of the danger of the infiltration of Nazi agents.[85] The Admiralty's resolve to attempt to use the C.C.S. was strengthened by the end of December when the Colonial Office convinced it that a conviction in Palestine courts

---

[80] Only two individuals arrived by sea (C.I.D. report, CO 733/430//76021/24(30).

[81] Rendel to FO, October 1939, various telegrams in FO 371/24095/W14672, 14965, 15040.

[82] Mathieson minute, 7 December 1939, CO 733/395//75113/2/9(39).

[83] Downie to Admiralty, 2 November 1939, CO 733/395//75113/2/2(39).

[84] Admiralty to FO, M/012830 (39), 5 November 1939, FO 371/24096/ W16266.

[85] Hoare to Halifax No. 348 (Despatch), 23 November 1939, and minutes FO 371/24096 W17753.

would be likely once a boat was actually brought into Haifa. Consequently the Admiralty agreed on 30 December to a 'test case,' instructing the Commander-in-Chief, Mediterranean Fleet, to intercept the *Rudnitchar* (which on 26 December had again left Varna carrying refugees) and divert her to Haifa.[86] But once again the Rudnitchar managed to avoid the naval patrols, and landed another 519 illegal immigrants on 9 January 1940, to the considerable chagrin of the Colonial Office.

By late 1939 the repeated failure to prevent boats leaving Europe, to intercept them en route or to deal with the refugees they carried once they succeeded in reaching Palestine was causing inter-departmental tension in London. Worse still, the British ambassadors in Sofia and Bucharest reported a general disbelief in the seriousness of Britain's intentions to curb illegal immigration,[87] while a Palestine Government Immigration Department official reported after a tour of the various countries of transit in the Balkans that it was widely believed that Britain was actually conniving in the traffic.[88] Meanwhile the numbers of refugees waiting in Danube ports for transport out of Europe grew, and the spectre of a German-inspired flood of refugees became more ominous.[89] The Colonial Office strategy in the campaign against the illegals relied increasingly on the cooperation of the Admiralty in using the C.C.S. But attempts to obtain this cooperation had from the beginning been complicated by the interest of the First Lord of the Admiralty, Churchill, and his sympathy with the refugees. Instructions issued by the Admiralty on 30 December agreeing to the use of the C.C.S. in intercepting the *Rudnitchar* had been issued without Churchill's knowledge. When he heard of it, he protested directly to MacDonald that the Navy could not make a practice of participating in the campaign against illegal immigration because of the wartime demands on its resources. Furthermore Churchill had wanted to know 'how you propose to treat these wretched people when they have been rounded up. Where are they to be sent, and what will be their fate?'[90]

In May 1939 Churchill had led the Parliamentary campaign against the White Paper with its restrictions on Jewish immigration

[86] Admiralty to C-in-C, Mediterranean Fleet No. 1110, 30 December 1939, CO 733/395//75113/2/10(39).

[87] Cf., for example, Rendel to FO 99 (Saving), 25 December 1939, FO 371/24097 W19334.

[88] Prosser Report, CO 733/396//75113/38(40).

[89] Hoare to FO, 27 December 1939 (unnumbered), FO 371/24097 W19349.

[90] Churchill to MacDonald, 4 January 1940, CO 733/429//76021/10(40).

and the Colonial Office recognised that in order to ensure the cooperation of the Navy in implementing that policy they would first have to overcome his objections. Thus the Middle East Department consulted Admiralty officials directly in order to gain their help in framing the next request for naval cooperation in a manner that the Lord Commissioners of the Admiralty would be least likely to refuse.[91] The next request came on 18 January 1940 when MacDonald wrote directly to Churchill asking that the C.C.S. make special dispositions to intercept the S.S. *Sakarya* (which had recently left Sulina) and bring it forcibly to Palestine where it was hoped that the courts would impose heavy penalties on the refugees, the ship and its crew.[92] However, the Admiralty refused to cooperate, agreeing only to bring the ship to Haifa should it be intercepted in the course of patrols already scheduled.[93]

Events in the Eastern Mediterranean overtook this rebuff. Independently of the efforts to obtain Admiralty cooperation in London, a naval patrol, on its regular route, intercepted the S.S. *Hilda* on 17 January, and brought it to Haifa with 729 refugees on board. Here at last was an opportunity for the Colonial Office to implement its new policy of taking tough action against a ship and crew while deporting or interning the illegal immigrants it carried. Future action by the government in its war against illegal immigration would depend largely on the success of the Colonial Office in carrying out this new policy.

Thus it was with considerable consternation that the Colonial Office reacted to a telegram from the High Commissioner stating that the new legislation was not yet ready, and that the chances of successful legal action in the Palestinian Courts against the *Hilda* were slim.[94] Reaction within the Foreign Office was extreme, and the Colonial Office was informed that if the Palestine Government failed to take punitive steps against the illegal immigrants on the *Hilda* (which it could not do under existing law) then the Foreign Office would not be able to continue to demand the cooperation of other

---

[91] Bennett-A. Ker (Admiralty) correspondence, and minutes, on *ibid.*

[92] *Ibid.*

[93] Admiralty to CO, 23 January 1940, *ibid.* The instructions which the Admiralty sent to the C-in-C Mediterranean Fleet very specifically ruled out special patrols. Ships suspected of carrying illegal immigrants were only to be challenged if intercepted in the course of ordinary contraband control (Admiralty to C-in-C Mediterranean Fleet No. 849 1116/24, 23 January 1940, *ibid.*).

[94] HCr to CO No. 48, 18 January 1940, CO 733/429//76021/1(40).

governments in suppressing the flow of Jewish refugees out of Europe.[95]

In the same week relations between the Middle East Department and the Refugees Section had been strained over another aspect of the problem. During the winter of 1939-40 the Danube froze and some 3,000-5,000 refugees were stranded on boats in terrible conditions.[96] This was a welcome respite for the Colonial Office, which asked the Foreign Office to prevent the American Jewish charity, the Joint Distribution Committee, from providing relief supplies for the refugees. As Bennett explained on an internal file, if no relief was forthcoming 'their chances of surviving to make the journey to Palestine would have decreased'.[97] The Foreign Office, however, refused to cooperate in what it called the Colonial Office's 'dirty work,' and inter-departmental relations soured even further.[98]

By the end of January the Foreign Office reaction to the failure of the Palestine Government to act on the *Hilda* case, and its refusal to block charitable aid to the refugees frozen up on the Danube, combined with Churchill's obstructionism in the Admiralty, forced the Colonial Office to find a way of compelling the other Departments to cooperate. The matter could have been taken to the War Cabinet for a decision, but during those weeks the Colonial Office was already embroiled in a Cabinet controversy over the implementations of the Land Regulations of the White Paper. No doubt MacDonald did not want to complicate matters further by introducing into Cabinet debates the difficulties of implementing the immigration provisions of the White Paper. The Middle East Department suggested a possible solution to the dilemma.

The High Commissioner in Palestine, when discussing the problems of taking action against the *Hilda* in the courts, had suggested using his executive powers to intern the captain, crew and passengers under Emergency Regulation 15b 'on the grounds of security' (allowing internment without trial for 12 months). He considered this expedient because action against the *Hilda* was necessary but could not be taken via the courts. As justification, however, he intended to cite the effects the refugees had on security,[99] by which

---

[95] Carvell to Downie, 25 January 1940, FO 371/25238 W1371.

[96] Jewish Telegraphic Agency Bulletin, 22 January 1940, C.Z.A. Z4/14/1241.

[97] Bennett's marginal comment on Carvell to Downie, 16 March 1940, CO 733/429//76021/1(40).

[98] Latham minute, 22 January 1940, FO 371/25238 W1087.

[99] HCr to CO No. 56, 20 January 1940, CO 733/429//76021/7(40).

he meant first the threat to internal security created by the likely reaction of Arab opinion to yet another boatload of Jewish refugees, and second the threat to general security since the refugees were enemy aliens.[100] An appeal to security requirements allowed the High Commissioner to circumvent the courts, and as the Middle East Department quickly realised, offered a potential solution to the problems of the Colonial Office too.

The risk that Nazi agents might be infiltrated into the Middle East amongst the illegal immigrants had been mentioned before in official correspondence, and was given a degree of plausibility by the fact, known to the Colonial Office since mid-1939, that the Gestapo often gave assistance to the organisers of illegal immigration in Germany and Austria in accordance with the current German policy of encouraging the emigration of as many Jews as possible.[101] There was no real evidence that agents had infiltrated by this means and up to 1940 the Colonial Office only occasionally referred to the security risk as a justification for the campaign against the refugee traffic. However, after Churchill's refusal to allow the Navy to become fully involved in measures against illegal immigration, the Colonial Office resolved to use all means possible to overcome his lack of cooperation. Thus on 1 February 1940 at a meeting between the Colonial Secretary and the Middle East Department, it was decided that new appeals to the Amiralty would be based on 'the fact that there may be a number of German agents amongst the Jewish illegal immigrants'.[102] The Colonial Office hoped that in war-time this would provide an incontrovertible defence of its policy, and before renewing the formal request for the aid of the C.C.S. Downie had private talks with Admiralty officials who assured him that the security risk would

[100]HCr to CO No. 56, 4 January 1940, CO 733/429//76021/7(40) and HCr to CO No. 80, 29 January 1940, CO 733/429//76021/6(40).

[101]Although originally the responsibility of the German Interior Ministry, from 1938 Jewish emigration came increasingly under the control of the Gestapo and the S.S.. At the same time the early German policy of orderly emigration was replaced by the policy of expulsion, until this policy in turn was replaced by the practice of mass murder. From 1938 to 1940 both the Gestapo and the S.S. attempted to regulate the growing number of organisations involved in illegal immigration, with the dual objectives of getting rid of as many Jews as possible and of exploiting the pecuniary possibilities of the traffic. However, during this period Nazi policy was inconsistent. At the same time as they were attempting to supervise illegal immigration, the Gestapo and the S.S. devoted much energy to disrupting the work of the Jewish relief organisations responsible for emigration, while other Nazi authorities organised anti-semitic (and therefore anti-immigrant) campaigns in the countries of immigration. Cf. A. Prinz, 'The Role of the Gestapo in Obstructing and Promoting Jewish Immigration', Yad Vashem Studies, 2, 1958, 205-18; E. Avriel, Open the Gates! (New York, 1975); J. & D. Kimche, The Secret Roads (London, 1954).

[102]Downie minute, CO 733/429//76012/10.

compel Admiralty cooperation.[103] Consequently the Colonial Office wrote officially to the Admiralty, and MacDonald wrote directly to Churchill, asking that all illegal immigrant ships be diverted to Haifa as a matter of principle due to 'the danger which may be involved to our position in the Middle East by the infiltration of enemy agents in this manner. . '.[104]

However, so vaguely worded a statement was not enough to convince the Admiralty, which replied that the danger of the infiltration of Nazi agents on ships 'carrying Jewish refugees from persecution to Jewish settlements in Palestine was not great enough' to warrant the diversion of ships to intercept them.[105] The use of this terminology (unusual for a Service department) convinced the Colonial Office that the refusal to comply with their request came directly from Churchill, especially as they knew that the Admiralty officials had recommended to the Board of the Admiralty that it agree to cooperate in the measures planned against illegal immigration.[106]

The only options now open to the Colonial Office were to bring the matter to the Cabinet or to actually discover Nazi agents among the illegal immigrants.[107] So far the claim that such enemy agents might exist had been deliberately couched in equivocal terms as none had been positively identified. In order to prepare as substantial a case as possible, the Colonial Office now asked the High Commissioner for whatever hard evidence on the presence of agents he could provide.[108] The reply was disappointing. MacMichael stated that interrogation of the refugees had not produced 'proof confirming suspicions,' i.e., agents. All he could do was to point out the logical possibility of the presence of agents amongst the refugees.[109] The Colonial Office had no alternative but to pass MacMichael's reply on to the Admiralty, which, on 29 April, again refused to use the C.C.S. to intercept illegal immigrant boats except when they were intercepted in the normal course of naval patrols.[110] The Colonial Office subsequently abandoned its efforts to employ the C.C.S., and the relevant file was closed a few days before Churchill became Prime Minister.

[103]*Ibid.*

[104]Downie to Ker, 7 February 1940; and MacDonald to Churchill, 3 February 1940, *ibid.*

[105]Admiralty to CO M. 02530/40, 14 March 1940, *ibid.*

[106]Bennett minutes, 24 February and 16 March 1940, *ibid.*

[107]Bennett minute, 16 March 1940, *ibid.*

[108]CO to HCr No. 201, 16 March 1940, CO 733/429//76021/7.

[109]HCr to CO No. 255, 18 March 1940, *ibid.*

[110]Admiralty to CO M. 06245/40, 29 April 1940, CO 733/429//76021/10.

66

While the debate on the use of the C.C.S. had been in progress the legal measures to be taken against ships which might be brought into Haifa were still being formulated. On 18 March, regulations were released allowing Palestinian courts to impose terms of eight years imprisonment on captain, crew and others organising any boatload of illegal immigrants, to seize any ship of up to 1,000 ton and to levy a fine of £10,000 on any ship over that weight.[111] These were severe punishments, and in order to forestall criticism in the House of Commons, the Colonial Office introduced the new legislation together with a reference to the security risk caused by the infiltration of enemy agents.[112] This was the first time the danger of Nazi agents had been mentioned in the House of Commons in connection with illegal immigration, and it provoked a number of Parliamentary questions. However, when pressed to give the number of interned illegals charged as agents, MacDonald replied that it would be 'undesirable' (for security reasons) to give the exact figures, thus giving the impression that such agents had already been identified, although he knew that this was not so.[113]

During the next six months, the flow of illegal immigration subsided, and with it the pressure on the Colonial Office. It was no coincidence that the issue of Nazi agents was shelved until Colonial Office policy was once more under debate in November 1940.

The question of deporting illegal immigrants — a fixed element in Colonial Office strategy throughout this period — was raised each time a boat was intercepted or landed its passengers. Practical difficulties, however, always frustrated the implementation of the policy. When arrested, passengers were usually without nationality documents so could not legally be returned to their country of origin. On 13 February 1940, when the S.S. *Sakarya* was intercepted (despite the Admiralty's refusal to make special arrangements to do so), the 2,228 passengers still held their passports.[114] The majority came from enemy or enemy-occupied territory and could not be deported, but 180 Hungarians and three from the Baltic States could, and the Colonial Office immediately instructed MacMichael to set about so doing.[115] As with his earlier stand during the debate on the

[111]Palestine Defence Order-in-Council, 18 March 1940, Palestine Gazette Extraordinary No. 994, Supplement No. 2. In September 1940 the 1,000 ton qualification was removed, allowing for the seizure of all ships involved regardless of size.

[112]358 HC/5s/Cols 1960-1962, 20 March 1940. Question by Stokes.

[113]359 HC/5s/Cols 147-148, 3 April 1940.

[114]HCr to CO no 143, 17 February 1940, CO 733/429//76021/11/(40).

[115]CO to HCr No. 176, 9 March 1940, *ibid.*

establishment of internment camps outside Palestine, the High Commissioner favoured the disposal of the refugees without ever bringing them to Palestine. Because of the great sensitivity of the Yishuv on the issue, MacMichael argued (as he had done in August 1939) that once landed it would be impossible to re-embark the refugees and forcibly deport them. Furthermore, unless the Admiralty was prepared to escort the boats back to their ports of embarkation (which it was not) the passengers would no doubt once more attempt to land in Palestine undetected.[116] As the Commander of British Forces in Palestine supported the High Commissioner's estimate of the unrest this policy would cause in the Yishuv, the Colonial Office was once again forced to abandon the idea of deportation (initially to internment camps outside Palestine, but now, once again, back to the country of embarkation) as a major deterrent.

However, in August, after the interception of the S.S. *Libertado* by a Palestine police launch,[117] the Colonial Office again suggested deportation.[118] This was the first time Lord Lloyd, MacDonald's successor as Secretary of State, had met the problem of illegal immigration and he warmly endorsed any determined measures which could be taken against the traffic.[119] But once again the High Commissioner opposed deportation, although this time for humanitarian reasons — during 1940 the situation of the Jews in the Balkans had deteriorated seriously.[120] While the Colonial Office was not impressed with MacMichael's humanitarian concern it did eventually agree to suspend the idea of deportation in this case because of the difficulty of finding the necessary shipping and because the rate of illegal immigration had dropped off substantially during the summer months of 1940.[121] In fact, although some Jewish refugees were returned to their countries of origin during the war, the numbers were small.[122] Of the passengers on the *Hilda* and *Sakarya,* only six were actually deported and proceedings against the rest were abandoned.

In the first twelve months of White Paper restrictions on Jewish immigration being in force some 10,529 legal immigrants and 15,489

---

[116]HCr to CO No. 273, 23 March 1940, *ibid*.

[117]HCr to CO No. 679, 19 July 1940, CO 733/430//76021/26(40).

[118]CO to HCr No. 649, 27 July 1940, *ibid*.

[119]Lloyd minutes on CO 733/430//76021/26(40), *passim*.

[120]HCr to CO No. 783, 16 August 1940, *ibid*.

[121]Luke minute, 21 August 1940, *ibid*.

[122]Draft Annual Report for 1940: in 1939, 43 Jews and 677 non-Jews; and in 1940, 72 Jews and 2,046 non-Jews were deported (CO 733/439//75126(41-43)).

recorded illegal immigrants had reached Palestine. Although the illegal traffic resumed towards the end of 1940, over half the total of Jewish immigrants (including about seventy per cent of the illegals) who were to reach Palestine during the five years of the White Paper immigration provisions, did so in the first twelve months. The circumstances of war and the campaign against illegal immigration made immigration into Palestine increasingly difficult. By August 1940, the High Commissioner had to inform London that of the certificates issued from the current quota (i.e., released in April), only one third of the immigrants had actually reached Palestine.[123]

In view of this lull the Jewish Agency appealed in August 1940 to have the ban on immigration from enemy territory lifted for adult refugees of special standing (community leaders, writers, scientists, Rabbis) to a maximum of 250 and for twenty-five Jewish Agency officials in Germany and Czechoslovakia who had stayed behind to help the last legal immigrants leave for Palestine.[124] Both the Palestine Government and the Colonial Office refused to consider these concessions, citing 'security risk' as excuse, although their records show that their real concern was not fear of Nazi agents but the need to adhere to the structure of policy and regulations that had finally, by the spring of 1940, brought all Jewish immigration into Palestine under control.[125] Thus when in early 1940 the Agency offered to introduce its own rigid security screen for immigrants the Colonial Office rejected the proposal without any internal discussion of its merits.[126]

As central and western Europe was all now enemy and enemy-occupied territory, and the Mediterranean was closed, the only potential source of legal immigration was the Balkans — a prospect which did not appeal to MacMichael. He therefore suggested that the last bi-monthly parcel of 3,000 certificates from the current quota period be withheld, not because of the pace of illegal immigration, but 'until there are prospects of getting the best type of immigrant again'.[127] MacMichael actually informed the Jewish Agency that he considered Balkan Jews to be 'undesirable',[128] while minutes were

[123]HCr to CO No. 1071, 20 October 1940, *ibid*.

[124]HCr to CO No. 830, 29 August 1940, CO 733/420//75113//58(40).

[125]*Ibid., passim.*

[126]Cf. minutes of Agency-CO meeting, 15 January 1940, on FO 371/25240 W2986. No discussion of this proposal has been found in CO files.

[127]HCr to CO No. 761, 10 August 1940, CO 733/419//75113(40).

[128]D. Trevor, *Under the White Paper* (Jerusalem, 1949), pp. 20-1.

circulated in the Colonial Office discussing whether Jews from the Balkans were 'the least desirable type of immigrant' or just an 'inferior type of Jew'.[129] The Colonial Office was also concerned that Arab attention was focussing on the fact that at least 26,000 Jews had entered Palestine in the first of the five years of the White Paper immigration provisions. So, on Lloyd's instructions, the High Commissioner was invited to consider suspending legal quotas for the forthcoming October 1940 to March 1941 quota period.[130] The High Commissioner duly responded by stating that economic circumstances prevented the issuing of any certificates in the next quota period. He did allow some exceptions — a few immigrants with capital and young children whose relatives could support them[131] — but Lloyd instructed him to ensure that these exceptions would be 'limited as strictly as possible'.[132]

The grounds for the suspension of the quota were, in London, purely political (concern for Arab reaction to the number of Jews who had entered Palestine in the past twelve months) and, in Palestine, idiosyncratic (MacMichael's desire to reserve the available certificates for 'good' non-Balkan immigrants). According to the White Paper, the only reasons for suspension were inadequate economic absorptive capacity or excessive illegal immigration. The problem was how to announce and justify the repeated suspension of the quota when illegal immigration was at its lowest level for eighteen months, and when, towards the end of 1940, Jewish unemployment sank 'to an insignificant figure'.[133] This question, however, was submerged by the events of the last few months of 1940 and a major conflict in London between Churchill and the Colonial Office over illegal immigration.

During the summer of 1940, illegal immigration slowed down considerably, and the question of the measures to be taken against it was not pressing. However, in October, German troops began to occupy Rumania, a process which ended with Rumania being added by the British to the list of enemy and enemy-occupied territory from which Jewish immigration was banned.

On 21 September, MacMichael warned the Colonial Office that the inevitable German occupation of the Balkans would probably

[129]Luke and Shuckburgh minutes, 21 August 1940, CO 733/419//75113(40).

[130]CO to HCr No. 756, 22 August 1940, *ibid*.

[131]HCr to CO No. 944, 25 September 1940, *ibid*.

[132]CO to HCr No. 1068, 5 November 1940, *ibid*.

[133]Draft Annual Report for 1940, CO 733/439//75126(41-43).

cause a resurgence of the flow of refugees and that the recently erected structure of legislation against the traffic would not be a sufficient deterrent. As with his previous arguments on deportation, MacMichael again suggested that the refugee boats be diverted at sea before reaching Palestine.[134] In mid-October the resurgence of the illegal traffic of which MacMichael had warned, materialised, and the High Commissioner informed the Colonial Office that five ships with nearly 6,000 refugees were reported to be at sea.[135] The Colonial Office succeeded in persuading the government of Mauritius to accept these refugees for detention under restraint,[136] but the High Commissioner's request that they be diverted at sea before they reached Palestine could not be met because of the time it would take to make the necessary arrangements in Mauritius. On 1 November, the first of the boats referred to by the High Commissioner, the S.S. *Pacific*, with 1062 refugees on board, was intercepted by a Palestine police naval patrol and brought to Haifa. The S.S. *Milos* with 709 refugees was intercepted and brought to Haifa three days later and a third boat, the S.S. *Atlantic* with almost 1800 refugees was expected shortly afterwards.

The Palestine Government answered enquiries from the Yishuv as to the fate of these refugees by stating that they would be deported — not back to Europe but 'south to a safe destination'. Because of the concern for their fate, MacMichael pressed for permission to announce publicly that the destination was Mauritius.[137] In its reply the Colonial Office added a new dimension to its deportation policy. In order to increase the deterrent nature of the deportation, MacMichael was instructed to announce that the destination was Mauritius, that the deportees would be interned there and that after the war they would be permanently banned from entering Palestine.[138] In London, Lord Lloyd recognized that the general policy of deportation should be brought to the attention of the Prime Minister before an announcement was made in Palestine. Thus, in mid-November 1940 Lloyd wrote at length to Churchill setting out the risk that Nazi agents would be introduced amongst the illegals, and detailing the effect that the revival of illegal immigration would have on Arab opinion. He did not, however, mention the punitive prohibition on their future legal

[134]HCr to CO 935, 21 September 1940, FO 371/25242 W11091.

[135]HCr to CO No. 1046, 15 October 1940, FO 371/25242 W11091.

[136]Govt. of Mauritius to CO. No. 297, 17 October 1940, *ibid*.

[137]HCr to CO No. 1142, 6 November 1940, *ibid*.

[138]CO to HCr No. 1093, 9 November 1940, *ibid*.

immigration to Palestine.[139] Even without being aware of this additional measure, Churchill was only prepared to endorse the principle of deportation under certain conditions: 'Provided these refugees are not sent back to the torments from which they have escaped and are decently treated in Mauritius, I agree.'[140]

On receipt of Churchill's reply, the Colonial Office extended its plans and also instructed the governor of Trinidad to construct camps similar to those being prepared in Mauritius, and to await the arrival of deportees from Palestine.[144] Unlike the earlier telegram to Mauritius, this telegram was passed on to Churchill's secretariat, where the Colonial Office specifications for the use of barbed wire and armed guards attracted the attention of Churchill's Principal Private Secretary, J.M. Martin. Martin brought the matter before the Prime Minister, asking him whether he had envisaged the establishment of 'a concentration camp'.[142] Churchill reacted strongly and withdrew his previous approval of deportation, instructing that the refugees awaiting deportation be allowed into Palestine, and that deportation be enforced only in future cases of illegal immigration.[143]

During the exchange of correspondence between Churchill and Lloyd the refugees in Palestine aboard the *Pacific* and the *Milos* were transferred to another boat, the *Patria*, for the trip to Mauritius. Before leaving for Mauritius, the boat remained in the port of Haifa awaiting the arrival of the *Atlantic*, whose passengers were also to be deported on the *Patria*. It took almost two weeks from the time it was first sighted for the *Atlantic* to make its way to Haifa and during this period the forthcoming deportations caused growing concern in the Yishuv. On 9 November, MacMichael discounted the possibility of serious incidents[144] but three days later he informed the Colonial Office that the elected representatives of the Yishuv were likely to proclaim a general strike and 'possibly the staging of acts'.[145] Under these circumstances MacMichael now advised the Colonial Office to wait until the *Patria* had sailed before announcing that the deportees were permanently banned from re-entering Palestine.[146] However, the

[139]Lloyd to Church, 13 November 1940, Prem 4/51/1.

[140]J.M. Martin to Eastwood, 14 November 1940, *ibid*.

[141]CO to Govt of Trinidad No. 804, 14 November 1940, FO 371/25242 W11091.

[142]Martin minute to Churchill, 17 November 1940, Prem 4/51/1.

[143]Churchill to Lloyd M324, 20 November 1940, *ibid*.

[144]HCr to CO No. 1160, 9 November 1940, FO 371/25242 W11091.

[145]HCr to CO No. 1176, 12 November 1940, *ibid*.

[146]HCr to CO No. 1183, 14 November 1940, *ibid*.

Colonial Office was concerned at the growing attention the matter was getting in the U.K., and on the 19 November told the High Commissioner to make the announcement the next day.[147] These instructions were despatched before Churchill countermanded his previous approval of the deportations, and consequently Lloyd was able to reply to Churchill's instructions of the 20 November by pointing out that the policy had already been made public and that to withdraw it would appear to be a surrender to Jewish pressure, the political effects of which in the Middle East 'would be altogether deplorable'.[148] In the circumstances Churchill authorised the deportations (he was as yet unaware of the permanent ban) but insisted that the deportees should not be 'caged up'.[149]

The presence of the refugees in Haifa presented a dilemma to the Zionist movement too. In the meetings of the London executive of the Jewish Agency, Chaim Weizmann was always hostile to illegal immigration, and feared that a conflict over the deportation of the refugees in Haifa would adversely affect the negotiations for a Jewish Fighting Force which were, at that time, at a delicate stage. In general the Jewish Agency, in London and Jerusalem, also feared Nazi agents, a further deterioration of Zionist-British relations, and the undermining of the orderly selection of immigrants. However, it recognised that to deport from Palestine immigrants who had already reached Haifa would gravely affect Yishuv opinion.[150] The Agency did not oppose the redirection of boats to Mauritius. It insisted, however, that the boats be diverted before they reached Palestine (as did the High Commissioner in his recommendations to the Colonial Office). It was the principle of deportation that the Zionists opposed. They also asked that the refugees sent to Mauritius or elsewhere be considered as a reservoir from which future legal immigrants could be drawn when certificates from the legal schedule became available. This was especially important in view of the difficulty the Agency was having during 1940 in finding enough potential immigrants for the certificates made available in the April-September quota. When Weizmann put these proposals to Lloyd in an interview on 14 November[151] he also offered to cable the Jewish Agency in Jerusalem to 'try [to] prevent rise of feeling which may complicate situation', and

[147]CO to HCr No. 1143, 19 November 1940, CO 733/431//76021/37(40).

[148]Lloyd to Churchill, 21 November 1940, Prem 4/51/1.

[149]Churchill to Lloyd M332, 22 November 1940, *ibid.*

[150]Cf. Minutes of Jewish Agency executive, London, 12 and 15 November, C.Z.A. Z4-302/24.

[151]*Ibid.,* and minutes of 26 November 1940.

to American Zionists to explain Britain's position.[152] In Jerusalem, the Jewish Agency approached the Palestine Government with the same proposal as Weizmann had made in London, adding that the Agency was willing to assist in the task of uncovering Nazi agents amongst the refugees so diverted.[153]

The latter point was significant as both the Colonial Office and the authorities in Palestine publicly justified their policy of deporting the refugees by referring to the risk of Nazi agents. But in an interview with the Agency in Jerusalem the Palestine authorities rejected the offer, explaining the real basis of the policy of deportation and the reasons for its deterrent nature. As Moshe Shertok, Head of the Agency's Political Department, later wrote to Weizmann: 'The Chief Secretary... told us frankly that it wasn't fear of spies that worried the Government. He explained that the main worry is that if those refugees are allowed into Palestine, others will follow them and the flood will become so great that it would endanger the White Paper. . .'.[154] The Colonial Office files relating to the rejection of the Jewish Agency's offer of cooperation in regulating the feared flood of refugees remain closed to research; however, its concern that the offer would become known was undoubtedly one of the reasons why MacMichael was instructed on the 19 November to release the official statement of policy as soon as possible.[155] In the event, the announcement that the refugees would not only be deported but also banned from ever applying to enter Palestine legally marked a major turning point in the attitude of the Agency towards the illegal immigration problem and to Britain's attempts to regulate it.

On 24 November the *Atlantic* was brought into Haifa with 1783 refugees on board, and preparations were made to transfer them to the *Patria,* which could then begin its trip to Mauritius. The following day, before the transfer could begin, the *Patria* sank as a result of an explosion on board and 252 lives were lost. The explosive charge had been smuggled on board by the Hagana in an attempt to prevent the

[152]CO to HCr (Private and Personal), 17 November 1940, FO 371/25242 W12017 and Minutes, 14-17 November, CO 733/430//76021/28(40).

[153]Shertok-MacMichael interview, 27 November 1940, *ibid*.

[154]Shertok to Weizmann, 17 December 1940, C.Z.A. S25/1716. This letter had been intercepted by Palestine Censorship and was seen in London (FO 371/29161-W339).

[155]Weizmann later said of his negotiations with the CO on this matter: 'Somebody, however, had been in a great hurry; had drafted the proclamation, and tried to bolt and bar the doors. . .' (Jewish Agency Executive Meeting, 26 November 1940, C.Z.A. Z4/302/24).

74

deportations, and was detonated by one of the refugees on board.[156] Churchill brought the sinking to the Cabinet's attention the same day[157] and initiated a Cabinet debate on the policy which had led up to it two days later. The Cabinet decided that despite the announcement of 20 November, the 1500 survivors of the Patria would be allowed to remain in Palestine, although the policy of deporting to Mauritius any illegal immigrants that might arrive in the future would continue.[158] The decision in favour of the survivors of the *Patria* was to be described as 'an exceptional act of mercy' and not as a principle guiding future policy. Nevertheless, General Wavell, Commander-in-Chief, Middle East Forces, and Sir Miles Lampson – both of whom were staunch supporters of the White Paper and would certainly have known that that policy was under attack in the Cabinet — decided to challenge that decision after it was taken. Wavell sent an urgent telegram to London arguing that from the military point of view it was disastrous. Claiming that it would cause widespread disorder in Palestine and elsewhere, Wavell said that unless the survivors of the *Patria* were deported he would have to withdraw his recommendation to open a supply route from Haifa to Basra via Iraq and Transjordan.[159] Lampson, in a separate telegram, strongly endorsed Wavell's opinion.[160]

Churchill sent a curt reply, describing the consequences of adopting Wavell's recommendation as an 'act of inhumanity unworthy of the British name'. He also dismissed Wavell's assertion that unless Arab opinion was met on this issue the reaction of the Arab world would be serious.[161] Wavell's cable was discussed by the Cabinet a few hours after Churchill's reply was despatched, together with MacMichael's statement of 20 November permanently banning the re-entry into Palestine after the war of the other refugees who were being deported to Mauritius. The latter had not been raised during the previous Cabinet debate on the *Patria*. After a lengthy and heated discussion, a compromise solution was adopted, and it was concluded that both the decision to allow the *Patria* survivors to remain in

[156]For a full account of this incident by the man responsible for smuggling the explosive charge on board, cf. M. Mardor, *Strictly Illegal* (London, 1964). The intention had been to disable the boat and thus prevent its departure, but the amount of explosives necessary had been miscalculated.

[157]WM 295(40) Cab 65/10, 25 November 1940.

[158]WM 294(40)5 Cab 65/10, 27 November 1940.

[159]Wavell to Secretary of State for War (0/28118), 30 November 1940, Prem 4/51/2.

[160]Lampson to FO No. 1646, 2 December 1940, Prem 4/51/1.

[161]Churchill to Wavell (WO to CiC, MEF 91193), 2 December 1940, Prem 4/51/2.

Palestine and the permanent banning of all other illegal immigrants should stand.[162]

As interventions by Wavell and Lampson had been rejected, the Middle East Department and Lloyd attempted to bring more pressure on Churchill to reverse the decision by asking the Australian Government to intervene.[163] However, this unorthodox ploy also achieved little as Churchill remained unmoved and insisted on inserting in the reply to the Australian Government references to British obligations to the Zionists and to the general humanitarian need to assist the refugees.[164]

The Cabinet decision to allow the refugees to stay in Palestine applied only to passengers from the *Milos* and the *Pacific* who survived the Patria tragedy. Passengers from the *Atlantic* were consequently placed in the detention camp of Athlit and then transferred to a boat for deportation to Mauritius on 9 December. As if to confirm MacMichael's apprehensions about bringing ships to Palestine before deportation, the transfer was accomplished with considerable violence, and further exacerbated relations with the Yishuv. Nevertheless, despite his warning in September, none of the other boats expected did arrive in Palestine in the months following the sinking of the *Patria*. One of them (the *Petcho*) ran aground on the Dodecanese and its passengers were taken by the Italians to Rhodes; another (the S.S. *Salvador*) sank with the loss of 107 lives in the Sea

---

[162]WM 299(40)7, Cab 65/10. Cf. also D. Dilks, (ed.), *Sir Alexander Cadogan Diaries 1938-1945* (London, 1971), p. 338.

[163]The Australian High Commissioner in London, S.M. Bruce, first cabled Prime Minister Menzies on 20 November, 'Being very worried as to the serious effect on Arabs if this illicit emigration [sic] cannot be stopped and knowing that I had strong views in regard to danger of arousing the Arab world against us, the Lord Lloyd approached me in the first instance to enlist my support behind him with the War Cabinet of whose attitude he was a little apprehensive owing to pro-Jew tendencies of some of its members. . . ' (Bruce to Menzies No. 1023, 20 November 1940, A.A. CRS A981 Palestine: Item 8). Following the failure of the Wavell/Lampson demarche Bruce asked Menzies to telegraph Churchill to protest at the *Patria* decision (Bruce to Menzies No. 1053, 4 December 1940, *ibid*) and Menzies compiled two days later (Menzies to Dominions Office No. 634, 6 December 1940, Prem 4/51/1). When these telegrams reached the Colonial Office, Shuckburgh minuted: 'I should surmise that the Australian Government's intervention has been prompted by Mr. Bruce with whom, as you know, we had some discussion recently on the subject of illegal immigration into Palestine. . . ' (CO 733/430//76021/28(40)).

[164]Dominions Office to Govt. of Australia No. 511, 24 December 1940 (*ibid*.). The last paragraph of the telegram, drafted by Shuckburgh, originally read: 'H.M.G. in the U.K. fully appreciate uneasiness felt by Commonwealth Government and share this view as to importance of retaining Arab goodwill. Circumstances relating of 'Patria' were regarded as quite exceptional and will not affect future policy. . . ' Churchill, on seeing this draft, personally inserted before the last sentence: 'They had also to consider their promises to the Zionists, and to be guided by general considerations of humanity towards those fleeing from the cruellest forms of persecution.'

76

of Marmora, where it had been towed by the Turkish authorities. As no other boats arrived in Palestine during the next few months, and only one further boat in the course of 1941, the Colonial Office policy of deportation remained in force, although not implemented, until early 1942. During this period the Colonial Office did all it could to keep matters related to illegal immigration 'as far as possible on the normal administrative plane and outside the realms of Cabinet policy'[165] in order to avoid further interventions by the Prime Minister.

The sinking of the *Patria* and the announcement by the High Commissioner on 20 November radicalised the Jewish Agency Executive in London, and Weizmann — who had till now been hostile to illegal immigration — in particular. The Agency now commenced an extensive lobbying campaign in London to gain support for its earlier offer of Jewish Agency-Colonial Office cooperation in handling the Jewish refugee-illegal immigrant phenomenon, an offer which it now elaborated. The problem, the Agency believed, was how to overcome the British Government's fear that the refugee phenomenon was part of a German engineered flood designed to overwhelm British capabilities in the Middle East. In a letter to the Colonial Office, the Agency wrote: 'We are prepared to cooperate with the Government in seeking a solution should the fears of the Colonial Office regarding continued refugee immigration of this type prove justified, even though such action is certain to create for us serious difficulties with regard to our own people.'[166] The Agency proposed diverting the ships at sea before they reached Haifa, allowing the Jewish Agency to select refugees with 'special claims' (e.g. the sick, people with close relatives in Palestine, holders of immigration certificates) for immediate admission, while the rest would be sent elsewhere and considered as potential immigrants when legal certificates became available. To facilitate their eventual immigration to Palestine, Agency workers should be allowed 'to cooperate in looking after the welfare, vocational training, education, etc' of the refugees so diverted.[167]

[165] Shuckburgh minute, 24 December 1940, CO 733/419//75113(40).

[166] Locker to G. Hall (Parliamentary. U-S, CO), 9 December 1940, C.Z.A. S25-2648.

[167] In the original document the categories to be allowed entry were left open for discussion with the CO. However, from the minutes of the London Executive it is clear that these categories would have been demanded by the Agency. It is probable that they would also have insisted on allowing the entry of children (Jewish Agency Memorandum, 4 December 1940, FO 371/25242 W12715. Also C.Z.A. S25-2648). The attitude of the Jerusalem Executive was slightly different. As Locker informed the London Executive: 'Jerusalem felt that they should not cooperate openly with the Government; but that the Government should carry out its own operations quietly, and with their tacit consent' (Locker to executive, minutes of 30 December 1940, C.Z.A., Z4/302/24).

The forced evacuation of the *Atlantic*'s passengers from Athlit internment camp and their deportation came a few days after the Jewish Agency offer was put to the Colonial Office. The suspension, on 26 December, of the legal quotas until March 1941 followed shortly afterwards. On 30 December the London Executive received a communication from Shertok in Jerusalem saying that relations between the High Commissioner and the Palestine Government, and the Jewish Agency there had reached their lowest ebb.[168] Although there is no record of the Agency offer of cooperation in Colonial Office files, the offer was presumably officially rejected and was certainly ignored in practice. The undesirability of cooperating with the Agency at any level if the White Paper was to be enforced was one reason why the Colonial Office and the Palestine Government failed to respond to the Agency's various offers of cooperation on the question of illegal immigration. Another was because the Colonial Office still held in late 1940 that the entire phenomenon was a political conspiracy by the Zionists against the British Government. Thus the Middle East Department advocated not only deportation but punitive detention as a deterrent: ' . . the conditions of their detention should be sufficiently punitive to continue to act as a deterrent to other Jews in Eastern Europe'.[169] Any measure designed to ameliorate the lot of the deported illegal immigrants, such as the suggestions put forward by the Agency in its offer of cooperation, was therefore rejected.

In the course of formulating immigration policy after the resumption of illegal immigration in October 1940, the Colonial Office had consulted the Eastern Department of the Foreign Office, bypassing the Refugee Section. This was, presumably, due to the various objections the Refugee Section had raised during the previous year to the Colonial Office's conduct of immigration policy. The Agency's offer of cooperation appealed to the Refugee Section, but as the Colonial Office had not invited its opinion, it decided not to intervene.[170] The element of punitive detention in Colonial Office policy troubled the Refugee Section and contributed to an open conflict between it and the Middle East Department over immigration policy in the months that followed. But the conflict began over another aspect of the problem altogether.

[168]Shertok to Weizmann, 17 December 1940, C.Z.A., Z4/302/24.

[169]Luke minute, 11 January 1941, CO 733/445//76021/31(41). A similar sentiment was expressed by Luke and Downie on 10-11 January on CO 733/445//76021 (Part 2)(41).

[170]Latham and Snow minutes, 9-10 January 1941, FO 371/25242 W12215.

The activities of the *Milos, Pacific* and *Atlantic* had been organised in central Europe with the cooperation of the German authorities, and this was known to the Foreign and Colonial Office.[171] As already mentioned, when Lloyd defended the policy of deportation to Churchill on 13 November he went beyond this information and claimed that the boats would most likely be carrying Nazi agents. The Eastern Department of the Foreign Office passed this 'fact' on to the British embassy in Washington to assist the embassy in defending the deportations in the face of critical American public opinion.[172] Following the sinking of the *Patria* an unattributed article appeared in the *New York News* stating that amongst the refugees aboard the *Patria* were '200 graduates of a special Jewish institution in Prague at which Gestapo agents and saboteurs are trained'.[173] The embassy, keen for any information which could be used to counter the anti-British feeling aroused in America by the sinking of the *Patria* asked the Foreign Office for further details.

Britain's growing dependence on American support in 1940-1 made American opinion a factor to be reckoned with by those responsible for colonial policy as much as by those responsible for the conduct of the war. The sinking of the *Patria* and the policy of deportation had attracted much critical attention in the U.S., and the Washington embassy said that a significant public relations coup could be achieved if the Colonial Office could cite concrete evidence of Nazi agents amongst the refugees. When the Washington embassy informed London that the *Saturday Evening Post*, encouraged by the U.S. State Department, wanted to publish a detailed article on the German tactic of 'war by refugee', the need for concrete evidence became even more pressing. Palestine would be only a small part of the article, but its author had asked the embassy, *inter alia*, for the 'number of Nazi agents detected amongst the refugees'.[174] The embassy pressed London for as much information as could be

[171]Memo by Palairet (Athens) to FO, 21 November 1940, CO 733/430//76021/20. In fact, these boats together with the *Petcho* had been organised by the Gestapo through their agent Storfer. Storfer, a Jew, was used by the Gestapo to coordinate the activities of the organisers of the illegal traffic (the independent operators, the Revisionists and the Mossad). Avriel, pp. 72-5, gives an account of the relations between these groups and the German authorities. According to Kimche (*Secret Roads*) the *Pacific, Milos,* and *Atlantic* were Storfer's last efforts (p. 54). Hannah Arendt, *Eichmann in Jerusalem* (London, 1963), pp. 45-6, drawing on Eichmann's testimony at his trial, quotes him as saying that Storfer then tried to escape but was caught by the Germans and shot (not gassed) at Auschwitz.

[172]FO to N. Butler (Washington) No. 3117(R), 19 November 1940, CO 733/430/-/76021/28.

[173]Quoted in Lothian to FO No. 2827(R), 27 November 1940, *ibid*.

[174]N. Butler, to FO No. 3238, 23 December 1940, FO 371/25242 W12759.

provided, and the Colonial Office was asked to reply. As there was no such concrete evidence, this was a difficult task. In its reply to the Foreign Office, the Colonial Office explained: 'We quite appreciate that it would be most useful if we could produce evidence of infiltration of enemy agents by this means. Unfortunately, it has so far not been possible for the Palestine Government to secure evidence establishing beyond doubt the fact that enemy agents have been introduced in this way.'[175] In lieu of real evidence, the Colonial Office suggested that general 'security reasons' be used to justify a refusal to provide any details. The Foreign Office passed this on to the Washington embassy, but the Refugee Section was sceptical about the existence of any agents at all. R.T.E. Latham commented: 'My inclination is to believe that the whole idea is a CO canard, begotten of their desire to fortify themselves in pursuing a policy which, however necessary on political grounds, is unavoidably inhumane to a degree.'[176]

So far the Refugee Section's reservations on Colonial Office policy had been expressed internally in the Foreign Office, and since the failure of the attempts made by Carvell and Baggallay to revive the British Guiana scheme in March to May 1940, the Refugee Section had had little impact on immigration policy. Now, however, prompted by the American situation, the Section proceeded to directly challenge the Colonial Office's use of the enemy agent argument suggesting that it had been unscrupulous in its insinuations about the presence of such agents and that this would rebound on Britain's credibility in America.[177] The Colonial Office, in its reply, was unable to do more than assert that logically it was highly likely that enemy agents were present and that this, together with the known role of the German authorities in encouraging the traffic, together justified their assertions even if no agents had in fact been identified.[178] This interdepartmental correspondence was brought to an end by the Eastern Department, which argued that 'no useful purpose' was being served by it,[179] but the

[175]Downie to Snow, 3 January 1941, CO 733/430//76021/25.

[176]Latham minute, 19 November 1940, FO 371/25242 W11823.

[177]Snow to Downie, FO 371/29160 W188. This letter prompted the CO to ask the Palestine government once again for any evidence on the presence of enemy agents (Downie to Macpherson (Jerusalem), 1 March 1941, CO 733/445//76021/41). Macpherson replied on 8 July 1941: 'The police have not been able to find any evidence showing individuals among the illegal immigrants to be enemy agents' (Macpherson to Downie, *ibid.* The CO decided not to forward this reply to the FO (Luke minute, 6 August 1941, *ibid.*).

[178]Downie to Snow, 8 February 1941, *ibid.*

[179]Baxter minute, FO 371/29160 W1639.

argument was taken up again in the drafting of a reply to the Washington embassy's request for a full explanation of Palestine immigration policy.

The Refugee Section welcomed the opportunity to make a statement on the Jewish refugee problem which distinguished its views from those of the Colonial Office. Thus the Foreign Office draft reply to Washington, compiled jointly by the Eastern Department and the Refugee Section, stated, in direct contradiction to the Colonial Office position, that the flow of Jews from Europe was a genuine refugee movement (not a political conspiracy of the Zionists) and the fact that the Gestapo had a hand in organising it did not discredit the motives of the refugees themselves nor mean that there were Nazi agents amongst them.[180]

If illegal immigration could not therefore be legitimately discredited by the Colonial Office, the question then was how to defend accepted government policy to the general public. As Latham stated:

> We must try and defend the White Paper policy (to which, whatever its merits, we are absolutely committed so long as the Middle East retains its present vital military importance) as representing actual justice. It is by no means impossible to show that it does represent justice — indeed, that it is even generous to the Jews — so long as one does not look (as the Colonial Office in effect does not) outside the borders of Palestine. It is impossible to represent it as remotely approaching justice if the position not only of all the Arabs in the world but also of all the Jews in the world, and the *lebensraum* available to them respectively, are taken into account. We have therefore in order to justify our Palestine policy, to prevent Palestine being the sole arena in which the crying needs of the Jews are allowed to be pitted against the less dramatic, but very real, interests of other peoples.[181]

This was a plea for the revival of the non-Palestinian territorial solution, which had last been considered in March to May 1940, and rejected by the Colonial Office. As an additional compelling reason for reviving consideration of these solutions, Latham pointed out that the Colonial Office's policy would create a post-war problem: how to dispose of the refugees in Mauritius. Furthermore, the future of the Jews in Europe would also have to be considered, and it would be better to prepare areas of immigration other than Palestine in

[180]Drafts and minutes, FO 371/27132 E204.

[181]Latham minute, 1 February 1941, *ibid.*

advance.[182] In another paper the Refugee Section examined other ways in which the Palestine government could keep the refugees away from Palestine, and concluded that:

> No deterrent device which British conscience at its broadest is likely to tolerate. . . is in the eyes of these Jews or in reality comparable to the cruelty and torture of living under Nazi anti-semitic measures. All deterrent measures against immigrants are therefore foredoomed to be useless so far as the suppression of the traffic is concerned. . . . Our prospects of putting a stop to the illegal immigration traffic within the four corners of the White Paper policy are poor. We can harass it in many ways, and thereby reduce the volume, but it seems most unlikely that we shall be able to prevent its continuing on a substantial scale.[183]

This realisation attracted the support of the Eastern Department for the Refugee Section's efforts to revive the British Guiana scheme, despite all its inherent difficulties. It was the only way, it argued, that British policy in Palestine could survive the inevitable post-war pressure of Jewish refugees on Palestine.[184]

However, Sir Horace Seymour, the Assistant Under-Secretary of State responsible, was sceptical, and it was not until March 1941, two months later, that he allowed the two departments concerned to consult the Colonial Office on the revival of the scheme. By then the German occupation of the Balkans had put an end to the flow of large-scale organised illegal immigration, and Foreign Office consideration of a non-Palestinian territorial solution was dropped. Consequently, despite internal Foreign Office reservations, the Colonial Office policy of non-cooperation with the Jewish Agency and of deportation remained in effect, unchallenged by either the Foreign Office or by the pressure of refugees. The problem of an agreed reply to the Washington embassy's request for an explanation of immigration policy remained, but before any reply could be sent, events provided a catalyst for yet another conflict between the Foreign and Colonial Offices.

In January 1941 violent anti-Jewish pogroms broke out in Bucharest and the anti-Semitic measures of the Antonescu regime there were intensified. On 7 February Weizmann wrote directly to Churchill asking that despite the current suspension of immigration quotas, special exceptions be made to allow the immigration to

[182]*Ibid.*

[183]Latham memo, 28 December, FO 371/29161 W2714. Snow, head of the Refugee Section, endorsed this memorandum (Snow minute, 10 January 1941, *ibid.*).

[184]Baxter minutes, 17 January 1941, *ibid.*; and 30 December 1940, FO 371/24568 E1063.

Palestine of limited numbers of Rumanian Jews.[185] Even though Rumania was not yet considered enemy territory (and therefore did not fall under the ban of 25 September 1939 on all immigration from such territory), the Colonial Office hoped to prevent any immigration from there — including the immigration of some 700 people who already held valid immigration certificates from the previous quota period — let alone make further concessions to the Jewish Agency.[186] But the appeal to Churchill attracted the attention of 10 Downing Street and of the Foreign Office and both pressed the Colonial Office for some accommodation of Weizmann's request.[182] In the course of the interdepartmental deliberations, Rumania was declared enemy territory (on February 1941) and the ban on immigration from such territory therefore applied to all categories of immigrant, including those who already held certificates. Thus the Colonial Office was able to inform Weizmann officially that nothing could be done for the Jews in Rumania.[188]

However, the plight of the Rumanian Jews had come to the attention of the U.S. Government, and as a result of pressure from the Washington embassy, the Colonial Office agreed to ask the High Commissioner whether it would be possible to reconsider.[189] The High Commissioner agreed on 28 February to allow holders of certificates issued before 15 February to proceed to Palestine, but he refused to contemplate the release of any further certificates or to make any other concessions.[190] The Foreign Office accepted this as a

[185] Weizmann to Churchill, 7 February 1941, Prem 4/51/8. In the various represent-ations made to H.M.G. and to the Palestine Government the following categories were mentioned: technicians capable of aiding the Allied war effort; families of Rumanian immigrants in Palestine who had enlisted in H.M. Forces in the Middle East; veteran Zionists; those with funds in Palestine; holders of valid immigration certificates.

[186] Cf. minutes on CO 733/437//75113/57(41).

[187] Peck to Eastwood, 12 February 1941, FO 371/29168 W1040.

[188] Downie subsequently informed Latham that 'He was anxious in a general way to keep Jews out of Palestine and he was in this sense happy that the German occupation of Rumania had given an opportunity to Palestine to make a 'profit on the immigration account' (Latham minute, 24 February 1941, FO 29169 W2120).

[189] CO to HCr No. 287, 25 February 1941, CO 733/437//75113/57(41). Another factor encouraging a reversal of the previous ruling was information from Sir Reginald Hoare, the Ex-Ambassador in Bucharest, that the British Embassy there had made a special effort to distribute the certificates and visas it still held prior to the Embassy's closure. As the Southern Department of the FO pointed out, 'No doubt Sir R. Hoare, who probably had first hand knowledge of the sort of treatment these people suffered, felt a personal obligation in arranging for their departure. . . ' (minute of 25 February on FO 371/29169 W2120). The Refugee Section applauded Hoare's action (FO 371/291168 W1175) and said that they would defend him against any protests from the CO.

[190] HCr to CO No. 263, 28 February 1941, CO 733/437//75113/57(41).

compromise and the Jewish Agency was informed accordingly.[191] The matter could have rested there, but the Colonial Office, having agreed to the entry of certificate holders, proceeded to oppose the release of blocked Rumanian funds to finance their transport (in case any of the funds were used to finance illegal immigration as well). The Refugee Section felt that the Colonial Office was being intentionally obstructive: its opposition was therefore ignored, and Halifax, now ambassador in Washington, was instructed to agree to the release of the funds by the American Government.[192] The general impression that the Middle East Department was attempting to make 'a profit on the immigration account' above and beyond the restrictions imposed by the White Paper was reinforced and relations between the two departments deteriorated further.[193]

In the course of 1941 the problem of certificate-holders who remained after the British embassy had withdrawn repeated itself in each of the Balkan States, and the Jewish Agency and the Colonial Office renewed negotiations on the number of Jews who would be allowed to enter Palestine in each case. Aware of the hostile attitude of the Middle East Department (and of Downie in particular), the Jewish Agency increasingly directed its representations on behalf of each category of refugee to the Foreign Office, invariably in the form of an approach by Lewis Namier to R.A. Butler. The Colonial Office attempted to prevent the Foreign Office becoming involved in its deliberations, arguing that most of the representations dealt with administrative questions, which were the proper province of the Department of Migration and Statistics in Jerusalem, and not of any ministry in London.[194] If the Foreign Office could have been excluded, the growing breach between the Colonial Office and the Refugee Section on the question of immigration policy would have been circumvented. The Eastern Department had suggested that Latham, the responsible official in the Refugee Section, meet the Colonial Office to attempt to resolve this breach, but Latham replied that he had done so many times before and had clearly achieved nothing.[195] In response to the Colonial Office's attempt to have the

---

[191] Moyne to Weizmann, 4 March 1941, FO 371/29169 W2593.

[192] FO to Halifax No. 1389, 15 March 1941, FO 371/29169 W2794.

[193] A sarcastic correspondence between the Middle East Dept. and the Refugee Section followed the instructions to Halifax (Downie to Snow, 14 March 1941, and Snow's reply of 17 March 1941, FO 371/29169 W2792). In fact about half the Rumanian certificate holders succeeded in reaching Palestine by early April 1941 (HCr to CO No. 444, 2 April 1941, CO 733/437//75113/57(41)).

[194] Downie to Snow, 18 April 1941, FO 371/29170 W4682.

[195] Minutes, April 1941, FO 371/29170 W3617.

Foreign Office agree not to receive representations from the Jewish Agency, Latham defended the Agency by pointing out that when it dealt with the Colonial Office it had to deal with Downie, who, Latham said, 'is anti-Semitic to a degree which prevents his conducting reasonable discussions with Jews'.[196] Butler also protested at the attempt 'to reserve all handling of the Jews to the CO', and the Foreign Office refused to exclude itself from matters brought to it by the Agency.[197]

The attack by the Refugee Section on the manner in which the Colonial Office was implementing the White Paper restrictions on immigration, and on the effectiveness of the policy of deportation, had not brought about any change. The Cabinet decision to deport all refugees who arrived after the sinking of the *Patria* was still in effect. Consequently when the S.S. *Darien*[198] with 791 passengers was intercepted off Palestine on 19 March 1941 the Colonial Office promptly announced that they too should be deported. In the atmosphere of controversy that now surrounded immigration policy, the Secretary of State, Lord Moyne, decided to explain in a paper to the Cabinet the reasons behind the Colonial Office's decision. In his paper Moyne eschewed reference to the security risk posed by the illegal immigrants and instead pointed to the need for resolute action in order to prevent the immigration provisions of the White Paper being destroyed under the pressure of 'a flood of gatecrashers'[199] (although when the fate of the *Darien* passengers was under consideration at least 2,500 certificates were still available from the previous schedule, that of April to September 1940). Moyne's paper was not discussed in the War Cabinet, and the Colonial Office instructed

[196]Latham minute, 24 April 1941, FO 371/29170 W4682.

[197]Minutes and correspondence, *ibid.*

[198]HCr to CO No. 368, 19 March 1941, CO 733/446//76021/40(41). The *Darien* had a unique history which had a profound effect on relations between the Jewish Agency and British Intelligence (in this case, S.O.E.). The ship had originally been purchased by the Mossad for the transport of illegal immigrants but the Jewish Agency agreed to sell the boat to the S.O.E. who planned to use it to block the Danube at the 'Iron Gates'. However the Mossad, to whom the ship belonged, preferred to take the chance of saving at least one load of refugees on the *Darien* rather than rely on the possibility of saving even more later as a result of S.O.E. – Agency cooperation which would, they hoped, have grown out of this joint venture. The Agency was unable to impose its will on the Mossad and the S.O.E. scheme did not materialize. Full details are given in Bauer, *From Diplomacy to Resistance,* pp. 116-18. These facts were not known to the Palestine government or the Colonial and Foreign Offices, and therefore did not affect the subsequent development of policy on the *Darien.* It is however an interesting illustration of the Mossad's ambivalent relations with the Jewish Agency.

[199]WP(41)74, Cab 66/15.

MacMichael to proceed with the deportation. For practical reasons, lack of accommodation in Mauritius and the conditions on board the *Darien*, this proved impossible and the refugees were disembarked and interned in Palestine, although the High Commissioner made it clear that he intended to deport them at the first possible opportunity.[200]

It was a *sine qua non* of immigration policy that an interpretation of the White Paper provisions on immigration which was more sympathetic to the refugees would have a serious effect on Arab opinion in general and on stability in Palestine. This understanding had previously been challenged when Churchill overrode Wavell's objections to the Cabinet decision on the *Patria* survivors. Churchill's curt response to Wavell's warnings of the unrest in the Arab world that the decision would cause was shown by events to be correct. Military intelligence in Palestine summed up the reaction of the Palestine Arabs to the *Patria* decision as 'remarkably small'.[201] However, at the level of the interdepartmental controversy the nature of the likely Arab reaction to any change in that policy was not seriously debated. Instead the Colonial Office felt that Britain's willingness to administer the White Paper provisions on immigration as rigidly as possible was a token of the British Government's intention to adhere to the White Paper as a whole in the face of Jewish opposition. The decision to deport the refugees on the *Darien* came shortly after Lord Moyne became Secretary of State for the Colonies, and he subsequently wrote privately to MacMichael asking whether deportation was in fact the only way of preventing a flood of refugees descending on Palestine.[202] MacMichael replied that the policy should be continued, and that Jewish opposition to deportation was essentially an attempt 'to assert the Jewish national will. . . . Jews would of course regard a revoke [sic] on our part as the first fruits of their campaign to undermine and destroy the White Paper root and branch'.[203] The conviction that the fate of the White Paper as a whole depended on a willingness to stand up to Jewish opposition, a willingness which could best be demonstrated in the conduct of the

[200]HCr to CO No. 404, 26 March 1941, CO 733/446//76021/40(41).

[201]Milpal Report 24/40, 14 December 1940, CO 732/86//79097.

[202]Moyne to MacMichael, Private and Personal letter, 28 March 1941, CO 733/449//P1/0/50.

[203]MacMichael to Moyne, Private and Personal No. 563, *ibid.* Prompted by this correspondence, Bennett sugested that the time had come to revive the policy of firing on refugee boats in order to keep them out of Palestine territorial waters. The threat of sinking the boats would be an even stronger deterrent than deportation. This suggestion was minuted at all levels in the CO and it was agreed that the idea be put to MacMichael. Moyne, however, refused to allow the telegram to be sent (minutes on CO 733/449//P1/0/20, May 1941, *passim.*).

immigration policy, entered the interdepartmental conflict in the reply to be sent to the Washington Embassy (still awaiting approval), which was resumed in March. In early April, Halifax wrote directly to R.A. Butler pressing London for a reply, and repeating that Jewish and Zionist influence in America was too important to be ignored.[204] The Colonial Office saw the sudden willingness of the Foreign Office to introduce the factor of American opinion into Palestine policy-making as a threat to the White Paper. When the Foreign Office draft reply to Washington was sent to the Colonial Office, Sir Cosmo Parkinson reacted by writing a minute to Moyne explaining:

> The day on which HMG go back on the White Paper of 1939 will be a very black day indeed for Great Britain in the Middle East and the whole Moslem world. American opinion may be important, and in the pressing circumstances is important; but we have a vast Moslem population in the Empire, and if Moslems or Arabs. . . mean nothing to the Americans they mean a very great deal to us. If ever HMG throw over the policy of the White Paper of 1939 that will be the last straw for the Arabs, and they could not (why should they?) repost any confidence whatever in the promises or assurances of HMG.[205]

Consequently the Middle East Department prepared a draft reply of its own setting out the Colonial Office case on the nature of the refugee problem, the motives of the illegal immigrants and of the Zionists who organized or encouraged their entry into Palestine, the security risks posed by the phenomenon, and the need for a deterrent policy.[206]

The Foreign Office reaction to this statement was scathing: 'It is only if one realises that the CO regards the Jews as no less our enemies than the Germans that certain features of this draft become explicable',[207] and it decided to terminate the controversy by sending its own exposition on Palestine immigration policy to Washington even though the Colonial Office had not concurred in it.[208]

In this interdepartmental conflict the Refugee Section won a futile victory. It had attempted to challenge the manner in which the Colonial Office and the Palestine Government administered Palestine policy, arguing that the way the immigration restrictions were administered was as offensive to the Jews, if not more so, than the policy itself. The

[204]Halifax to R.A. Butler (FO), 4 April 1941, CO 733/444//75872/102.

[205]Parkinson minute addressed to Moyne, 26 March 1941, CO 733/445//76012/25(41).

[206]Downie to Baxter, 1 April 1941, CO 733/445//76021/25(41).

[207]Latham minute, 22 April 1941, FO 371/27132 E1240.

[208]Seymour to Butler, N. 26 May 1941, CO 733/445//76021/25.

Refugee Section doubted the effectiveness of deportation, challenged the need for punitive detention and supported cooperation with the Jewish Agency in diverting the flow of refugees from Palestine. Even more significantly it advocated positive planning on alternative sites of settlement as a contribution to the solution of the entire Jewish problem in Europe. All this was feasible in the context of Britain's given policy in Palestine, the White Paper, and was in fact intended to facilitate that policy. Otherwise, the Foreign Office, (and here the Refugee Section was supported by the Eastern Department) feared that the entire policy would be overwhelmed not by irresolution on the part of the British Government (as the Colonial Office feared) but by the sheer size of the post-war Jewish refugee problem. However, in the debate with the Middle East Department, the Refugee Section had succeeded in altering only the terms in which the Colonial Office policy was defended. The policy itself, of being as inflexible as possible in the administration of the White Paper restrictions on immigration, remained intact during 1941.

In 1941 the Foreign Office came to appreciate the impact that the massive post-war Jewish problem would have on Britain's freedom of manoeuvre in Palestine. This was one of the reasons put forward for reviving the British Guiana scheme. In Palestine itself the government also appreciated that the Jewish question would be taken up again after the war. However, there this fact was seen as another reason for the meticulous administration of the White Paper restrictions. As the Director of Migration explained in a lengthy memorandum to the High Commissioner when the problem of the Rumanian certificates was debated, the Palestine government would be well advised to conserve as many of the 75,000 certificates as were still available, so that they could be used after the war.[209] Although the Colonial Office did not agree to the suggestion that all immigration should therefore cease for the duration of the war (because, they argued, the Arabs would not accept any Jewish immigration after 1944, that date when, according to the White Paper, all such immigration would cease unless the Arabs agreed otherwise), it did agree to continue the suspension of the quota.[210] Thus for the first half of the April to September 1941 quota period, no legal certificates were issued. In July MacMichael suggested a quota of 750 certificates for the second half of the quota period,[211] but refused to consider a request by the Jewish Agency for additional certificates to be used for the survivors

[209]Mills Memorandum, 4 February 1941, CO 733/436//75113 Part 1(41).

[210]CO to HCr No. 443, 27 March 1941, *ibid.*

[211]HCr to CO No. 1057, 21 July 1941, *ibid.*

of the large scale anti-Jewish rioting that broke out in Baghdad in June 1941 prior to the entry of British forces into that city.[212] Moyne personally suggested that 750 certificates might be inadequate, especially in view of Army recruiting needs in Palestine but MacMichael insisted that larger numbers could not be absorbed without disruption to the economy.[213]

The end of the quota period on 30 September marked the end of the first half of the five years of Jewish immigration allowed under the White Paper (1 April 1939 to 30 September 1941). By then just over 35,000 Jews had actually arrived in Palestine — legally or illegally — i.e. slightly less than half of the 75,000 total. The Palestine Government and the Colonial Office had in effect not only balanced the 'immigration account', but were beginning to show a small 'credit' balance — as the Refugee Section had accused them of trying to do.

[212]HCr to CO No. 1111, 5 August 1941, CO 733/438//75113/63(42).

[213]CO to HCr No. 1350, 30 July 1941, ibid., and HCr to CO No. 1111, 5 August 1941, ibid.

4

THE SEARCH FOR AN ALTERNATIVE POLICY

The Colonial Office originally believed that when the British Government's firm resolve to implement the White Paper became apparent, moderate opinion amongst the Arabs and Jews would prevail and the new policy would thus gain general support. Its failure to gain such support, together with Churchill's stated opposition to it, inevitably resulted in doubts being raised as to the permanence of the 1939 policy. Such doubts were encouraged by war-time developments in the Middle East, while the deteriorating circumstances of European Jewry changed the entire context in which the White Paper had originally been conceived and in which it was to be implemented. These facts, as well as the difficulties the authorities were facing in implementing the White Paper, encouraged political circles in England to consider possible alternatives which were closer to the ideas evolving amongst the Zionists.

As the Arabs had shown themselves hostile to the possibility of partitioning Palestine when it was first suggested in 1937, the only feasible alternative solutions to the Palestine problem were variations on the theme of federation. This could be viewed in two different ways. The first, best described as 'cantonisation', advocated the creation of semi-autonomous, separate Arab and Jewish cantons in a bi-national federal state. The second called for the creation of a wide Arab federation consisting of Palestine, Transjordan and Syria (and perhaps other Arab states as well – the scope varied with each proposal) in which a Jewish state, province or otherwise defined autonomous region in all or part of Palestine would be included. The principle underlying this approach was that in meeting the central demands of Arab nationalism by the promotion of Arab unity and the ending of Mandatory control in Syria and Palestine, the Arabs might be persuaded to accept some degree of Jewish autonomy in Palestine as a *quid pro quo*. Where the proposal called for the creation of a Jewish province or region only, the Jews were to be persuaded to give up their hopes of statehood in exchange for the possibility of expanding Jewish settlement and commerce throughout the wider Arab federation of which it was to be a part.

In the course of the negotiations on the White Paper, the Colonial Secretary, Malcolm MacDonald, had favoured a federal (cantonal) solution and attempted unsuccessfully to have the proposal written into the White Paper itself.[1] When he was replaced as Secretary of State in May 1940 the cantonal approach was put aside. During the next few years almost all discussion of a federal solution to the Palestine problem concentrated on the wider approach, the inclusion of Palestine in a large Arab federation. The Zionists turned to the concept of federation when Britain abandoned the partition plan during 1938. Although initially sceptical of the idea and uncommitted to any specific proposal, during 1938-9 they turned increasingly to federation in order to prove that there were other ways out of the Palestine quagmire than the White Paper, ways which did not require an end to the development of the Jewish National Home.[2]

While the Jewish Agency was attempting during 1939 to interest influential English circles in a solution through federation, Weizmann (together with Lewis Namier, who acted as a political adviser to the offices of the Agency in London), was actively engaged in attempting to interest the Arabs directly in a specific federation proposal. The opportunity to do so came from Hugh St. John Philby, the controversial Arabist who was a confidante (and self-appointed agent) of King Ibn Saud.

Philby advocated the creation of an Arab federation under the Saudi Arabian Monarchy, the granting of independence to all Arab states not yet fully independent (including Syria and Lebanon but not Aden), and the creation of a Jewish state in all of western Palestine which could also be included in the federation under the Saudi Monarchy. To encourage Ibn Saud's support, the Zionists were to pay him £20 million, which was presumably (the point remained unclear in Philby's proposal) to be devoted to the resettlement of landless Palestinian Arabs outside Palestine.[3] Philby arranged a meeting between the Saudi Ambassador in London, Fuad Hamza, and Weizmann during the St. James Conference, but the Saudi avoided a further meeting called shortly afterwards and nothing came of this initial attempt to gain acceptance of Philby's proposal.[4] Some months later Philby again tried to interest the Zionists in his plan and

---

[1] Cf. M. J. Cohen, *Palestine: Retreat from the Mandate. The Making of British Policy 1936-1945* (London, 1978), p. 83; and CO to HC No. 250, 21 April 1939, CO 733/410//75872/78(1939).

[2] During the St. James Conference Ben Gurion proposed a 'Semitic Federation' in the Middle East which would include a Jewish State (Rose, *Gentile Zionists,* p. 185), and in March 1939 Weizmann told MacDonald that he would be prepared to 'consider cantonisation, with a view to a federal state' *ibid,* p. 191).

[3] Philby gave an account of the details of his proposal in his *Arabian Jubilee* (London, 1952), pp. 212-13.

[4] According to Elizabeth Monroe, *Philby of Arabia* (London, 1973), p. 219, Ben Gurion was also present at the luncheon of 28 February 1939, although Philby's own

at a meeting on 6 October 1939 with Weizmann, Shertok and Namier, it was mutually agreed that Philby should try to obtain Ibn Saud's endorsement of his plan while the Zionists, through their political connections as well as through public opinion, would attempt to 'create circumstances which would favour such a scheme'.[5] Philby hoped that Ibn Saud would endorse the proposal as it would not only ensure full Arab independence but would also guarantee Zionist support for the promotion of the Wahabi dynasty to the kingship of the Arab federation and would provide £20 million at a time when Saudi funds were depleted because of the wartime interruption of the pilgrimage.

Philby returned to Saudi Arabia shortly after his October meeting with Weizmann, Shertok and Namier in London, and for the next half year he attempted unsuccessfully to gain Ibn Saud's support for his scheme. He subsequently claimed that the Saudi Monarch was prepared to consider the scheme seriously should it be proposed to him by the British and American Governments,[6] and in April 1940 he informed Weizmann that the King was 'just thinking out how it can be worked without producing a howl of anger among certain Arab elements'.[7] In fact, it appears that Philby greatly overestimated his success in promoting the scheme, and nothing further developed on the Saudi side until 1943, when Ibn Saud vehemently denied that he had ever favoured Philby's proposals.

Amongst the Zionists only Weizmann and Namier paid serious attention to Philby. Shertok was sceptical and did not refer to Philby's efforts again after participating in the October 1939 meeting,[8] even though the principle of federation as a possible alternative to the White Paper was discussed a number of times – if only as a *pis aller* – by the Agency in Jerusalem during 1940 (as MacMichael had warned the Colonial Office).[9] Weizmann remained convinced that contacts with Ibn Saud through Philby might eventually provide a break-

account does not mention this meeting, claiming that he made his proposal first in September of that year (Philby, p. 213).

[5] Minutes by Namier of meeting of 6 October 1939, in Philby Papers, Box 10 File 3, Middle East Centre, St. Anthony's College, Oxford.

[6] Philby, p. 113.

[7] Dora Philby, (for H. St. J. Philby) to Weizmann 16 April 1940 and subsequent correspondence. Philby Papers, Box 10, File 3.

[8] Bauer, *From Diplomacy to Resistance,* pp. 226-7.

[9] The Palestine Military Intelligence Summary for early May 1940 reported:

At a recent meeting of the Jewish Agency Executive, Mr. Shertok spoke on the subject of federation and expressed doubts as to the practicality of the scheme, but stressed the importance of not allowing this to pass without enquiring into the possibilities of finding through in the Palestine impasse and he attempted to gain British and later American support for Philby's proposals several times during the war. Undeterred by the lack of any early success in his efforts to deal with Ibn Saud, Weizmann wanted to keep alive the idea that the White Paper was not the only possible British policy on Palestine, and that an alternative might be found in federation.

Prior to 1939 the concept of Arab federation had not attracted serious attention within either the Foreign or the Colonial Offices. Although it was to become a major issue in Middle Eastern affairs during and after the war years, the Eastern and Middle East Departments first began to consider their respective departmental positions on Arab federation only when various proposals were made during 1939 linking federation with possible solutions of the Palestine problem.[10] Shortly after the outbreak of war the Eastern Department prepared the Foreign Office's first comprehensive memorandum on federation in an attempt to define Britain's policy.[11]

The memorandum agreed, with the Arab nationalists, that there was nothing inherently permanent about most of the borders between the Arab states, and that the desire for Arab solidarity, 'stimulated enormously in all Arab countries by the troubles in Palestine', was

an outlet from the impasse in which the Palestine question finds itself if such an outlet showed any prospect of nullifying the White Paper. Generally speaking, the members of the Political Department of the Jewish Agency seem to be ready to discuss the federal arrangement provided that the scheme assured the Jews free immigration into Palestine and colonisation without artificial restrictions. (Palestine Military Intelligence Summary, No. 10/40, 10 May 1940, CO 732/86//79097(1940).
In early September 1940 Shertok and Zaslani went to Cairo and, according to a Military Intelligence report, one of their intentions was 'to try and get in touch with King Ibn Saud in order to find out his attitude towards the Jewish problem in Palestine' (Summary No. 18/40, 18 September 1940, *ibid.*). By October 1940, Eliahu Epstein, a member of the Political department of the Agency (but a man whose views did not reflect a widespread attitude) advocated 'coming to terms with the Arabs and encouraging the union of Palestine, Syria and Transjordan'. He appeared to favour 'crystallisation' of the National Home, presumably by cantonisation or local autonomy, and to hope for the possibility of limited immigration into the remainder of the union' (Summary No. 20/40, 15 October 1940, *ibid.*). Following a further visit by Shertok to Cairo in 1941 and his talks there with Iraqi and Egyptian politicians, Shertok prepared a Jewish Agency internal report which discussed Arab federation in general (i.e., not just its Palestine aspect). He concluded that the leaders of the Arab world were not seriously interested in federation as an immediate objective and that therefore a major reconstruction of the Middle East could not be expected for a long time (Report by Political Department of Jewish Agency, Arab Affairs, 27 December 1941, on Macpherson to Boyd, 16 January 1942, CO 732/87(i)//79238(1942)).

[10]Cf. Eyres' minutes on proposals of Prof. A.F. Lawrence, January 1939, FO 371/23245 E1274; and Vansittart to Lawrence, 29 March 1939, FO 371/23246 E1573; minutes on FO 371/23194 E2655 (Bagallay – Comte de Caix de St. Aymour interview, 5 April 1939) and Bagallay to Sir E. Phipps (H.M. ambassador, Paris) 17 March 1939, CO 733/398//75156/14(39).

[11]Bagallay memorandum, 28 September 1939, FO 371/23239 E6357.

growing. However, the counterbalancing forces of local nationalism, the practical difficulties of administering a federation, the suspicions of France and perhaps also of Turkey, all made Arab federation unrealistic. Furthermore, the memorandum argued, Britain's own interests (communications and oil) might be adversely affected by a federation of Arab states: '. . .a single State embracing all the Arab countries would not be amenable to British influence in the same way as a number of small and weaker States.'[12] The Eastern Department did not believe that by endorsing federation Britain would obtain Arab support for any solution to the Palestine problem which might meet Zionist demands for increased or continued Jewish immigration (which was the lowest common denominator of Zionist demands). However, as federation *per se* (i.e., independently of its Palestine aspect) was supported by Arab nationalism with its demands, vague and inchoate at that stage, for Arab unity, the British government did not want to be seen to be an obstacle to Arab nationalist ambitions. The memorandum therefore concluded that if the Pan-Arab movement gained wide support then the only policy which Britain could adopt was to 'endeavour to guide the movement along lines which would ensure that the ensuing federation or union was friendly to Great Britain' and that in the meanwhile 'a positive declaration on the subject should be avoided as long as possible'.[13] The views set out by the Eastern Department in this memorandum were accepted by the Foreign Office, and its recommendations determined Britain's attitude, both to Arab federation and to the attempts to solve the Palestine problem through federation, until the whole question came under official review once again three years later.

Before then, however, a passing reference in favour of federation as a possible solution to the Palestine problems made by Lord Lloyd to Weizmann in July 1940,[14] encouraged the latter to take the question up with the Foreign Secretary, Lord Halifax, in an interview on 28 August 1940. At their meeting, the possibility of finding an alternative solution was discussed in very general terms, and in their respective accounts of the interview each attributed the idea to the other. Halifax thought the suggestion sufficently interesting to inform Churchill of Weizmann's thinking,[15] and he also discussed it with Lord Lloyd. Lloyd was interested in Arab federation both because of

[12]*Ibid.*

[13]*Ibid.*

[14]Protocols of Jewish Agency Executive in London, 12 July 1940, C.Z.A. Z4/302/23.

[15]Halifax to Churchill, 28 August 1940, FO 371/24567 E2387. Weizmann's account is on Protocols, 29 August 1940, Z4/302/24.

its possible bearing on Palestine (as he had mentioned to Weizmann) and because of his general sympathy with Arab nationalism. He recommended to Halifax that Britain seize the opportunity created by France's defection from the Allied cause to grant Syria independence, encourage Arab federation and dictate a peace settlement for the Middle East.[16] In the course of his talks with Halifax, Weizmann told the Foreign Secretary of his indirect 'contacts' with Ibn Saud via Philby. Although he expressed little faith in Philby personally as an intermediary, Weizmann did report Philby's assessment that for the sum of £20 million Ibn Saud would be prepared to promote an Arab federation which included an autonomous Jewish area in Palestine.[17]

Halifax put both Weizmann's and Lloyd's ideas to the Eastern Department, which immediately advised him not to encourage Weizmann any further. In a lengthy minute, Baggallay explained Foreign Office policy on Arab Federation as a whole – that Britain should not encourage the idea but, on the other hand, should not appear to be an insuperable obstacle to Arab unity if the Arab world wanted it. As for endorsing a Jewish autonomous area within an Arab federation or making Britain's support for federation conditional on the Arabs' acceptance of Jewish autonomy, Baggallay likened such a position to the Balfour Declaration, the consequences of which he considered 'little short of disastrous'.[18] Halifax accepted the conclusion that whatever merits a Jewish autonomous area might have, the British Government must not give any indication that it was prepared to advocate it, and he instructed that Lord Lloyd also be informed of Foreign Office thinking on this question.[19]

Weizmann's talks with Halifax had taken place at a time when relations between the Zionists in London and the British Government were better than they had been since the publication of the White Paper fifteen months earlier. Despite the introduction of the restrictions on land sales in February 1940, no apparent steps had been taken subsequently towards the introduction of the Heads of Department scheme, and illegal immigration was at its lowest level since the outbreak of war. The deterioration of relations caused by the events related to the sinking of the *Patria* were some months in the future. Furthermore, progress was being made on the Jewish Army question. On 13 September, two weeks after Weizmann had discussed federation

[16]Departmental minutes of Halifax's account of his discussion with Lloyd (Bagallay minute, 5 September 1940, FO 371/24569 E2635).

[17]*Ibid.*

[18]*Ibid.*

[19]Halifax minute, 7 September 1940, *ibid.*

with Halifax, Anthony Eden (then Secretary of State for War) told Weizmann that Halifax, Lloyd and himself were prepared to accept in principle the Jewish Agency's proposal for a Jewish Fighting Force (a decision which was subsequently reversed a year later). In the friendly atmosphere of the meeting on 13 September, Weizmann recounted his talks with Halifax to Eden and to Lloyd (who was also present). Baggallay, who was representing the Foreign Office at the meeting, subsequently resolved that the time had come to carry out Halifax's instructions and inform Lloyd of Foreign Office thinking on the matter and to caution him (via his private secretary) against encouraging the Zionists to think that the Government might be prepared to endorse Weizmann's federation proposals.[20]

Lloyd accepted the Foreign Office reminder of the need for caution, but he remained interested in the concept of a solution through federation and engaged in a lengthy private correspondence with the High Commissioner during the period under discussion, in which he expressed his own feelings on the idea. He told MacMichael that 'Jewish minds are thinking on the lines of a self-contained Jewish unit in a federation', and added: 'The idea is not without its attraction. I have always felt that there can be no real solution of the Palestine problem within the present territorial limits of Palestine, and it may be that, with the position as fluid as it is at present in Syria, an opening will occur which will make big political alterations possible in your part of the world.'[21] MacMichael replied that he felt that such a solution was possible, but only if the Jews were prepared to accept a token area in Palestine and a refuge for European Jews somewhere else.[22] However, the sudden deterioration in the Zionists' relations with the Colonial Office which followed the *Patria* incident, and Lloyd's death a few months later, cut short his tentative efforts to explore possible alternatives to the White Paper, while within the Foreign Office the Eastern Department had successfully convinced Halifax that the question should not be pursued any further.

[20]W.I. Mallett, Halifax's private secretary, to C. Eastwood, Lloyd's private secretary, 19 September 1940, FO 371/24569 E2635.

[21]Lloyd to HCr, 24 September 1940, CO 733/444//75872/115(1940).

[22]HCr to Lloyd, 4 October 1940, *ibid*. The private correspondence between Lloyd and MacMichael continued for some time, and was paralleled by correspondence between Shuckburgh – the longest serving 'Palestine hand' in the civil service – and MacMichael. The opinions expressed in both these series of letters (and in correspondence between MacMichael and the other Secretaries of State during the war) were frequently referred to in the files and occasionally quoted. However, the communications themselves have either not survived or (more likely) have not yet been opened for research. That the Lloyd-MacMichael correspondence on the federation question continued into November 1940 at least can be seen from HCr to CO, Most Secret and Personal, 12 November 1940, CO 733/426//75872/85(40).

Within a few days of Lord Lloyd's death, the Middle East Department prepared a lengthy memorandum on the question of federation (presumably intended for Lord Moyne, Lloyd's successor as Secretary of State), dismissing the notion that the Arabs would accept any degree of Jewish autonomy in exchange for support of Arab unity.[23] Not only was discussion of federation unrealistic therefore, but there were also, the memorandum argued, specific reasons why the British Government should reject it – the risk of becoming involved in the dynastic and party rivalries of the Arab world, and the problem of relations with the French in the Middle East. But, and herein lay the Middle East Department's central message to the new Colonial Secretary, the most significant objection to federation from the British point of view was 'the danger of re-opening the Palestine controversy'. The Arabs had always doubted Britain's willingness and ability to stand up to Zionist pressure against the White Paper and the Colonial Office was particularly sensitive to this fact. To raise, however cautiously, the question of Jewish autonomy within the context of Arab federation would, the memorandum argued, be enough to confirm Arab doubts: 'Any suggestion that we still have an open mind and are toying with alternative policies, e.g. "federation," would have the disastrous effect of reviving the [Arab] fears, uncertainties and apprehensions which the White Paper has done so much to allay.'[24] In effect, this memorandum argued that even though it was becoming increasingly apparent that the major provisions of the White Paper (on immigration and constitutional development) were unworkable, there could be no 'open mind' on Palestine and no consideration of alternative policies.

It would seem that the 'fears, uncertainities and apprehensions' which would be revived in the Arab world if alternative policies were discussed were shared by the departments responsible for Palestine affairs in London. As subsequent events were to show, these departments adhered to the White Paper not because they had faith in that policy's specific provisions but because it was the concrete expression of the redirection of Palestine policy which took place in 1938-9. To re-open debate on the White Paper would inevitably have meant a reconsideration by Churchill's Government of the whole policy on Palestine – and this was something which both the Eastern and Middle East Departments wished to avoid.

Despite an initial interest in federation proposals shown by Lloyd and Halifax during 1940, by the end of that year it seemed that

[23]Downie memorandum, 12 February 1941, CO 732/87(i)//79283(1941).
[24]*Ibid.*

Weizmann had failed to gain any meaningful political support. In March 1941, just prior to his departure for the United States, he was able to discuss directly with Churchill ideas which were very similar to those put forward by Philby. According to Weizmann's subsequent account of the talks (which he did not confide to the Agency executive in London at the time), Churchill supported the main outline of Weizmann's own thinking regarding a federal settlement with the Arabs, with Ibn Saud taking a leading role.[25] However, after Weizmann left for America the concept of a Jewish autonomous area within an Arab federation received no further attention in London until political developments in the Middle East revived the entire question of Arab policy three months later.

The Rashid Ali coup in Iraq in April 1941 not only created a crisis in Anglo-Iraqi relations but also brought the question of Britain's relations with the Vichy regime in Syria to the forefront, for it seemed that the Axis powers were about to gain a foothold in both Iraq and Syria. The fall of France in June 1940 and the subsequent alignment of the French authorities in Syria and Lebanon with Vichy created political as well as strategic problems for Britain. It was initially decided that in the interests of post-war Anglo-French relations, Britain would respect France's position in its Syrian and Lebanese Mandates and would consequently discourage any Arab attempts to exploit France's difficulties in order to extract political concessions or to expel her altogether. It was also resolved that, as stability in Syria was in Britain's own interest, the government would be willing to deal with the Vichy authorities there.[26] However, the deteriorating position in Iraq, and the appearance of German aircraft in Syria en route to assist the Rashid Ali regime, convinced the authorities in London that the Vichy administration would have to be replaced as soon as possible by Free French forces, with British military assistance if necessary. This decision had first been taken by the Defence Committee on 8 May,[27] but was not discussed by the Cabinet for a further eleven days. In the interim the High Commissioner in Palestine also took up the question of a declaration to the Arabs by the British Government, pointing out that for such a declaration to be

[25]Weizmann to S. Gestetner, 15 March 1941, *Letters and Papers of Chaim Weizmann* (Jerusalem, 1979), Series A, vol. XX, p. 125. Additional references to this meeting with Churchill can be found in Weizmann's autobiography *Trial and Error* (London, 1966), p. 525; and Gilbert, *Churchill and Zionism,* p. 24.

[26]Foreign Office Memorandum to M.E.(O) Committee, ME(O)(41)21, 26 June 1940, and HCr to CO No. 621, 3 July 1940, Cab 21/1439.

[27]Sir Llewellyn Woodward, *British Foreign Policy During the Second World War,* History of the Second World War, Civil Series, Volume I (London, 1962), p. 564.

effective it must meet Arab aspirations for an independent Syria without reservations designed to guarantee French (Free or Vichy) interests there.[28]

MacMichael's cable attracted Churchill's attention, and he appended it to a memorandum he wrote to Sir John Dill, Chief of the Imperial General Staff, in which he suggested a policy for the forthcoming incursion into Syria and at the same time formulated a radically new departure in Britain's general policy towards the Arab world. Churchill advocated ending the French Mandate for Syria, proclaiming an independent Arab state there, under British auspices, and forming a federation of Arab states under Ibn Saud with whom some settlement would be reached about the Jews.[29] Churchill instructed the C.I.G.S. to consider these suggestions 'as a background', but added that he considered them important and invited Dill to discuss them with him after the immediate military tasks in the Middle East had been accomplished one month hence.[30] Immediately afterwards, however, Churchill prepared a fuller memorandum which elaborated on the steps to be taken to declare Syria independent of France.[31] He also suggested that Britain take advantage of its sponsorship of Syrian independence by offering some Syrian territory to the Turks and settling Turkish-French disputes over Syria generally in Turkey's favour as a means of countering German influence in Turkey and binding her more closely to the Allies.[32] Churchill also proposed making Ibn Saud 'general overlord' of Iraq and Transjordan, and obtaining his agreement to an autonomous Jewish state in western Palestine, to form part of the Arab Federation.[33]

This second memorandum was printed as a Cabinet paper, presumably for circulation to the War Cabinet in anticipation of the debate that day on Syria – the first time that the Cabinet was scheduled to discuss the Defence Committee's recommendations of 8

[28] HCr to CO No. 669, 16 May 1941, Prem 3/296/17.

[29] Churchill Memorandum to C.I.G.S. M557/1, 18 May 1941, Prem. 3/296/17.

[30] Ibid.

[31] 'Syrian Policy', Memorandum by the Prime Minister, 19 May 1941, Prem 3/422/2. This document was first published in Cohen, Churchill, pp. 82-4, where it is available in full, together with many other documents cited in this work.

[32] The sudden introduction of Turkish affairs into Churchill's proposals may be explained by a memo, addressed to him by Eden on the same day that Churchill's own memorandum was prepared. Eden warned of an increase in German pressure on Turkey and commented: 'the only way to ensure that Turkey holds fast is to deal at the earliest possible moment with the situation in Syria and Iraq' (Eden to Churchill, PM/41/12, 19 May 1941, FO 371/27043 E2476).

[33] 'Syrian Policy', Memorandum by the Prime Minister.

May, that British Forces assist Free French forces in an armed invasion of that territory. However, final copies of the paper were never circulated,[34] and in the brief Cabinet debate on Syria that did take place, Churchill (according to the Cabinet Conclusions) mentioned only that he had formulated a proposal of his own and would submit it to the Foreign Secretary.[35]

The proposals for Palestine which Churchill detailed in his memorandum embodied, no doubt, the 'plan' he had discussed with Weizmann in March, and was the first time since 1939 that he had actually put forward an alternative to the White Paper he disliked so much. That alone would have ensured the opposition of the responsible officials, but the memorandum did not deal only with Palestine. By suggesting that Britain actively exclude France from Syria, Churchill was advocating that the Government abandon its traditional policy towards the French Levant, a policy which had been reconfirmed less than a year earlier. Promoting Ibn Saud as head of a wide Arab federation would have meant abandoning the long-established policy of the Colonial and Foreign Offices of maintaining balance between the Wahabis of the Arabian Peninsula and the Hashemites of Iraq and Transjordan. Consequently Departmental opposition to Churchill's proposal was massive.

The Foreign Office considered Churchill's recommendations to be positively alarming. The Eastern Department argued that concessions to the Arabs on Syria would not guarantee Arab opinion, let alone provide a pretext for solving the Palestine problem in favour of the Zionists. As for the proposal that a Jewish state be created as part of an Arab federation, the Eastern Department repeated its earlier conclusion reached when the idea had been put forward in 1940 – that Britain could only endorse a settlement reached directly between the Arabs and the Jews, and could not impose a Jewish state on an unwilling Arab world. Churchill's suggestion that Ibn Saud become monarch of a British-sponsored Arab federation was dismissed as impractical.[36]

These views were first expressed by the Eastern Department, but the official Foreign Office reply to the Prime Minister's proposals could not be purely departmental and was consequently determined at a meeting between the Eastern Department, the Permanent Under

[34]Martin minute, 21 May 1941, Prem 4/32/5.

[35]WM 51(41)3, 19 May 1941, (Confidential Annex) Cab 65/22.

[36]'Minutes on Prime Minister's Note on Syrian Policy', by Baxter, 22 May 1941, FO 371/27043 E2685.

Secretary (Cadogan) and the Secretary of State (Eden).[37] Each of Churchill's proposals was considered in turn and a memorandum was drafted, designed originally as a direct reply to him. However, this memorandum ended up being printed and circulated as an official Cabinet paper.[38] Starting with Palestine, the paper argued that Britain's conduct of policy there had 'facilitated the present rebellion of the Iraqi military leaders, which is directed against our position in the Middle East'. The Foreign Office stated in an allusion to the *modus vivendi* within the Cabinet on Palestine affairs, that for its part it was not asking for a reconsideration of Palestine policy at that stage, and agreed that a unique opportunity existed for Britain to sponsor Syrian independence. It suggested, however, that the Free French first be given a real chance to do this themselves. Should they fail 'to win over Syria to our side' by not promising Syria and Lebanon their independence, or should such a promise fail 'to bring Syria over to us', Britain should take military and diplomatic action to promote Syrian independence. As for the question of federation, the overlordship of Ibn Saud and the solution to the Palestine problem which Churchill had proposed, the Foreign Office commented that while an Arab federation was not practical politics at that time, Britain should express its support for it whenever the opportunity arose.

As this Cabinet paper was intended to be a direct reply to Churchill, Eden himself carefully amended the first draft prepared by the Eastern Department, contrary to his general practice on papers emanating from that Department. However, as Churchill's memorandum had not been circulated to the Cabinet, the Foreign Office could not take direct issue with the specific proposals made by the Prime Minister. The paper was therefore entitled 'Our Arab Policy' and made passing reference to Saudi Arabia and Iraq so as to give it the appearance of a general survey of Middle Eastern affairs.[39]

---

[37] Minutes, *ibid.*

[38] WP(41)116 'Our Arab Policy', 27 May 1941, Cab 66/16.

[39] As the Foreign Office paper was in fact a reply to Churchill and not a statement reflecting a basic review by officials of British policy in the Middle East, the Foreign Office had not bothered to consult the Colonial Office when it was drafted. (The Colonial Office was still not aware of Churchill's original memorandum.) When they saw the Cabinet paper, Parkinson endorsed the views it expressed but complained of the lack of consultation, writing sarcastically: 'I was wondering whether you would like to see in draft and have an opportunity to comment on a Cabinet Paper from the Colonial Office about relations with Venezuela?' (Parkinson to Cadogan, 31 May 1941, FO 371/27043 E2716).The Foreign Office apologised, explaining that their paper was a reply to a paper from the Prime Minister and was not intended to initiate a review by the Foreign Office alone on Arab policy. Cadogan added that Eden himself had, at the last moment, decided to circulate it as a Cabinet paper (Cadogan to Parkinson, 5 June 1941, *ibid.*). It is interesting to note that when it referred to

In a brief conclusion the paper set out the Foreign Office's policy recommendations:

    (a) Palestine. No change
    (b) Syria. If the Free French can do nothing we should declare ourselves in favour of Syrian independence. . .
    (c) Public support of the idea of Arab federation, the terms of which it must be left to the Arabs to work out.[40]

The Cabinet considered the paper on 2 June 1941, and after a brief debate on Syrian policy it endorsed the Foreign Office's recommendations.[41] The Foreign Office had therefore effectively forestalled the possibility of any radical new departures in Middle Eastern affairs such as those proposed by Churchill. On Palestine the Cabinet accepted the Foreign Office's principal point – that there should be no change in the *status quo* concerning the White Paper. As for the rest, the Cabinet paper's recommendations on Syrian independence were sufficiently vague to leave the Foreign Office entirely free in its conduct of the ongoing talks with the Free French on that territory's political future; while on Arab federation, the Foreign Office obtained explicit authorisation to make to the Arab World a declaration of British policy (which by then had been under consideration for some weeks) expressing Britain's sympathy towards Arab interest in the question of unity.[42] By adding the phrase 'the terms of which it must be left to the Arabs to work out' the Foreign Office succeeded, at the same time, in gaining the Cabinet's implicit (and perhaps unwitting) rejection of Churchill's proposal that Britain should actively sponsor such a federation under the leadership of Ibn Saud, and, as *quid pro quo,* obtain Arab support for an autonomous Jewish state in Palestine.

The solution of the Palestine impasse embodied in Churchill's proposal (which was so similar to the ideas actively advocated by

Churchill's memorandum the Foreign Office did not take the opportunity of informing the Colonial Office of its contents.

[40] WP(41)116, 'Our Arab Policy', 27 May 1941, Cab 66/16.

[41] WM 56(41)4, Cab 65/18.

[42] Shortly after the Eastern Department had met Eden to discuss Churchill's memorandum, it was instructed that the Secretary of State wanted 'to say something about "Arab Federation"' in his forthcoming Guildhall speech (minutes, FO 371/27043 E2793). The Department thus drafted the following passage in Eden's celebrated Mansion House Speech delivered on 29 May 1941: 'Many Arab thinkers desire for the Arab peoples a greater degree of unity than they now enjoy. In reaching out towards this unity they hope for our support. No such appeal from our friends should go unanswered. It seems to me both natural and right that the cultural and economic ties between the Arab countries, and the political ties too, should be strengthened. His Majesty's Government for their part will give their full support to any scheme that commands general approval' (draft and final text of this speech are *ibid.*).

Weizmann during the previous eighteen months) was basically a by-product of the search for a policy on the future of Syria. It was that Mandate, and not Palestine, whose fate was in question during mid-1941, and the ideas on Palestine which Churchill had recommended to Dill and then to Eden depended on Britain first being able to offer Syrian independence to the Arab world. In the negotiations with the Free French during the period under discussion (i.e. in the weeks preceding the invasion of Syria) this possibility was foreclosed, and any thought that Britain might abandon its traditional support for France's role in the Middle East in favour of Syrian independence was soon put aside. While Britain did force the Free French to issue a statement prior to the invasion which promised Syrian and Lebanese independence, it also agreed to a number of reservations which limited that independence and protected France's interests.[43] A few months later, when it seemed that the Free French were not fulfilling their commitments to the Syrians, the question was revived, but the potential in May-June 1941 for reshaping the Middle East, on which Churchill's proposals were based, no longer existed, and for the time being he did not press them.[44] While it had rejected Churchill's proposal (and obtained Cabinet authority to do so), the Foreign Office did not oppose the principle of finding a solution to the Palestine problem through federation. What it strongly rejected was that a solution to the Palestine problem be imposed on the Arab world, or that Britain take the initiative in advocating any solution on behalf of the Zionists. Either position would have gone against the redirection of policy embodied in the White Paper – that Britain was no longer prepared to impose on the Arab world, or even to recommend, any solution to the Palestine problem which the Arabs did not want.

Churchill's initiative was not the only attempt to exploit the opportunity afforded by developments in Syria in mid-1941 to find a solution to Palestine's problems. As a member of the Middle East (Ministerial) Committee, Leo Amery received copies of MacMichael's correspondence relating to Transjordan in which the High Commissioner pointed to the impact which the invasion on Syria was having on Britain's other Mandate in the Middle East, and to the Emir

[43] Woodward, *British Foreign Policy*, Volume 1, pp. 566-7, and Kirk, *The Middle East*, pp. 106-9.

[44] Churchill was also, no doubt, diverted from his proposal to Eden by military developments. Between the time he sent his memorandum to Eden (19 May) and the Cabinet discussion on the Foreign Office's reply (2 June), Crete fell to the Germans.

Abdullah's interest in the Syrian throne.[45] Amery wrote to Eden suggesting, *inter alia*, that the incursion into Syria be matched by the granting of full independence to Transjordan, the creation of an Arab federation and the partitioning of Palestine along the lines recommended by the Peel Commission. The Jewish unit thereby created ('whether called State or Province') would form part of the Arab federation.[46] Amery's proposal was similar to Churchill's, but Amery gave Emir Abdullah the throne of Syria which Churchill had reserved for Ibn Saud. Amery succeeded in having his proposal placed on the agenda of the Middle East (Ministerial) Committee and it was discussed in mid-July.[47] Although no conclusions were reached, and the Committee was disbanded shortly thereafter, Amery's letter to Eden, unlike Churchill's, did reach the Colonial Office as Lord Moyne was also a member of the Committee.[48]

Moyne was interested in Amery's ideas and insisted that the proposal be put to the High Commissioner.[49] Thus the letter, which had originally been put aside together with the Middle East (Ministerial) Committee, paradoxically achieved the one thing which the Middle East Department had tried to avoid when Lloyd raised the question in late 1940 and the Eastern Department had tried to avoid when Churchill raised it in May 1941 – it re-opened at official level the debate on Palestine policy and on the White Paper. For although MacMichael personally opposed Arab federation (both on its own account and as a means of solving the Palestine problem[50]), he was concerned that Britain might actually favour a Jewish autonomous unit in Palestine and might be intending to create one in the immediate future. Consequently, he responded to Moyne's communication with concrete proposals of his own for changing the White Paper.

MacMichael warned that any attempt to establish a Jewish unit as large as that suggested by the Peel Commission in 1937 'would undoubtedly lead to a fresh Arab revolt'. However, 'a small token

[45] HCr to CO No. 822, cited in Amery to Eden, 11 June 1941 (Amery Papers, Box 140).

[46] Amery to Eden, 11 June 1941.

[47] ME(M)(41) 3rd meeting, 11 July 1941, Cab 95/2.

[48] Thus a copy of Amery to Eden, 11 June 1941, is on CO 733/444(1)//75872/115(41).

[49] Bennett minute, 25 June 1941, *ibid.*

[50] MacMichael took every opportunity to discredit the concept of Arab unity. Cf. his 'Note on the Prospects of "Federation" as a Solution of the Palestine Problem,' which he prepared for the Minister of State in Cairo and copied to the Colonial Office in September 1941 (CO 732/87(1)//79238(41)).

Jewish state' would, he argued, be acceptable to the Arabs 'if it was coupled with steps towards Arab independence', and 'would provide an ideal solution' to the Palestine impasse. MacMichael believed that such a state, as part of the Britain Empire, would be 'entirely consonant with the views of the vast majority' of the Jews although it would no doubt be opposed by the 'professional politicians of the Jewish Agency', whom he considered to be 'the real bar to any kind of progress along the road of conciliation and commonsense'. If the Jews did not accept such a state, then Britain should seize the opportunity to revise the Mandate, abolish the Jewish Agency, abandon the constitutional provisions of the White Paper (which he disliked almost as much as he disliked the Agency) and turn Palestine into a Crown Colony 'until its people can manage to live together in amity'.[51]

Although MacMichael's proposals were different from anything which had been suggested by Churchill or Amery, the difference between a Jewish state occupying the whole of western Palestine (as proposed by Churchill), or within the borders recommended by the Peel Commission (as proposed by Amery) and a 'token state' (as proposed by the High Commissioner) was only one of size. MacMichael had come to believe that some form of Jewish autonomy was necessary, contrary to the policy of the White Paper, if only, as he later made clear, in order to give to the Jewish authorities themselves the invidious task of selecting the refugees who could enter 'their' state. Furthermore, MacMichael had repeated his dislike of the constitutional provisions of the White Paper and wanted to use the chance afforded by a re-examination of Palestine's future to have these provisions put aside, thus undermining the White Paper as a whole.

The Middle East Department was alarmed by MacMichael's telegram, and prepared a lengthy and detailed critique of each of his proposals. It pointed out that regardless of what the Arab world as a whole would gain by Syrian independence and Arab federation, the Arabs of Palestine would not gain anything directly by it and would not therefore be any more yielding in their attitude towards the Jews than they had been in the past. Furthermore, the Jewish world as a whole (and not just the 'professional politicians of the Jewish Agency', as MacMichael claimed) would not accept a token state especially since it already anticipated that 'they can secure powerful political support in this country in their post-war campaign for the

[51] HCr to CO No. 1021, Most Secret and Personal, 13 July 1941, CO 733/444(1)//75872/115(41).

smashing of the White Paper policy'.[52] The Department also dismissed MacMichael's suggestion that the constitutional provisions be abandoned and Palestine be turned into a Crown Colony as an inadmissible breach of faith. Instead, the Department argued, Britain could only continue to adhere to the White Paper, using the phrase 'perseverance, not partition' as a concise expression of its advice. Commenting on the differences between the High Commissioner and the Middle East Department Moyne said that further discussion would not be fruitful,[53] and as the Colonial Office had prevented the terms of MacMichael's telegram going beyond itself and the Eastern Department of the Foreign Office,[54] the debate appeared to be at an end.

However, Amery's interest in the Palestine question had by now been fully revived and, despite his earlier failure to interest the Middle East (Ministerial) Committee in using the Syrian situation as a lever for reviving partition, he set about mobilising support for his proposals. First he wrote to Sir Reginald Coupland,[55] the senior surviving member of the Peel Commission and the author of the Commision's proposals on partition, asking for his views on the suggestions that the Palestine problem be solved through Arab federation.[56] Coupland responded at once, pointing out that although the Peel Commissioners had themselves been precluded in 1937 from considering any changes in Palestine's frontiers, the Commissioners had favoured a solution based on partition within a wider federation incorporating Syria, and had tried unsuccessfully to interest the incumbent Colonial Secretary (Ormsby-Gore) in it.[57] Shortly after the release of the White Paper in May 1939, the surviving members of the Commission had put their proposal in a letter to *The Times* and Coupland had tried various means to gain support for his ideas.[58] At Amery's suggestion Coupland once again took the matter up and in August 1941 he sent a lengthy memorandum to Moyne strongly

[52] Luke minute, 21 July 1941, *ibid*. Boyd, Shuckburgh and Parkinson each endorsed this very long minute.

[53] Moyne minute, 4 August 1941, *ibid*.

[54] Boyd to Baxter (Most Secret) 17 July 1941: 'This telegram, HCr to CO No. 1021, has so far not been distributed outside the Colonial Office, and copies are not being sent to any Committees. . .' (FO 371/27044 E3937).

[55] Beit Professor of the History of Colonial Empire, Oxford, 1920-48.

[56] Amery to Coupland, 19 July 1941, Amery Papers Box 135.

[57] Coupland memorandum, in Coupland to Amery, 6 August 1941, *ibid*.

[58] The surviving members of the Peel Commission were Coupland, Sir Horace Rumbold, Sir Walter Crane and Sir Harold Morris. Their letter appeared on 22 May 1939.

favouring the establishment of two separate provinces in Palestine linked with Syria and Lebanon in a pan-Syrian federation.[59]

This memorandun reached the Colonial Office shortly after the Middle East Department had attempted to convince Moyne that both Amery's original proposal to the Middle East (Ministerial) Committee and MacMichael's subsequent suggestions were not worth pursuing. But the Department was aware that the Colonial Secretary remained interested in possible alternatives to the White Paper, that he had discussed the question with, amongst others, Brendan Bracken and Bevin, and that he intended to take the matter up with the Prime Minister.[60] MacMichael's and Amery's suggestions had been dealt with by Departmental minutes, but now Sir Cosmo Parkinson, the Permanent Under Secretary, intervened, writing a critique of Coupland's proposals and appealing to the Colonial Secretary to discuss the matter with his own advisers and to invite the views of the Foreign Office before he pursued the question in political circles.[61] Moyne agreed.[62] This time we must assume that the Colonial Office succeeded in impressing its reservations on Moyne for two days later he minuted that the time was not yet ripe for raising the question of Palestine and Arab federation.[63] Later that same week the question of Syrian independence was again discussed by the Cabinet, for it had become apparent that the Free French did not intend to make the immediate concessions to the Syrian Arabs that Britain had hoped for. Churchill again suggested in Cabinet that Britain break with the French over Syria and reach a general settlement (which would include Palestine) with the Arabs on the basis of granting Syrian independence. But both Eden and Moyne (now presumably convinced by Departmental hostility to the idea) spoke against it, and with the discussion going against him, Churchill succeeded only in preventing any final decision on his proposal being taken.[64] The Colonial Office greeted this conclusion with considerable relief, hoping that the question had finally been put aside until after the war, and that the accepted policy towards Palestine set out in the White Paper was not about to be challenged by any radical new initiative.[65]

---

[59] Sir R. Coupland to Moyne, 7 August 1941, CO 733/444(1)//75872/115(41).

[60] Parkinson minute, 20 August 1941, *ibid.*

[61] *Ibid.*

[62] Thornley (Private Secretary to Secretary of State) minute, 21 August 1941, *ibid.*

[63] Moyne minute, CO 875/9//6281/73(1941).

[64] WM 87(41)2, 28 August 1941, Cab 65/19.

[65] Boyd and Luke minutes, 3 September 1941, CO 733/444(1)//75872(41).

In fact, the possibility of finding a solution to the Palestine impasse through Arab federation remained alive. Despite the Foreign Office rebuff to his memorandum in June, Churchill was determined to have his proposals on Ibn Saud, Syria and Palestine considered more fully, and the opportunity to do so came during a visit to London by Oliver Lyttelton, the recently appointed Minister of State Resident in Cairo. On 10 September, Amery, who had so far failed to interest official circles in his own proposals, wrote to Churchill directly advocating a scheme almost identical to that which Churchill had himself proposed in his memorandum of May 1941.[66] Churchill warmly endorsed Amery's ideas, calling them 'full of interest and indeed the best I can think of,'[67] (there is evidence that Churchill himself was responsible for Amery having raised the question again)[68], and he instructed Eden, Moyne and Lyttelton to discuss the matter with Amery directly.[69]

The Prime Minister's instructions again placed the question on the agenda. The Foreign and Colonial Offices had managed to have it

[66] Amery to Churchill, 10 September 1941, Prem 4/52/5 Part 2 (Amery also wrote to Moyne, 10 September 1941, Amery Papers Box 135).

[67] Churchill minute M 923/1, 23 September 1941, Prem 4/52/5 Part 2.

[68] Amery's letter to Churchill was prompted by a letter that the former, as Secretary of State for India, had received from the Indian High Commissioner, Sir Firaz Khan Noon. Sir Firaz Khan suggested that Ibn Saud be made King of the Arabs, Syria be given independence and a Jewish autonomous unit be set up in Palestine – i.e. Churchill's own proposals (Firaz Khan Noon to Amery 3 September 1941, Amery Papers Box 135). As a leading Moslem politician Firaz Khan Noon's support for any solution to the Palestine problem was an asset, and that fact was the excuse Amery gave for bringing the matter before Churchill (Amery to Churchill, 10 September 1941). However, Churchill himself was responsible for Noon's sudden interest in the question. He had lunched with the Indian High Commissioner in mid-August and had discussed Palestine with him. Churchill advised him to meet Weizmann 'to talk the matter over', which he did on 2 September. Weizmann and Noon discussed the federation and the Ibn Saud proposal at length and Noon was left with the impression that the proposal was his own and that he had only convinced Weizmann of its feasibility with some difficulty (Firaz Khan Noon to Amery, 3 September 1941, Amery Papers Box 135). It was Noon's account of his meeting with Weizmann and the agreement that they had reached which prompted Amery to write to Churchill on 10 September in support of a proposal which was different in some of its details from Amery's own proposal. Amery's letter, in turn, provided Churchill with an excuse to bring the matter up again at an inter-ministerial level. Smuts wrote from South Africa also advocating that Amery take up a federal solution to the Palestine question. He urged that Britain exchange its support for an Arab federation for Arab agreement that such a federation 'be open to Jewish immigration and equal rights in land holding and otherwise'. (Smuts did not mention the possibility of Jewish autonomy within the Arab federation. He concluded: 'I hope you will find some time to explore it with your colleagues in the Foreign Office and Colonial Office. . .' (Smuts to Amery, 9 September 1941, Amery Papers Box 141). This letter would have arrived in London too late to have influenced Amery's decision to write to Churchill, but it does reflect the interest that Zionist sympathisers had in a solution through federation at that time.

[69] Churchill minute M 923/1, 23 September 1941, Prem 4/52/5.

glossed over each time it had appeared during the past five months, but this time Churchill's insistence on having his proposals considered resulted in the most far-reaching re-examination of British policy in the Middle East by the Civil Service since the deliberations in 1938 which had led up to the convening of the St. James Conference and the subsequent release of the White Paper in 1939. Churchill's persistence, however, was not the only factor in the debate.

In August the Saudi Arabian ambassador in London, Sheikh Hafiz Wahba, asked the Foreign Office for information concerning British intentions on Arab federation in view of the interest in the question that Eden had expressed in his Mansion House speech at the end of May. In the course of an interview with Eden he recommended that Britain take the initiative and come forward with a scheme for federation as soon as possible, adding that the Arabs 'would be deeply disappointed' if Britain intended to delay the question until after the war.[70] Copies of this interview were widely distributed[71] and observations were invited from British ambassadors in the various Arab capitals. At the same time MacMichael's lengthy telegram, in reply to Moyne's query of July on Palestine policy, was under discussion within the Foreign Office, where it evoked a more positive response than it had received in the Colonial Office.[72] The Foreign Office was interested in MacMichael's comments on the need to replace the Heads of Department scheme by the Advisory Councils which he had always advocated. But, more significantly, in the minutes on MacMichael's proposals the Eastern Department for the first time suggested that 'we must now recognise that Palestine cannot be considered by itself and that we must be prepared to find a solution in some form of federation. We must equally recognise that the White Paper will not be the final solution of the Palestine problem.'[73] What was now needed, the Eastern Department believed, was 'a far wider survey of the situation, taking Palestine, Transjordan, Syria and the Lebanon as a single unit, and trying to clear our own ideas regarding the future of this area'.[74] On 19 September, four days before Churchill's minute instructing that Amery's (and consequently his own) proposal be reconsidered, the Foreign Office wrote to the Colonial Office setting out the case for formulating a general Middle

[70]FO to Sonehewer-Bird No. 44, 15 August 1941, FO 371/27044 E4761.

[71]The King, Cabinet and Dominion Governments were, *inter alia*, sent telegrams.

[72]The telegram was actually discussed twice, first on 21-3 July 1941 (FO 371/27044 E3937) and again during August 1941 (FO 371/27137 E4536).

[73]Eyres minute, 12 August 1941, FO 371/27137 E4536.

[74]Baxter minute, 29 August 1941, *ibid.*

Eastern policy which took the recent political developments there into account. Pointing out that in the Mansion House speech Eden had stated his general sympathy with Arab unity 'without having any precise idea of how far we would be prepared to go to bring this about', the letter argued that this question should now be resolved. As for Palestine, the Eastern Department put forward a number of alternative policies for the Jewish National Home and for the Arab population (none of which included the White Paper) and suggested that they also be considered in the context of a general discussion of Middle East policy.[75]

This request alarmed the Colonial Office, where it was feared that the Foreign Office was about to revive the debate of the early 1930s on Britain's attitudes to the conflicting ambitions of the Hashemite and Wahabi dynasties.[76] Indications of a significant shift in Zionist thinking on the Jewish problem in Europe and its impact on the future of Palestine had prompted the Colonial Office itself to formulate new proposals, which it now sought to bring into any forthcoming debate on policy which might affect Palestine.

Zionism's political objectives were formally limited to the establishment of a Jewish National Home in Palestine, an objective which had been confirmed at the Twenty-first Zionist Congress in August 1939. Ever since the debate on the Peel Commission's recommendations on partition the possibility of going beyond a 'National Home' in a British Mandated territory had been discussed in Zionist circles. Furthermore, as had been indicated, in his discussions on Arab federation Weizmann talked of a Jewish state or province. However, the question was not felt to have any immediate import in the early years of the war and the terms 'state' and 'province' were used without distinction or precision. Moyne held a series of interviews with Weizmann and Ben Gurion in August 1941, when the question of Palestine policy was under active consideration in London. At a meeting with the Colonial Secretary on 1 August, Weizmann ventured the opinion that the position of the Jews in Europe was becoming hopeless, that the scope of the post-war refugee problem would be larger than ever imagined, and that, as the only solution to the problem, the Zionists hoped to bring 1,500,000 Jews to Palestine in the next twenty years.[77] Three weeks later Ben Gurion, who was in London *en route* to America, told Moyne that Palestine

[75] Caccia to Boyd, 19 September 1941, *ibid.*

[76] Parkinson, Shuckburgh and Boyd minutes, 22-4 September, CO 732/87(1)// 79238(41).

[77] Moyne-Weizmann interview, on FO 371/27128 E4474.

would have to absorb three million Jews within ten years. In addition, Ben Gurion explicitly stated a fact only implicit in Weizmann's comments: 'settlement on so large a scale, and within so short a time, could only be achieved by a Jewish state...'[78]

Although the Middle East Department (and the Eastern Department) had frequently expressed the belief that the Zionists' ultimate objective was a Jewish state in Palestine, they had not previously received such direct confirmation of the ideas around which Zionist policy was crystallising from two of Zionism's most authoritative leaders. Open advocacy of a Jewish state had previously come only from the Revisionists. Following these interviews, however, the Colonial Office considered that the only difference between Zionist moderation (as represented by Weizmann) and Zionist extremism (which the Colonial Office felt Ben Gurion represented) was that Ben Gurion 'doubles the number of post-war immigrants that Palestine must absorb and halves the time in which to do it'.[79] What Weizmann and Ben Gurion proposed concerning the future fate of Jewish refugees was clearly impossible under the White Paper, and would normally have been dismissed on those grounds by the Colonial Office. However, as even the Colonial Office was beginning to understand something of the scale of the Jewish tragedy in Europe, it recognized that the Zionist attitude to the refugee problem might gain wide support after the war. In order that steps might be taken against such an eventuality the Colonial Office resolved to bring the matter to the Cabinet.[80] In a draft Cabinet paper prepared during September 1941, the Colonial Office argued that the size of the post-war Jewish refugee problem would be even larger than Weizmann thought, and that Ben Gurion's figure of three million refugees was probably more accurate. But such large numbers of refugees could be resettled in Palestine only if 'the whole of the Middle East is held down by British arms', and the Colonial Office suggested that Britain should instead plan alternative territorial solutions outside the Middle East. It even suggested a possible site: 'Would, for instance, a substantial Jewish enclave in a reconstituted Poland not be possible?' But whatever the

[78] Moyne-Ben Gurion interview, 21 August 1941, CO 733/446//76033(41).

[79] Moyne to MacMichael, 29 August 1941, semi-official letter, CO 733/446//76033/3(41).

[80] The Colonial Office files relating to the Moyne-Weizmann interview of 1 August, the Departmental reaction to the subsequent Moyne-Ben Gurion interview, and the papers relating to the drafting of the Cabinet paper referred to here are on 75872/26 (1941) which remains closed. However, a copy of the draft and the interdepartmental correspondence relating to it are available on Foreign Office files at FO 371/27128 E6188. The Cabinet paper (with some amendments) was later circulated on 30 September 1941 by the Colonial Office as WP(G)(41) 104, 'Jewish Policy'.

post-war solution of the Jewish problem, the draft Cabinet paper argued that Britain's first priority should be to deflate the Zionists' extravagant expectations concerning Palestine. This could best be done by a public reaffirmation by the Government of the White Paper.[81] Thus, at the same time as Churchill was reviving the debate on a solution to the Palestine problem through Arab federation, and the Foreign Office was independently suggesting a major inter-departmental re-appraisal of the whole of British policy in the Middle East, the Colonial Office, alarmed at the direction that Zionist thinking was taking, wanted the Cabinet to reaffirm the White Paper as a means of asserting one of the basic principles on which that policy was based – that the Jewish problem would not be resolved within the confines of the Palestine Mandate. Before submitting its paper on Jewish policy to the Cabinet, the Colonial Office placed it on the agenda of the meeting with the Minister of State and the Secretaries of State for Foreign Affairs, Colonies and India which Churchill had instructed was to convene to consider the possibility of finding a solution to the Palestine problem through Arab federation. Thus the meeting of Ministers had before it one proposal (formally from Amery but endorsed by the Prime Minister) for replacing the White Paper, and another (from the Colonial Office) calling for its public re-affirmation.[82]

Lyttelton was not unfamiliar with the proposals made in London relating the Palestine problem to Arab federation,[83] and at his request MacMichael had written a lengthy memorandum arguing against federation in general and as a possible solution to the Palestine problem.[84] Furthermore, two days prior to the meeting with Eden, Moyne and Amery, scheduled for 26 September, the Colonial Office had an opportunity to put its own case against federation and in favour of a re-affirmation of the White Paper directly to Lyttelton at a meeting in the Colonial Office.[85] Churchill may have insisted that Amery's (and his) proposal be discussed with Lyttelton in the hope

[81] *Ibid.*

[82] All papers are on Cab 95/8. The Colonial Office submitted another paper on the Jewish Army question which recommended that it be abandoned (MSC(41)17 *ibid.*). This paper was later circulated to the Cabinet as WP(G)(41) 105 (Revise) (Cab 67/9) and endorsed by it.

[83] Amery had sent a copy of Coupland's memorandum to the Colonial Office to the Commander-in-chief, Middle East Command C. Auchinleck, with whom he frequently corresponded. Auchinleck replied that he had discussed it with Lyttelton, Lampson, the three Commanders-in-Chief and MacMichael in Cairo (Auchinleck to Amery, 20 August 1941, Amery Papers Box 140).

[84] MacMichael to Moyne, 14 September 1941, CO 732/87(1)//79238(41).

[85] The meeting is recorded on the Minister of State's itinerary, Cab 95/8.

that the Minister of State would not share the hostility to it already expressed by both Eden and Moyne. However, by the time the meeting took place the Colonial Office had had ample opportunity to convince Lyttelton of its point view.

On 26 September, Amery was the only person to defend the attempt to find a solution to the Palestine problem through Arab federation under Ibn Saud.[86] The majority resolved that such federation was impracticable. As for the wider question of the various other forms which an eventual Arab federation might take, the Ministers decided that the question should be examined by the Middle East (Official) Committee, which would also be instructed 'to pay special regard to the help which such a scheme would afford to the solution of the Palestine problem'.[87] Eden wrote to Churchill three days later communicating these conclusions,[88] and a meeting was proposed between Churchill and the four Ministers concerned so that the Prime Minister could discuss their recommendations further.[89]

Churchill no doubt recognised that as his proposals had failed to gain the support of Lyttelton, Eden and Moyne, they were not likely to be endorsed by the officials who made up the Middle East (Official) Committee either. Consequently there was now no possibility of gaining meaningful political support for a solution to the Palestine question which would allow for a significant area of Jewish autonomy within the context of an Arab federation under Ibn Saud. Presumably as a result, he declined to meet Lyttelton, Eden, Moyne and Amery to discuss the question further, and instead he recorded his strongest minute of the war years endorsing a Jewish state in general and attacking the existing policy on Palestine:

> I may say at once that if Britain and the United States emerge victorious from the war, the creation of a great Jewish state in Palestine inhabitated [sic] by millions of Jews will be one of the leading features of the Peace Conference discussions. The Liberal and Labour Parties will never agree to the pro-Arab solutions which are the commonplace of British Service circles; nor, so long as I remain in British public life, will I. . .[90]

There is no record that Churchill ever raised the federation proposal again during the remainder of the war years, and we must

---

[86]Entry for 26 September 1941, Amery Diaries 1941.

[87]Minutes of meeting, MSC(41) (14)5 Cab 95/8.

[88]Eden to Churchill, 29 September 1941, FO 371/27045 E6190.

[89]Martin minute, 1 October 1941, Prem 4/52/5 Part 2.

[90]Churchill minute C 79/1, 1 October 1941, *ibid.*

assume that he had finally put it aside. The Colonial Office paper on Jewish policy, which had been revised so that in its final form it called only for a private rebuke to the Zionists for their statements on post-war immigration to Palestine, came before the Cabinet on 2 October 1941.[91] Churchill succeeded in delaying (permanently, as it turned out) any conclusive discussion on the Colonial Office recommendations, and instead used the occasion to convey to the Cabinet his belief that 'the creation of a great Jewish State in Palestine would inevitably be one of the matters to be discussed at the Peace Conference'.[92]

Churchill's proposals for a solution to the Palestine problem, which he had first communicated to Weizmann in March 1941, raised with the Foreign Secretary and the Chief of the Imperial General Staff in May, and revived in September, had been successfully contained by the Ministers involved together with their officials. Seen together with Moyne's failure to obtain Cabinet approval for either a public re-affirmation of the White Paper (which the Colonial Office had originally planned to request from the Cabinet) or even a private rebuke to Weizmann, the outcome of the discussions on Palestine during 1941 conform to the *modus vivendi* which had effectively governed debate on the question at the highest political levels ever since Churchill joined the War Cabinet on the outbreak of war. The White Paper would remain in force until it could be reconsidered after the war. Meanwhile, nothing would be done in implementing its provisions which might prejudice reconsideration. In November the Colonial Office had occasion to believe that Churchill was still pursuing his proposals on federation. It received minutes of a talk Philby had had, at Weizmann's instigation, with John Martin at 10 Downing Street. Moyne subsequently wrote to remind the Prime Minister that the question was formally under discussion by the Middle East (Official) Committee.[93] But Churchill had already put the matter aside, and he replied to Moyne that 'All this talk is premature. I remain wedded to the Balfour Declaration as implemented by me... It is much better now however to get on with the war.'[94]

Although the issue was thus effectively dormant at the political level, the Middle East (Official) Committee began a lengthy examination of the question of Arab federation in general and its

[91] WM 99(41)5 Cab 65/19.
[92] *Ibid.*
[93] Moyne to Churchill, 6 November 1941, CO 732/87(1)//79238.
[94] Brown (PM's office) to Thornley, 9 November 1941, *ibid.*

relation to the Palestine problem. Churchill's proposal was rejected as
completely impracticable by the Committee at its first meeting.[95]
Once that was done the officials of the Middle East Department and
the Eastern Department were able to devote themselves to the
questions which had remained unanswered in the discussions of the
past few months – what Britain's policy to Arab federation in general
should be,[96] what was to be done about the growing expectations of the
Zionists, and whether any possible alternative to the White Paper
could be found which, while preserving its basic principles, would be
acceptable to both Arabs and Jews.

[95]ME(0)(41) 5th meeting, 8 October 1941, Cab 95/1. The Committee's detailed
deliberations on Arab federations *per se* are not relevant here, but the manner in which
the Committee rejected Churchill's proposal is of some interest. The first draft of the
memorandum was prepared by Shuckburgh, the Committee's chairman, and in
discussing the Palestine aspect of the various federal schemes which were under
consideration he stated: 'The Palestine solution must be looked for outside the federal
scheme, and it must be recognised that Palestine cannot be worked satisfactorily into
any federation until its own peculiar problem has been solved.' (Draft on CO
732/87(i)//79238(1941)). However, the Foreign Office countered with a draft of its
own which was more forthright. Referring specifically to the Weizmann-Philby plan
which Churchill had put forward, the Foreign Office draft stated: 'This is a fantastic
suggestion. It is quite certain that a man of Ibn Saud's high spirit and honourable
character could not be bribed or cajoled into taking a step which every Arab would
regard as a shameful surrender of Arab interests' (*ibid.*). When this was received in the
Colonial Office, Luke pencilled the marginal comment that as the 'Prime Minister
regards [this] as the "best solution" this paragraph is rather tactlessly worded'.
Consequently at an inter-departmental meeting of the Colonial and Foreign Offices
(held on 12 December 1941 to resolve a number of differences) the reference to the
Weizmann-Philby plan was moderated to state that the plan was not 'deserving of
serious consideration'. The draft agreed upon at this inter-departmental meeting was
subsequently adopted (with only minor changes) as the final draft of the Report.

[96]Despite the rejection in the Report on Arab Federation of the specific proposal
which Churchill had endorsed, there was increasing departmental interest in the
possibility of resolving at least some of Palestine's problems by incorporating it in an
eventual federation of Arab states (cf. footnotes 86 and 87 above; minutes by Baxter,
11 November 1941, FO 371/27137 E7150; Luke and Reilly memoranda, 12-13
November 1941, CO 732/87(i)//79238(1941)). The Report reflected this interest,
stating that Palestine's inclusion in an Arab federation would offer such advantages to
both Arabs and Jews that it might encourage them to settle their differences, and that it
might also provide a structure of government which would eventually allow the
termination of the Mandate. Nevertheless, the Report made it clear that an Arab-
Jewish settlement would have to come about independently of and prior to Palestine's
participation in a federation. The notion that Britain should sponsor any particular
scheme of federation and enforce Palestine's participation in it as a means of bringing
about an Arab-Jewish settlement was firmly rejected (Report on Arab Federation).
Compiling this Report was Shuckburgh's last major project within the Colonial Office,
and Moyne described it as 'a fitting conclusion to the many years of work and study
which Sir J. Shuckburgh has given to the affairs of the Middle East Department.'
(Moyne minute, 31 January 1942, CO 732/87(i)//79238(1942)). The accolade was
ironic, as Churchill had lost interest in the question and the Report was never
considered at a political level. The Minister of State in Cairo asked to be allowed to
submit a paper of his own on Palestine when the Report was considered by the Cabinet,
and thus further consideration was delayed in anticipation of his paper. By the time

Lyttelton's paper arrived there was no political interest in the question of federation, and the four ministers, whose meeting of 26 September 1941 initiated the Report, 'postponed indefinitely' a further meeting to consider it. (Caccia minute, 23 April 1942, FO 371/31337 E2583). Lyttelton's paper on Palestine eventually materialised in April 1942, but was not considered by the Cabinet until July 1943 (cf. chapter 6).

5

IMMIGRATION POLICY 1942-5

At the beginning of 1942 it seemed that the problem posed by illegal immigration had been contained by the rigorous measures taken during the three years since the introduction of White Paper immigration restrictions. No further boatloads of refugees had succeeded in reaching Palestine since the arrival of the *Darien* in March 1941. Although the wartime shortage of shipping and the closure of escape routes as the Germans gained control of the Balkans during 1941 were the main causes of the decline in the traffic in refugees, the Colonial Office was content that its efforts to close the frontiers to Jews attempting to leave Europe and the punitive measures it had taken against refugees who did manage to escape towards Palestine were finally proving to be effective. Furthermore, by propagating the belief that the refugee traffic was a proven, as opposed to theoretical, security risk, and by discrediting the whole phenomenon of illegal immigration as a Zionist-sponsored campaign with political ends, the officials concerned had effectively contained any humanitarian concern for the consequences of Britain's policy, both in the Cabinet and in public opinion. Moyne's attempt to bring the future implications of the refugee question for post-war policy to the attention of the Cabinet had not been successful, but in late 1941 and early 1942 the matter did not seem urgent. After all, as a result of the continued application of the ban on immigration from enemy and enemy-controlled territory, there were by 1941 more certificates available under the White Paper quotas than there were immigrants eligible to apply for them and capable of reaching Palestine.

In these circumstances the Colonial Office felt itself able to make a significant concession. Ever since February 1941, when Rumania had been declared enemy-occupied territory, the Jewish Agency had sought to have the ban on immigration from enemy territory lifted for those prospective Rumanian immigrants who had been approved for immigration to Palestine by the British authorities and had already received immigration certificates before the withdrawal of the British legation. When the Palestine Government refused to consider this request the Jewish Agency then asked that the children of these certificate holders who were under sixteen years of age be allowed to proceed to Palestine. The High Commissioner refused this request, again for reasons of security,[1] but the Colonial Office would not

[1] HCr to CO No. 60, 15 January 1942, CO 733/437//75113/57(1942).

accept that children of fifteen and younger could pose a threat to the security of Palestine, and they asked MacMichael to reconsider the ban, which was subsequently lifted.[2] Although only 271 children were involved (the scheme was eventually extended to include Hungary too), this action marks a significant turning point in the attitude of the Colonial Office. While there had been concessions in 1940 relating to the ban on immigration from enemy territory, these had all been made at the instigation of the then Secretary of State, Malcolm MacDonald. In this instance it was the Middle East Department which challenged the decision of the Palestine Government and cast doubt on the supposed security risk created by the refugees.

Shortly afterwards, the fate of the 793 passengers of the *Darien*, who remained in internment in Athlit pending an opportunity to deport them to Mauritius, came under discussion in London. Their continued internment despite the availability of unused immigration certificates had become a source of continued tension between the Jewish Agency and the Palestine Government, and in February 1942 the Agency succeeded in bringing the matter to Churchill's attention.[3] Churchill raised the question with Moyne, pointing out than when the original decision to deport the *Darien* passengers had been taken it seemed likely that the scale of illegal immigration would be greater than it turned out to be, and advised that the passengers be released from internment and allowed to remain in Palestine.[4]

The release of the *Darien's* passengers would have established a precedent which, in turn, would have meant the effective abandonment of the policy of deportation, and in his reply to Churchill, Moyne argued that 'any relaxation of our deterrent measures is likely to encourage further shipments of the same kind'.[5] Furthermore, the fate of the *Darien's* passengers was seen as a 'test case of the Government's determination to adhere to their proclaimed policy', and any concession, Moyne argued, would cause great damage to Britain's 'reputation in the Middle East for trustworthiness and firmness'.[6]

Churchill considered the question of sufficient importance to bring

[2]Minutes by Luke and Boyd, 20-21 January 1942 and CO to HCr No. 109, 24 January 1941, *ibid.*, cf. also F.B. Chary, *The Bulgarian Jews and the Final Solution, 1940-1944* (Pittsburgh, 1972), p. 137 and chapter 5, *passim.*

[3]Through lobbying of Randolph Churchill, Randolph Churchill to Churchill, 4 February 1942, Prem 4/51/1.

[4]Churchill to Moyne M27/2, 5 Feburary 1942, *ibid.*

[5]Moyne to Churchill, 7 February 1942, CO 733/446//76021/40(1942).

[6]*Ibid.*

to the Cabinet, where it was discussed on 16 February.[7] Opinion within the Cabinet was divided, and it was resolved that Lyttelton in Cairo be consulted for his views on the matter. The Cabinet did not reach a final decision either on the future of the *Darien* refugees or on the wider principle of deportation as a deterrent to illegal immigration. However the very fact that these questions had been raised in London, taken together with the Colonial Office's earlier instructions to MacMichael to reverse his decision on the children of certificate holders from Rumania and Hungary, alerted the Palestine government to the possibility London might not now be as 'firm' on immigration policy as it had previously been. The deliberations on immigration policy in London during January and February 1942 formed the background to decisions reached at the same time on yet another boatload of refugees — decisions which in turn led to a major upheaval in policy.

In October 1941 the High Commissioner informed the Colonial Office that a refugee boat, the M.V. *Struma*, carrying 769 passengers, was preparing to leave Constanza for Palestine.[8] MacMichael's first reaction was to request H.M. ambassador in Ankara, Sir Hughe Knatchbull-Hugessen, to ask the Turkish Government to turn the boat back under a pretext. The Foreign Office supported this request, but as it did not anticipate Turkish compliance, the Admiralty was also asked to prepare to intercept the boat before it reached Palestine.[9]

The *Struma* left Constanza on 12 December 1941, and eight days later Hugessen told the Foreign Office that it had arrived at Istanbul and that the Turkish Ministry of Foreign Affairs would turn it back to the Black Sea unless the Palestine Government was prepared to allow its passengers to enter Palestine. Hugessen added that he had told the Turks that, on humanitarian grounds, he himself did not approve of the boat being turned back and consequently had advised that the boat be sent on to the Dardenelles in the hope that 'if they reach Palestine, they might despite their illegality receive humane treatment'.[10] Both MacMichael and the Colonial Office protested vigorously at Hugessen's action.[11] As the Middle East Department pointed out, Hugessen had

[7]It is interesting to note that the fate of the *Darien* refugees was debated despite the Government's preoccupation with the fall of Singapore, which was discussed at the same Cabinet meeting.

[8]Minutes and correspondence, FO 371/29163 W12180 (October 1941).

[9]*Ibid.*

[10]Knatchbull-Hugessen to FO No. 2960, 20 December 1941, on CO 733/449//-P3/4/30.

[11]HCr to CO No. 1792, 22 December 1941, *ibid.*

missed a 'heaven-sent opportunity'[12], and: 'This is the first occasion on which, in spite of numerous efforts, the Turkish Government has shown any signs of being ready to help in frustrating these illegal immigrant ships, and the Ambassador then goes and spoils the whole effect on absurdly mis-judged humanitarian grounds.'[13] In a letter requesting that the Foreign Office instruct Hugessen to reverse his position, Moyne wrote to Richard Law, Parliamentary Under Secretary of State at the Foreign Office, arguing, *inter alia,* that if the ship was sent towards Palestine other illegal immigrants would be encouraged to make the journey.[14] The next day, Moyne, Sir Cosmo Parkinson and Boyd met officials of the Foreign Office in an attempt to undo the 'damage' done by Hugessen's gesture to the impression of consistency in Palestine immigration policy. Together they drafted countervailing instructions to Ankara which stated: 'We should leave Turkish authorities in no doubt that His Majesty's Government's policy is unmodified in respect of this illegal immigration. Please make this clear accordingly to the Turkish Ministry of Foreign Affairs, and ask them to send the ship back to the Black Sea as originally suggested by the Ministry.'[15] On reflection, however, the officials concerned felt that the last sentence would allow the Turks to blame Britain in the likely event that the boat would have a disastrous end, and the words following 'Foreign Affairs' were deleted in favour of: 'There seems no good reason why the Turks should not take the measure they themselves suggested.'[16] On 28 December the embassy at Ankara was able to reply that the message had been conveyed to the Turkish Government.[17] Meanwhile the Refugee Section did make tentative efforts to find a refuge for the *Struma's* passengers elsewhere in the British Empire, but these were perfunctory and not pursued.[18]

On 9 February Hugessen reported that the Turkish Minister of Foreign Affairs had raised the *Struma* question once again, stating that unless an 'alternative solution could be found he would be forced to send the vessel and passengers back in the direction from which they came'. To this Hugessen had replied that: 'this was a matter in

[12]Boyd minute, 23 December 1941, *ibid.*

[13]Luke minute, 23 December 1941, *ibid.*

[14]Moyne added that he found it 'difficult to write with moderation about this occurrence' (Moyne to Law, 24 December 1941, *ibid.*).

[15]Draft on FO 371/29207 W15571.

[16]FO to Angora No. 2651, 24 December 1941. The telegram, as it was finally despatched, is on FO 371/29207 W15313.

[17]Morgan to FO No. 3000, 28 December 1941, *ibid.*

[18]Boyd minute, 12 February 1942, CO 733/446//76021/42(1942).

which it was quite impossible for His Majesty's Government to be of any assistance or to take any action. They had no means of doing so and [the] decision must rest with him.'[19] Hugessen added that action would probably be taken by the Turkish authorities on 16 February.

By this time London had been fully informed of the appalling situation on board the *Struma,* and had received details about the refugees it carried.[20] In Palestine the fate of the *Struma* was being followed closely by the Yishuv, and the Jewish Agency made constant representations to the Palestine Government on the passengers' behalf. Those few passengers who held valid immigration certificates had been allowed off the boat, and on the basis of information they provided the Palestine Government was informed that amongst the *Struma's* passengers:

> There is a large number of able-bodied men, including skilled craftsmen. There is (sic) also a number of professional people, including over 20 doctors. Many of the passengers have close relatives in Palestine. Quite a number have property or capital in Palestine, and there are some to whom immigration permits had been despatched before Rumania was declared enemy territory. Most of the refugees hail from Bukovina and Bessarabia — the provinces particularly affected by the anti-Jewish outrages.[21]

Hugessen's cable informing the Foreign Office that the Turkish authorities intended to return the boat to the Black Sea on 16 February arrived in London on 10 February and was circulated for consideration the next day. With the deadline only five days away the Refugee Section debated Britain's role in the matter at length and with some anguish. While recognising what the probable fate of the refugees would be once they returned to German-controlled territory (if they did not sink on the return journey), Alec Randall noted that allowing them to enter Palestine would not only entail a 'security' risk, but even more significantly, 'what is perhaps worst of all, they will have succeeded in breaking through our policy, and this would certainly open the way for frequent repetitions of the same procedure'. As an alternative to having the refugees sent back, Randall suggested that they be sent to Cyprus 'pending provision of shipping to remove

[19]Knatchbull-Hugessen to FO No. 284, 9 February 1942, FO 371/32661 W2093.

[20]The boat is variously reported to have been between 180 and 210 tons, it measured 16 by 6 metres and lacked almost all facilities. A Naval Intelligence report stated that half the passengers were women and children, and that amongst the men were 10 doctors, 30 engineers, seamen and labourers. The report concluded: 'Understand majority are anxious to serve war effort against enemy in any capacity' (SO(I) (Istanbul) to Admiralty No. 1055B, 4 Feburary 1942, *ibid.*).

[21]Shertok to Macpherson, 13 February 1942, C.Z.A., Z4/14645.

them to Mauritius'.[22] However the Eastern Department considered that 'it would be unwise to intervene' with the Colonial Office by putting this idea forward, and that if Britain were to offer any sort of refuge 'there would of course be more and more shiploads of unwanted Jews later!'[23] This was the central dilemma of the refugee problem as a whole, and Departmental opinion within the Foreign Office was thus inclined to support the 'extremely strong line'[24] which the Colonial Office had adopted towards the *Struma* refugees (and all others) in accordance with the White Paper.

Moyne and Eden discussed the *Struma* case on 12 or 13 February, and Moyne argued that as Cyprus was on a war footing it was not possible to send the *Struma* passengers there. He added that he knew from 'secret sources' that the *Struma* was only the first of several ships being organised to resume the traffic in illegal immigration. Eden then wrote to Churchill, putting forward the points made by Moyne and joining Moyne in advocating (as Moyne had already done in his reply to Churchill on the internment of the *Darien* refugees) that the general policy of deporting the illegal immigrants to Mauritius be allowed to stand. Concerning the fate of the *Struma,* Eden wrote: 'The position is that the Turks will send it back unless we can admit them into Palestine.' Eden did not explain that the Foreign Office had instructed H.M. ambassador in Turkey to encourage them to do so. In fact the only comment in Eden's minute to Churchill which referred to British policy was an appeal that the Cabinet decision on deportation, taken at the time of the *Patria* incident (i.e. in November 1940) be allowed to stand. Eden quoted the decision in full in his minute, including the operative clause: 'in future all other illegal immigrants attempting to enter Palestine should be directed to Mauritius or elsewhere.'[25]

Thus, intentionally or otherwise, Eden's minute created the impression that while the Turkish government was threatening to return the *Struma* to occupied Europe, the Foreign and Colonial Offices wanted to send its passengers to Mauritius. At the very least the minute confused the issue, and gave no indication that despite the German occupation of Rumania and the existence of a violently anti-Semitic regime there, the Foreign and Colonial Offices were still pursuing their earlier policy of 1939-40 — i.e. of forcing the boats off

[22]Randall minute, 12 February 1942, FO 371/32661 W2093.

[23]Baxter minute, 12 February 1942, *ibid.*

[24]Randall minute, 12 February 1942, *ibid.*

[25]Eden to Churchill PM/42/22, 13 February 1942, *ibid.*

whenever possible — as did appear possible in the case of the *Struma* — and deporting to Mauritius only those who managed to overcome the obstacles and reach Palestine. As the *Struma* was the first instance, since the outbreak of war and the subsequent adoption of the policy of deportation, where the return of a boat to Europe could be enforced, it cannot be expected that the Colonial Office's determination to proceed with the policy, despite the changed circumstances of 1942, was widely appreciated. The fact that the *Darien* case, and the policy of internment and deportation which were central to it, had been taken up in London just at the moment when the return of the *Struma* refugees to Europe was under consideration, created great scope for confusion amongst those not intimately familiar with the day to day administration of Palestine's immigration laws. By combining the two cases, Eden and Moyne succeeded in diverting attention from the likely consequences of their policy towards the *Struma*.

Despite the Government's pre-occupation with military developments during the second week of February, Churchill referred Eden's minute to the Cabinet, where it was debated on 16 February. However, the Cabinet discussion focused on the *Darien* and the policy of deportation. The *Struma* was cited only as an instance of continuing illegal immigration, countering Churchill's claim that deportation could be abandoned in view of the decline in the refugee traffic. The problem of the *Struma* itself was not discussed.[26]

The Middle East Department of the Colonial Office felt that Eden's minute to Churchill was 'rather misleading'[27] and recognized that the question of policy on the *Struma per se* had not been dealt with by the Cabinet. It was assumed that the question would be taken up separately as soon as the Minister of State's reply on the *Darien* had been received,[28] a belief which both the Refugee Section of the Foreign Office[29] and Churchill's Secretariat also shared.[30] However

[26] WM 21(42)11, Cab 65/25. The day after the Cabinet debate, Boyd minuted: 'I understand that the fate of the "Struma" was *not* discussed after all at the meeting of the War Cabinet yesterday.' (Minute of 17 February 1942, CO 733/446//76021/42-(1942)). In a subsequent minute by Luke reviewing the events which led up to the *Struma*'s sinking, it was noted that: 'The matter was not however specifically discussed in Cabinet when another problem connected with illegal immigration to Palestine (i.e. the disposal of the passengers from the S.S. "Darien") came before the Cabinet on the 16th February.' (Luke minute, no date, *ibid.*)

[27] Luke minute, 20 February 1942, *ibid.*

[28] Luke minute, 20 February 1942, *ibid.*

[29] Thus Randall minuted: 'it is clear we can't come to any decision about the "Struma" in general until we hear from the Minister of State.' (Minute of 19 February FO 371/32661 W2483).

[30] Rowan to Lawford (FO) and Thornley (CO), 17 February 1942, Prem 4/51/1.

Lyttelton's reply did not reach London until 27 February, by which time the *Struma* had already met its fate. Given that nowhere in Eden's minute to Churchill, in the record of the Cabinet debate, in the query to the Minister of State or in his reply, is reference made to the Foreign and Colonial Office policy that while the *Darien* passengers were to be deported, the *Struma* was not to be sent to Mauritius but rather was to be sent back to occupied Europe, it is doubtful whether the question of policy towards the *Struma* was discussed at all outside the inter-departmental deliberations of the Foreign and Colonial Offices.

On 15 February — three weeks after MacMichael had been instructed (against his wishes) by the Colonial Office to allow the entry into Palestine of the children of Rumanian and Hungarian certificate holders — the Palestine government told Hugessen that it was prepared to admit children aged between eleven and sixteen from the *Struma*.[31] In view of this, the Turkish Government agreed to an extension of the 16 February deadline, but immediately informed the British Government that it would not permit the children concerned to travel to Palestine overland across Turkey.[32] Despite pressure from London,[33] the Turkish Government refused to reconsider this decision and for the next week the matter remained deadlocked. During that period Hugessen reported that the Turks were preparing to tow the *Struma* into the Black Sea where it was to be cut adrift.[34]

News of this alarmed the Refugee Section, and Randall minuted: 'The Black Sea is rough at this time of the year and the Struma may well founder. I do not [at] all like the idea that we may be acting as accessories in bringing about the death of these miserable people.'[35] In the hope that policy towards the *Struma* would be considered by the Cabinet once Lyttelton's reply on the *Darien*'s passengers had arrived, Randall sent a request to the Minister of State in Cairo asking him to reply as soon as possible,[36] and another to Ankara asking the Turkish authorities to delay their action until the question of the transit of the children had been resolved.[37]

[31] HCr to Knatchbull-Hugessen No. 13, 15 February 1942, on FO 371/32661 W2483.

[32] Morgan (Angora) to FO No. 340, 18 February 1942, FO 371/32661 W2483.

[33] FO to Angora No. 311, 20 February 1942, *ibid*.

[34] Knatchbull-Hugessen to FO No. 378, 23 February 1942, FO 371/32661 W2810.

[35] Randall minute, 24 February 1942, *ibid*.

[36] FO to Knatchbull-Hugessen No. 339, 24 February 1942, *ibid*.

[37] FO to Lyttelton No. 199, 24 February 1942, *ibid*.

The Refugee Section's disquiet was not, however, shared by the Palestine Government, which remained consistently hostile to any concessions to the *Struma's* passengers. Conscious of the general concern for the fate of the *Struma*, which was increasing all the time the boat was at Istanbul,[38] MacMichael referred to the 'general security objection' to allowing refugee aliens into Palestine 'on account of the risk of leakage into the Middle East of persons working in Axis interests'. In the particular case of refugees from Rumania, MacMichael stated that information had been received that the Gestapo had been directly involved in organising illegal immigration and that the *Struma* carried Nazi agents.[39] He also anticipated supply difficulties in Palestine, which the reception of over 700 refugees would only worsen, and mentioned the 'practical difficulties' of selecting certain refugees (other than children) for possible immigration.

The Colonial Office considered that MacMichael's telegram provided 'an unanswerable case against any arrangement for the acceptance of the 'Struma' passengers in Palestine'.[40] and recommended that it be circulated to the Cabinet and to the other ministeries concerned in anticipation of a Cabinet debate on the situation once Lyttelton's reply on the *Darien* had arrived. However, before this happened the Turkish authorities towed the *Struma* into the Black Sea beyond Turkish territorial waters.[41] As its engines had failed, the boat was immobilised, and on 25 February it sank with only one survivor. Most accounts, including that of the lone survivor, claim that the boat had been struck by a torpedo.

The sinking of the *Struma* marked a major turning point in Britain's campaign against illegal immigration, and in order to understand the decisions taken in London and Jerusalem which led up to the tragedy it is necessary to consider the general development of refugee policy at that time. Despite the Palestine Government's stated concern at the security risk which would be created if the *Struma's* passengers were allowed into Palestine, or the 'practical difficulties' which such a concession would cause, it is doubtful whether these

---

[38] Lord Wedgwood intended to raise the question in the House of Lords on 16 February (CO 733/446//76021/42 PQ(1942)). The plight of the *Struma's* passengers was described in *The Times* on 17 February 1942.

[39] HCr to CO No. 190, 17 February 1942, CO 733/446//76021/42(1942).

[40] Luke minute, 20 February 1942, CO 733/446//76021/42(1942).

[41] According to Y. Slutzky, *Sefer Toldot Hahagana* (History of the Hagana) (ed. *B.-Z. Dinur*) (Tel Aviv, 1976), Vol. 3 Part 1, p. 159, the boat was towed out on 23 February without water, food or fuel.

were the issues which really exercised the authorities in Jerusalem.[42] In early February the Chief Secretary of the Palestine Government, J.S. Macpherson, wrote to the Middle East Department about their concern at the apparent shift of policy manifested in the decision (unrelated to the *Struma*) to allow the 271 children of certificate-holders in Rumania and Hungary to proceed to Palestine. That decision had been made possible by the recent agreement of the Swiss Government (which represented British interests in German-occupied territory) to undertake the task of identification and documentation in the countries of emigration. The Palestine Government was concerned that this new factor might presage a wider lifting by the Colonial Office of the ban on legal immigration from enemy territory.[43] The decision on the 271 children was followed almost immediately by the debate over the continued internment and eventual deportation of the *Darien* refugees, a debate which threatened to undermine the policy of deporting and permanently excluding from Palestine all refugees who succeeded in reaching that country illegally. The ban on immigration from enemy territory (which the Palestine Government feared might be in question) and the deterrent policy of deportation and exclusion (which had recently been challenged in the Cabinet) were cornerstones of Britain's defence against the spectre of 'a flood of gatercrashers', an endless stream of Jewish refugees fleeing Nazi Europe. In February 1942 it seemed that both policies were being questioned in London. Furthermore, whatever was happening to attitudes in London, the deterrent policy of deportation and exclusion became less effective as the circumstances of European Jewry deteriorated. Even Mauritius and a permanent ban on re-entering Palestine were better than remaining in Europe. Thus in order to prevent 'more and more shiploads of unwanted Jews later' it was understood that, whenever possible, Jewish refugees would be returned to Europe before they reached British-controlled territory. This policy could be implemented only with the cooperation of the Turkish authorities, and explains why the Foreign and Colonial Offices considered the Turks' original statement of their intention to

---

[42]When the Palestine Government informed the Jewish Agency that 'practical difficulties' made any concessions impossible, Moshe Shertok (Head of the Agency's Political Department) replied:
  the Jewish community of Palestine as a whole, and each Jewish town and village in particular, would be quite ready to have its ration cut short in order to provide a margin for feeding the refugees. As regards selection, invidious as the task may be, the Jewish Agency is quite prepared to undertake it in order to save at least a part of the transport from certain death through starvation, disease, drowning or delivery into the hands of the enemy. (Shertok to Macpherson, 20 February 1942, Z4/14645, C.Z.A.).

[43]Macpherson to Boyd, 10 February 1942, CO 733/437//75113/57(1942).

126

turn the boat back as 'a heaven-sent opportunity' towards which British policy had been working for the previous three years.

Thus, for a number of reasons the authorities both in Jerusalem and the Colonial Office wanted the Government to demonstrate its resolve to pursue the campaign against illegal immigration to its logical conclusion. Consequently the decision was taken to encourage the Turkish Government in its determination to turn the *Struma* into the Black Sea, despite the availability of legal immigration certificates under the White Paper and despite the calculable cost of doing so in terms of British and American public opinion. The risk of Nazi agents being infiltrated should the *Struma* refugees be allowed into Palestine was more imagined than real, and the constant references made by the Palestine Government (and repeated by Moyne and Eden to Churchill[44]) to concrete evidence of the presence of Nazi agents amongst the refugees were, in 1942 as in 1939-41, a canard.[45]

In Palestine the news of the sinking caused a definite hardening of anti-Government feeling and open hostility towards the High Commissioner personally. From Washington, Halifax cabled that Britain's role in the affair was viewed critically and that American opinion could not understand why the *Struma*'s passengers were refused entry into Palestine at a time when many unused immigration certificates were available.[46] The State Department, through the American embassy in London, also asked the Foreign Office for an explanation of its policy.[47] In Britain, Parliamentary opinion was critical.[48]

[44] Eden to Churchill PM/42/22, 13 February 1942.

[45] In November 1942, M.I.2a (that Military Intelligence department of the War office which dealt with the Middle East) stated that no German agents had been identified amongst the large number of Jewish illegal immigrants who had been interrogated since the start of the war (cf. 90). Whether or not the Gestapo were actively engaged in organising the illegal traffic in 1942 — as MacMichael's telegram of 17 February (No. 190) implied they were — is a separate question. However, it is equally doubtful whether the Palestine Government was in possession of any evidence that proved this assertion either, as the Germans had abandoned the policy of expulsion in favour of a policy of extermination during 1941. In accordance with this latter policy the Germans attempted to close the borders for Jews in territories which they controlled rather than expel Jewish refugees across them.

[46] Halifax to FO Nos. 1278 & 1279, 4 March 1942, FO 371/32662 W3371.

[47] Shantz to FO, March 1942, FO 371/32662 W3401.

[48] Wedgwood raised the matter in the Lords almost immediately (H.L. Debs/Vol 122/Cols. 159-160/26 February 1942). A week later the fate of the *Struma* was discussed in the Commons when S.S. Silverman (Labour M.P. for Nelson and Colne, 1935-68) asked why the *Struma*'s passengers were 'refused admission to Palestine although the immigration quota has 3,000 unallotted vacancies' (H.C. Debs. 5s/378/Cols 638-641/4 March 1942).

The Colonial Office recognized that it now faced the severest challenge so far to its conduct of Palestine immigration policy, and that concessions would have to be made. At the same time, it was determined that such concessions should not affect the central principle of the White Paper restrictions on Jewish immigration — i.e. that it should not exceed 75,000 by March 1944 and that it should cease altogether after that date. Shortly after the sinking of the *Struma*, the Middle East Department, together with the Permanent Under-Secretary, formulated a series of proposals which Parkinson placed before Lord Cranborne,[49] Moyne's successor as Secretary of State, on 1 March. These proposals, in the form of a draft Cabinet paper, listed all the reasons why *no* change of policy should be made: the undesirability of changing a policy which in large part had already been made public, the impact on Arab opinion, the security risks, and, finally, the risk that: 'If we relax now our deterrent measures, we may release a flood, organised by the Nazis for their own convenience and for our embarrassment.' If, nevertheless, the Cabinet resolved that it did want to liberalise immigration policy, then the officials recommended that the ban on immigration from enemy countries be partially lifted for those refugees who succeeded in reaching Palestine, and that immigration certificates be provided for them from the balance of the 25,000 refugee certificates made available under the White Paper. This was to apply to the *Darien* internees too. However, in order to maintain some deterrent, the Colonial Office wanted to retain the legislation, intended to deter the masters and owners of vessels involved in the refugee traffic, which was introduced in 1939-40.[50] In effect, the officials within the Colonial Office advocated changes which did not affect the central components of immigration policy, hoping to weather the storm of criticism which followed the *Struma* tragedy by making concessions which were more apparent than real. The measures they proposed applied only to those refugees who succeeded in running the gauntlet of the difficulties involved in getting to Palestine, including those difficulties specifically created by the government: these the Colonial Office wanted to maintain.

Cranborne and Harold Macmillan (the new Parliamentary Under-Secretary of State) discussed the Departmental draft proposals shortly after they were presented, and, while accepting the general principles put forward, subsequently rewrote the paper. Their most

[49]Harold Macmillan replaced George Hall as Parliamentary Under-Secretary of State on 4 February 1942 (a post which he retained until 1 January 1943), and Viscount Cranborne replaced Lord Moyne on 22 February 1942. Both of the new incumbents were more sympathathic to the Zionists than their predecessors.

[50]Draft Cabinet paper, CO 733/445//76021(1942).

significant additions included an introductory paragraph explaining
that while the White Paper as a whole was, for various reasons,
'already gravely imperilled', 'to tinker with the White Paper policy,
to suggest modifications here or there, or still more, to scrap it and
start afresh (during the war) would lay us open to new incalculable
dangers'.[51] Their version of the Cabinet paper suggested two alternatives — either the government stand by its previous policy, or illegal
immigrants be allowed into Palestine 'so long as their numbers were
deducted from the annual quota, and so long as under no circumstances
did they exceed that quota'. Cranborne added that he 'inclined
slightly' towards the second option. In fact his formulation went
significantly beyond the recommendation of his officials. By referring
to the 'annual quota' rather than the 'refugee quota' (to which the
Departmental draft referred) Cranborne was advocating that *all* the
outstanding immigration certificates under the White Paper — over
18,000 per year for the next two years — be made available to
refugees from occupied Europe, and not just the 6,000 outstanding
refugee certificates.

Cranborne submitted his draft paper to Churchill[52] and obtained
his approval for circulating it to the Cabinet. It was discussed on 5
March. However for the first time since the release of the White Paper
the Cabinet actually took a harsher line than that advocated by a
Colonial Secretary, maintaining that if illegal immigrants were
admitted to Palestine, there was little hope of deporting to Mauritius
any refugees who did not pass a security check in Palestine or who
might arrive in excess of the number of certificates available. On the
other hand the Cabinet recognized that it must avoid a second *Struma*
tragedy. Thus while it rejected the concessions advocated by Cranborne,
the Cabinet deferred consideration of whether future boatloads of
refugees would be allowed into Palestine until such a boat next
reached Istanbul. In the meantime 'nothing should be said. . . to
encourage the view that such a request would be granted'.[53] The
Government came under attack once again in the Lords on 10 March
and Cranborne announced that, subject to general policy on
immigration not being affected, the Government 'will do all that is

---

[51] WP(42)108 'Illegal Immigration into Palestine', 4 March 1942, Cab 66/22. In a
paper which Cranborne circulated to the Cabinet in May 1943, some months after he
had left the Colonial Office, he stated that he still opposed the White Paper as a whole
(as he had in 1939) and that he believed that the planned termination of the Jewish
immigration was contrary to the terms of the Mandate. He added, however, that he felt
that the White Paper should not be altered *during* the war. (WP(43)187, Cab 66/36).

[52] Cranborne to Churchill, 3 March 1942, CO 733/445//76021(1942).

[53] WM 29(42)1, Cab 65/25.

practicable to prevent [a Struma-like] tragedy happening again'.[54] Macmillan gave a similar commitment the next day in the Commons.[55] In fact it took over two months of complex and controversial debate before a new policy on immigration emerged.

The Colonial Office debated the question of future policy on 19 March and decided that of the various options open to it, the most practicable was that which Cranborne had advocated to the Cabinet — i.e. allowing refugees who reached Turkey to proceed to Palestine, where they would be given immigration certificates as long as such certificates remained available under the White Paper.[56] These proposals were then put to the High Commissioner for discussion, with the comment that public reaction in the U.S. and U.K. to recent events was 'causing considerable embarrassment to His Majesty's Government', and that it was 'essential to avoid repetition of Struma disaster'.[57] MacMichael replied to the Colonial Office's recommendations the next day. While Cranborne had referred to public opinion in the U.K. and U.S. as a reason for making concessions, MacMichael provided an even more urgent reason: 'I take the view that there is quite a likelihood of a Jewish insurrection in Palestine unless some concession is made to them. The difficulty is to find a concession which does not constitute a landslide.' MacMichael firmly rejected Cranborne's recommendation that the refugees be permitted entry into Palestine as long as the supply of immigration certificates lasted, arguing that if such a policy were adopted the stream of refugees would swell. As an alternative, MacMichael recommended that future boatloads of refugees be intercepted by the Navy and diverted 'through the canal for safe conduct to Mauritius or else where'. This, of course, was what the Jewish Agency had advocated in 1940, and although he had opposed the policy then, MacMichael now acknowledged that leading personalities (he did not mention the Agency) 'had consistently urged' it.[58]

MacMichael's statement represented the most candid statement so far by the Palestine government of its real concerns on the refugee problem. In his telegram MacMichael had not even bothered to employ the 'Nazi agent' argument, as he had done to such good effect only a month earlier. Furthermore, neither the Palestine Government

[54] House of Lords Debates, Vol. 122 Cols 200-223, 10 March 1942.

[55] H.C. Debs./5s/378/Cols.1048-1049/11 March 1942.

[56] Minutes, CO 733/446//76021/41(42).

[57] CO to HCr, Most Secret and Personal, 19 March 1942, *ibid.*

[58] HCr to CO, Most Secret and Personal, 20 March 1942, CO 733/445//76021-(1942).

nor the the Colonial Office were referring to the phenomenon of illegal immigration as a 'Zionist conspiracy' any longer. By 1942 the authorities concerned had accepted that the motives of the refugees, and of the Jewish Agency, were honest. However, one final misconception about the circumstances of the refugee problem still persisted — that their flight was 'being facilitated by the Nazis themselves in order to rid themselves of encumbrance, ease their food difficulties and embarrass us politically'.[59] This had been substantially true in the period 1939-40, but during 1941 the Germans had abandoned their hopes of expelling significant numbers of European Jews. Instead, they attempted to close the borders of territories they controlled to Jews and commenced the programme of genocide. By March 1942, when MacMichael warned that the refugee problem was 'being facilitated by the the Nazis themselves', the Germans were bringing into operation the first four gas-chamber equipped death camps. For the moment this fact was unknown, or at least unrecognized by the Allied governments, as a whole, and was clearly not known to the lesser authorities responsible for immigration into Palestine.[60]

Pending the conclusion of the general review of policy there had been only one significant change resulting from the *Struma* affair — as the Colonial Office informed the Jewish Agency and Cranborne informed Churchill, in future the British government would 'do nothing to prevent [the refugee] ships from proceeding on their way'.[61] In other words, the policy of encouraging their return to Europe had been abandoned. If the boats were intercepted by Royal Navy patrols they would be escorted to 'some destination outside Palestine', although exactly where remained uncertain. If they succeeded in reaching Palestine without being intercepted, the passengers would be interned pending deportation sometime in the future.

During April 1942 MacMichael came to London for talks with the Colonial Office, and the opportunity was used to resolve the question of immigration policy. This time MacMichael finally agreed to the Colonial Office's initial proposal — that refugees who landed in Palestine should be interned for strict security checks, and, if cleared be issued with legal immigration certificates and released. As no shipping was available for deportation, as the Palestine authorities did

---

[59]*Ibid*.

[60]For a detailed discussion of the growing awareness amongst the Allies of the German treatment of the Jews see W. Laqueur, *The Terrible Secret* (London, 1980) and M. Gilbert, *Auschwitz and the Allies* (London, 1981).

[61]Cranborne to Churchill, 27 March 1942, CO 733/445//76021(1942).

not have the means to intern large numbers of refugees until such shipping became available, and as an attempt to find an alternative site nearer to Palestine to which the refugees could be diverted at sea or deported if they reached Palestine had failed, there was probably no alternative but to release the refugees in Palestine. This policy was also to apply to the *Darien* internees. However, MacMichael insisted, and the Colonial Office agreed, that for the sake of Arab opinion nothing should be done to facilitate the journey of refugees from Turkey to Palestine.[62]

The Colonial Office wanted to present its new policy for Cabinet approval as soon as possible, and shortly after the talks with MacMichael it submitted a draft Cabinet paper to the Foreign Office for its concurrence. As a result of the High Commissioner's proviso that nothing be done to facilitate the onward journey of refugees who were stranded in Turkey, the new policy's concessions were in effect limited to those refugees who travelled in larger boats capable of the journey from the Balkans to the Middle East. Those who crossed the Bulgarian-Turkish border by land and those who arrived in Turkey on lesser craft would not be given refuge. The draft paper warned the Cabinet that the Turks might deport such refugees back to occupied Europe, which might mean further public criticism.[63] Nevertheless the distinction between those refugees who could escape enemy territory and those who could, in addition, make their own way to Palestine, was central to the new policy. As the Colonial Office subsequently explained when the Foreign Office complained that it had conceded too much, it was counting on the fact that the numbers would be low, because of the lack of shipping.[64] Furthermore, the Colonial Office added that 'all practicable steps should be taken to avoid publicity for the new arrangements' lest the Germans decide to provide the necessary shipping and the refugees be tempted to risk the journey.[65] The Foreign Office agreed to support the new policy, adding only the *caveat* that if the concessions did lead to a serious increase in Jewish immigration, they would be reviewed when the remaining immigration certificates available under the White Paper were exhausted.[66] With this additional provision the policy was

[62] Protocols of MacMichael-Colonial Office talks, 23 April 1942, CO 733/448//76155. Paradoxically MacMichael also insisted that people who received legal certificates in this way should still be served with deportation notices.

[63] WP(42)209, 15 May 1942, 'Illegal Immigration into Palestine', Cab 66/24.

[64] Randall minute, 13 May 1942, FO 371/32665 W7459.

[65] WP(42)209.

[66] Eden comment at Cabinet meeting of 18 May, WM 64(42)6 Cab 65/26.

endorsed by the Cabinet on 18 May 1942, ending a period of almost three months of uncertainty concerning immigration policy.

The new policy made a virtue of necessity by 'legalising' those illegal immigrants who had reached Palestine and could not be disposed of in any other way. Britain still refused to countenance the orderly exodus (i.e. legal immigration) of Jews from occupied Europe, even within the limits of the remaining immigration certificates, and refused to issue certificates to Jewish refugees stranded in neutral or Allied territory (a more liberal policy in this regard was pursued for non-Jewish refugees). The fear of opening the floodgates remained and the ban on immigration from enemy-controlled territory was thus kept in force. Nevertheless the liberalisation of policy in May 1942 marked the end of the deterrent and punitive period of immigration policy which had inspired official thinking in 1939-1941.

The changes in policy had been necessary primarily because public opinion needed to be reassured that a *Struma* tragedy would not occur again. However, there were other reasons for change as well. MacMichael's warning that, unless concessions were forthcoming, there would be serious Jewish unrest in Palestine, alarmed the Colonial Office. Furthermore, as the Germans occupied more and more of Europe in 1940-1, the ban on immigration from enemy-controlled territory meant that increasingly large numbers of European Jews were no longer eligible for legal immigration certificates. As a result, almost all Jewish immigration into Palestine had to be illegal (a point which the Jewish Agency had repeatedly made to the Colonial Office) and under the previous policy there was, therefore, no way in which the Palestine Government could distribute the very large balance of immigration certificates which had been promised under the White Paper but were still unused. This was not only politically embarrassing as the plight of European Jewry worsened, but it also threatened to undermine the immigration provisions of the White Paper, which were based on the assumption that there would be no legal certificates available at the end of March 1944 when all Jewish immigration was to end. Thus, concessions which allowed the distribution of legal certificates to illegal immigrants were not only desirable but had become necessary. The final factor which contributed to the change of policy was a perceptible change of attitude within the Colonial Office. The appointment of Lord Cranborne as Colonial Secretary and the replacement of Sir Cosmo Parkinson by Sir George Gater as Permanent Under-Secretary, during the months under discussion, marked the completion of a changeover of personnel dealing with Palestine affairs, at all levels within the Colonial Office. Bennett had been sent to Cairo in July 1941 as the advisor on

Palestine affairs in the newly created office of Minister of State Resident in the Middle East, and although he continued from Cairo to oppose any liberalisation of an immigration policy which he personally had done much to formulate,[67] he had little influence within the Colonial Office. Downie had been transferred out of the Middle East Department and Shuckburgh retired. E.B. Boyd and Sir William Battershill — their respective replacements — had not been personally involved in formulating the policies which had emerged during 1939-40 and were consequently less rigidly committed to them.[68] Although the new officials shared the belief of their predecessors that the immigration restrictions of the White Paper were both equitable and necessary for the good government of Palestine, they did not (judging from their minutes on the whole range of Palestine-related matters) share their anti-Zionist animus.[69]

Between May and August no further boatloads of refugees were able to leave Rumania, but in early September the Turkish Government informed Hugessen that four more boats were preparing to leave, and that if they were unable to proceed beyond Turkey for any reason their passengers would be returned to occupied Europe.[70] Perhaps because the upsurge in illegal immigration expected after the introduction of the new policy in May had not occurred, both the Colonial Office and the Refugee Section were concerned lest the decision not to allow entry to Palestine of refugees stranded *en route* would contribute to the Turkish intention to send them back to Europe and therefore to another *Struma*. At the specific request of the Colonial Office, and in the face of opposition from the Eastern Department of the Foreign Office,[71] Hugessen was instructed to ask the Turks to delay sending

[67]FO 921/10, *passim*.

[68]Luke was on sick-leave from April to August 1942, and was transferred to a different Department within the Colonial Office when he returned. Downie was made Head of the West Indian Department in mid-1941. Shuckburgh, the longest serving 'Middle-East hand' of either the Colonial or the Foreign Office, retired in early 1942 but was given the task of collating material for the Colonial Office volume in the Civil Series of the Official Histories of the Second World War. Battershill had previously been Chief Secretary to the Palestine government (1937-9) and was selected to replace MacMichael as High Commissioner when the latter's term of appointment expired in 1943. However illness prevented him from taking up the post (CO 850/188//20410/6 and MacMichael Papers, St. Anthony's College, Oxford).

[69]The protocols of the London executive of the Jewish Agency for the period following the sinking of the *Struma*, make frequent mention of 'a new atmosphere in the Colonial Office' on matters relating to immigration (Z4/302/25,*passim*., C.Z.A.). Cf. also Conclusion.

[70]Knatchbull-Hugessen to FO No. 1672, 12 September 1942, FO 371/32666 W12420.

[71]Caccia minute, 15 September 1942, FO 371/32666 W12420.

any of the refugees back in the event of shipwreck so that the British Government could consider the situation.[72]

Within the Colonial Office, where the problem was discussed at all levels, a radical and more generous understanding of policy had developed. Cranborne stated the new attitude forthrightly: 'If in fact we have made up our minds — as I think we must — to do everything in our power to prevent Jews being sent back to Axis-occupied territory, we had better make this clear (to the Turkish Government) as soon as possible. . . .'[73] The problem, once again, was to find a suitable formula which embodied the new resolve to prevent deportations from Turkey but at the same time avoided creating an open-ended obligation concerning refugees who might arrive in the future. The solution decided upon was that the Turkish Government would not be informed of Britain's intention of finding a refuge for all the refugees who became stranded. Instead they were told that each case would be dealt with separately. In accordance with the Cabinet decision of 18 May that only those refugees who made their own way to Palestine would be given immigration certificates, the refugees stranded in Turkey were to be sent to Cyprus.[74] This arrangement worked smoothly for a few weeks, and during September sixty-four refugees were sent to Cyprus. However, the appearance of a further 120 shipwrecked refugees in early October prompted the Cyprus government to protest that the island was not able to absorb many more,[75] while Hugessen cabled from Ankara that the Turkish authorities were losing patience with the apparently *ad hoc* arrangements and would probably start to turn all refugees back to Rumania unless Britain made a clear statement of policy.[76] To compound the problem, there were reports of four to six more boats preparing to leave Rumania with a further 250 refugees, and others were expected to follow.[77]

The Cabinet decision of 18 May and the *ad hoc* arrangement adopted in September had both been based on the assumption that the number of refugees who might be stranded in Turkey would be small, as most of the boats were expected to reach Palestine successfuly. However, of the seven vessels which had carried Jewish refugees from Rumania since the *Struma*, only two manged to complete their

[72]FO to Knatchbull-Hugessen No. 1441, 19 September 1942, *ibid.*

[73]Cranborne minute, 17 September 1942, CO 733/445//76021.

[74]Minutes *ibid.*

[75]Governor, Cyprus to CO No. 493, 11 October 1942, FO 371/32667 W13746.

[76]Knatchbull-Hugessen to FO No. 1874A, 13 October 1942, FO 371/32667 W13686.

[77]Randall to Boyd, 3 November 1942, FO 371/32667 W14413.

journey. The others had all been stranded in Turkey and it became apparent that the Rumanian crews were scuttling their boats and abandoning their passengers, and that therefore all future refugee boats would be stranded in Turkey too. As Randall pointed out to Boyd, the choice facing Britain appeared to lie between 'giving the Turks a free hand to deal with this question, which involves the possibility of further "Strumas" [or the] jeopardising of British policy in the Middle East by the arrival of a more or less continuous stream of Jews'.[78] However, an inter-departmental meeting, called on 17 November with representatives of the Foreign, Colonial and War Offices to consider the problem, concluded that there was no alternative but to continue to send stranded refugees to Cyprus.[79]

In July 1942 the Polish government-in-exile released a report to the Allied governments giving a detailed account of the massacre of 700,000 Polish Jews by the Germans. In August 1942 the Foreign Office received evidence that these activities were not confined to Poland and that the Germans were in fact bringing into effect a plan for the total destruction of European Jewry. In the weeks that followed confirmatory reports were received and in early December *The Times* published a full account under the heading 'Deliberate Plan for Extermination'. On 17 December Eden made the first official response to the news in a statement to the Commons.[80] Although the Foreign Office attempted to suppress public debate through the press on what Britain's response to the revelations should be,[81] Eden's statement evoked widespread public sympathy, and as the Refugee Section noted 'this is not the moment to raise objections of any kind to facilitating the escape of refugees. . . '[82] In general, the official

[78]*Ibid.*

[79]Minutes of inter-departmental meeting, 17 November 1942, CO 733/445//76021-(1942).

[80]H.C. Debs/5s/385/Cols.2082-87/17 December 1942. This statement served the purpose, *inter alia,* of confirming publicly that the situation was as bad as the Jewish Agency and other organisations had been claiming in their representations on matters relating to refugees. An Allied Declaration condemning German policy was released on the same day. Reacting to a statement on the Final Solution by the Va'ad Le'umi (the elected National Council of the Yishuv), Bennett minuted: 'Familiar stuff. The Jews have spoilt their case by laying it on too thick for years past.' (Marginal note of 7 December 1942, on Scott to Bennett, 2 December 1942, FO 921/7). Elsewhere Bennett complained at the response of Colonel Stanley to the news of the Final Solution: 'What is disturbing is the apparent readiness of the new Colonial Secretary to take Jewish Agency "sob-stuff" at its face value.' (Minute of 7 December 1942, FO 921/10). It is not possible to trace the growing realisation within the Colonial Office of the full extent of German anti-Jewish policy as the relevant files (76198 (1942) and (1943)) have been destroyed under statute.

[81]Minutes for 22-4 December 1942, FO 371/32682 W17575.

[82]Walker minute, 28 December 1942, FO 371/32668 W17422.

136

response to the public demands for action to save European Jewry was that there was little if anything that Britain could do. However, late in 1942 MacMichael informed the Colonial Office that in the three and a half years since the introduction of the White Paper quotas only slightly more than half of the 75,000 immigration certificates had been used, and that over 37,000 remained to be distributed within the next eighteen months.[83] The officially acknowledged fact of the plight of European Jewry, together with the availability of significant numbers of immigration certificates even within the framework of the Government's declared Palestine policy, represented a major challenge to the continuation of the ban on immigration from enemy-controlled territory.

On 9 November 1942 MacMichael passed on to the Colonial Office a request by the Jewish Agency offices in Jerusalem that Britain revoke its ban on immigration from enemy-controlled territory so that Jews from Bulgaria might be allowed to depart for Palestine under the White Paper quota. As the Jewish Agency had pointed out in its representation, the Bulgarian authorities had recently (in August 1942) implemented a series of anti-Semitic decrees which were to be 'the first step in the planned destruction of Bulgarian Jewry'. However, according to the Agency, the Bulgarian authorities were 'at present prepared to allow the Jews to immigrate (sic), and that Jewish Banking accounts have been confiscated, and are to be used [to] finance such immigration'.[84] Together with this information, MacMichael passed on a strong plea of his own that it be rejected on the grounds that such a concession would encourage Bulgaria and other Axis countries to despatch vast numbers of Jews to Palestine.[85] MacMichael's cable was discussed at the interdepartmental meeting of 17 November called to discuss the fate of Rumanian Jews stranded in Turkey. The Bulgarian proposal does not appear to have been debated at any length,[86] and the general consensus supported MacMichael's view that 'to accede to the Jewish Agency's request would mean that we should be opening the floodgate'.[87]

[83]HCr to CO No. 1541, 2 December 1942, CO 733/436//75113(1942).

[84]HCr to CO No. 1449, 9 November, CO 733/438//75113/57A(1942). The claim that Bulgarian Jewish funds had been confiscated to finance the emigration of Jews was, in an inverted manner, correct. However, the confiscated funds were to be used to deport Jews not to Palestine but to the extermination camps in Poland, as the German authorities demanded re-imbursement for their services. (Chary, *Bulgarian Jews, passim*).

[85]HCr to CO No. 1449, 9 November, CO 733/438//75113/57A(1942).

[87]'This question was taken towards the end of the meeting this morning, in fact nearly at 1 o'clock, and there was not much time to discuss it.' (Boyd minute, 17 November 1942, CO 733/438//75113/57A(1942)).

[87]*Ibid.*

Apparently, the only problem which the proposal posed was that of finding publicly acceptable grounds for rejecting it. It was now widely known that there were many certificates available under the quota. Furthermore, following the Cabinet decision of 18 May and the subsequent release of the *Darien* passengers, a procedure had been established for checking the credentials of refugees in Palestine before they were released, thus overcoming the obvious security difficulties. The War Office had even informed the inter-departmental meeting that 'no evidence had come to light from the examination of the large numbers of illegals who had previously entered Palestine of the presence of enemy Axis agents'.[88] As the Colonial Office did not consider that it could use its fear of 'opening the floodgates' as a public justification for its intention to reject the Jewish Agency's proposal, some other excuse was necessary, and the only one which remained was the 'security argument'. Consequently it was decided that, as MacMichael had not mentioned the security factor as a reason for rejecting the Agency's request, he would be instructed to discuss it with G.O.C. Palestine, presumably in the hope that General McConnel would oblige by doing so.[89] As had been anticipated, McConnel did indeed raise security objections to acceding to the Agency's request,[90] and they were reinforced by the views of the military and intelligence authorities in Cairo[91] and the opinion of the Minister of State Resident there.[92]

Nothing further developed on the question for almost two weeks. On 23 November, Lord Cranborne was replaced by Colonel Oliver Stanley as Secretary of State, and on 4 December (the day of *The Times* revelations on the Final Solution) a Jewish Agency delegation met the new Colonial Secretary and all the Colonial Office officials who dealt with Palestine affairs. At this meeting the Agency modified their earlier request (made from Jerusalem) and now asked that as many as possible of the small Bulgarian Jewish community be brought to safety in any refuge available — i.e. not only to Palestine. The

[88] Clark minute, quoting Captain Jones, MI 2a, War Office, 17 November 1942, *ibid*.

[89] CO to HCr No. 1343, 19 November 1942, *ibid*. The Middle East Department's intentions in dispatching this telegram were later explained in a minute to Boyd: 'It will be very useful to us if, in fact, the G.O.C., Palestine, certifies that on security grounds it will be inadvisable to arrange for large-scale immigration into Palestine of Jews from Bulgaria.' (Minute of 21 November, *ibid*.).

[90] HCr to CO No. 1508, 23 November 1942, *ibid*.

[91] Lt-General Lindsell (i/c administration, G.H.Q., M.E.F., Cairo) to Minister of State, 18 November 1942, FO 921/10, and Brigadier I.N. (Clayton M.E.I.C.) to Secretary, Minister of State 16 November 1942, *ibid*.

[92] Minister of State Resident to CO No. 54, 22 November 1942, CO 733/438/-/75113/57A.

Agency even suggested Mauritius as a possible site. As the Jewish community in Bulgaria was not large (70,000) the Agency felt that something might be done for them without evoking British fears of a flood of refugees. The Jewish communities of Hungary and Rumania numbered well over a million and clearly nothing could be done to evacuate them. However, as there was some hope that the pro-Axis governments of those countries too might still allow Jewish emigration, the Agency also asked that at least Jewish children from Hungary and Rumania be allowed entry into Allied-controlled territory.[93]

The Agency's representations on behalf of the children from Rumania and Hungary were ignored by the Colonial Office, but the desire to give children preference provided the Colonial Office with the means to make a significant symbolic concession while at the same time avoiding any risk of 'opening the floodgates'. In a cable sent to the High Commissioner giving information about the interview the Colonial Office made a very strong recommendation that he allocate 4,500 immigration certificates to children and a further 500 certificates to adults from Bulgaria alone.[94] This telegram was so sympathetically worded and the recommendation so emphatically put that the Palestine Government had little choice but to accept, which they did at once.[95]

The decision to allow 4,500 children and 500 accompanying adults to proceed to Palestine was a concession made necessary by the public response to the news that the Germans were already implementing their policy of genocide. Nevertheless, it was a significant breach of the ban on immigration from enemy-controlled territory, and the Colonial Office therefore decided to obtain the approval of higher authority. Thus on 9 December Stanley put the proposal to Churchill, explaining that: 'So long as the proposal is limited to a definite number of children I do not think it presents any serious dangers from our point of view.'[96] Churchill replied enthusiastically ('Bravo!') and suggested that the proposal be put to the Cabinet to 'obtain, as you will, its hearty endorsement. . .'[97] The Cabinet discussed and approved the scheme on 14 December.[98] In the meantime, the Colonial Office pressed MacMichael to expedite

[93] Protocols of the Colonial Office – Jewish Agency meeting of 4 December 1942, *ibid*.

[94] CO to HCr No. 1418, 4 December 1942, *ibid*.

[95] HCr to CO No. 1565, 6 December 1942, *ibid*.

[96] Stanley to Churchill, 9 December 1942, *ibid*.

[97] Churchill to Stanley, 11 December 1942, Prem 4/51/2.

[98] WM 168(42)9 Cab 65/28.

arrangements, and on 16 December the Foreign Office was requested to inform the Swiss Government (which acted as intermediary with the Bulgarian authorities).[99] On 9 January 1943 MacMichael reported that he had approved the Jewish Agency's detailed plans for the settlement of children in Palestine,[100] and shortly afterwards the Turkish Government approved in principle their transport overland across Turkey.[101]

In the weeks that followed Eden's announcement of 17 December, the question of 'rescue' was mentioned a number of times in Parliament and in the press, influential delegations demanded action and numerous representations were made to the Foreign Office. Eden raised the question of refugee policy in Cabinet on 23 December, arguing that the Government 'should consider very carefully whether there was anything we could do to assist these people'.[102] As a result of this Cabinet meeting, a special Cabinet Committee on the Refugee Problem was formed to consider: 'What arrangements could be made for the reception and accommodation of such Jewish refugees as might be able to find their way out of enemy-occupied territory through Bulgaria or Portugal.'[103] Although this Cabinet Committee (consisting of Attlee, Morrison, Stanley and Eden) did not limit itself strictly to these terms of reference, its purpose was to find ways of dealing with the problem of refugees (Jewish and non-Jewish) who were filtering through to neutral countries on the edges of occupied Europe, and not to consider the rescue of those who remained within German-controlled territory. In fact the Committee was concerned to prevent any dealings with the German authorities on the Jewish question (in accordance with Allied policy on all other matters)[104] and to prevent any large scale movements of population into areas under the control of the Allies. Thus the Committee at first resolved to exclude the possibility of using the outstanding immigration certificates for purposes of rescue. As Stanley explained: 'there was reason to believe that it was the policy of certain Axis countries, notably Rumania, to extrude Jews from their territories as an alternative to the

[99] Boyd to Randall, 16 December 1942, CO 733/438//75113/57A.

[100] HCr to CO No. 38, 9 January 1943, *ibid*.

[101] Knatchbull-Hugessen to FO No. 113, 18 January 1943, *ibid*.

[102] WM 172(42)5 Cab 65/28.

[103] *Ibid*.

[104] In February 1943, when the Norwegian Government-in-Exile asked H.M.G. to agree to exchange 500 German prisoners-of-war 'unfit for military duties' for 500 Norwegian Jews who were about to be deported to Germany, the request was refused and the Committee resolved to refuse all similar requests which might be made in the future (J.R. (43) 4th meeting, 19 February 1943, Cab 95/15).

policy of extermination. This made it all the more necessary that the
policy of His Majesty's Government to accept into Palestine only the
limited number of Jewish children with a small number of accompanying women from Eastern Europe should be firmly adhered to'.[105] As a
result it was decided at the Committee's first meeting that Palestine's
contribution to any refugee relief programme would be limited to the
5,000 immigration certificates which the Colonial Office had already
made available for the Bulgarian children.[106]

However, the policy of limiting as far as possible the number of
people who could leave occupied Europe was soon overtaken by
events. Following the Allied military successes against the Germans
in the Western Desert in late 1942, the pro-Axis Balkan Governments
attempted to re-insure with the Allies by offering concessions
concerning their respective Jewish populations. The Bulgarian
Government's willingness to allow the departure of Jewish children
was one such concession. In late December 1942 the British Embassy
in Ankara reported a rumour that the Rumanian Government was
preparing a similar concession — a scheme to allow 70,000 Rumanian
Jews to emigrate in exchange for a substantial sum per head.[107]
Shortly afterwards, the Jewish Agency (who had learnt of the scheme
through its representatives in Istanbul) approached the Foreign
Office with a request that the matter be further investigated.[108] Both
the Foreign and the Colonial Offices considered the proposal highly
embarrassing, and the Foreign Office immediately cabled to Washington
in to attempt to dissuade the State Department from taking the matter
up should it be aware of it.[109] The proposal not only conflicted with the
economic blockade of Axis countries, but it presaged exactly the sort
of large-scale population transfer which had always been feared.

On 14 January 1943, shortly after the Foreign Office cable to
Washington arguing against any positive response to the Rumanian
proposal, the Bulgarian authorities confirmed (though the Swiss
Government) their willingness to allow the 4,500 children and 500
accompanying adults to leave. In addition, the Bulgarians added that
they were prepared to allow even more than that figure to emigrate if
the Allies were prepared to receive them. However, they anticipated

[105]J.R. (43) 2nd meeting, 7 January 1943, Cab 95/15.

[106]J.R. (43) 1st meeting, 31 December 1942, *ibid*. The Cabinet endorsed this
resolution of the Committee on 11 January 1943 (WM 6(43)4, Cab 65/33).

[107]Sterndale-Bennett to FO No. 2318, 23 December 1942, FO 371/32668
W17422.

[108]Randall to Boyd, 5 January 1943, CO 733/446//76021/44(1942).

[109]FO to Washington No. 1304, 26 February 1943, *ibid*.

German opposition to the scheme (contrary to the anxieties of the Foreign Office) and pressed Britain for an early response.[110] The possibility of the rescue of significant numbers of people created by the developments in Bulgaria and Rumania would, were it known publicly, have increased the pressure on Britain and would have highlighted the discrepancy between the numbers of Palestine certificates outstanding and the few which the Government had resolved to make available.[111] The Jewish Agency in London was at the time aware of the scheme concerning the Bulgarian children and also knew of the rumoured willingness of the Rumanian Government to ransom large numbers of Jews. It did not however, yet know that the Bulgarian Government had formally expressed its willingness to proceed with the scheme or indeed to extend it significantly. Its current policy was to bring pressure to bear on the Colonial Office to abandon the ban on immigration from enemy-controlled territory, i.e. to allow the immigration of adults as well as of children. If the full extent of the rescue possibilities (as they appeared in January 1943) became known and was set against the Cabinet Committee's very limited plans for the reception of small groups of refugees, the Colonial Office feared a public outcry which might engulf not only the ban on immigration from enemy-controlled territory but also the White Paper's general restrictions on Jewish immigration into Palestine.

Thus, in its most significant concession on immigration policy so far, the Colonial Office attempted to forestall such pressure by reversing the initial decision of the Cabinet Committee taken a few weeks earlier and making all the outstanding certificates available for Jewish children from enemy-controlled territory, together with a proportion of accompanying adults (which was to include a small number of 'veteran Zionists', Rabbis and doctors). As Stanley subsequently explained to the High Commissioner, such a concession was necessary in order to avoid the wider restrictions on Jewish immigration into Palestine coming under attack.[112] The Colonial Office's proposal was debated by the Cabinet on 25 January 1943, and on 3 February, in response to a Parliamentary question Stanley

---

[110]Berne to FO No. 205, 14 January 1943, on CO 733/438//75113/57A, Part 1 (1943).

[111]Randall to Boyd, 23 February 1943, *ibid*. The proposal had, in fact, already been made public. The *New York Times* published an account in mid-February together with an appeal by a Jewish organisation under the heading 'Buy a Jew, $50'.

[112]CO to HCr No. 94, 26 January 1943, CO 733/438//75113/57A(1942). MacMichael accepted the Colonial Office's recommended concession shortly afterwards (HCr to CO No. 108, 28 January 1943, CO 733/436//75113(1943)).

[113]WM 16(43)6 Cab 65/33.

142

was able to reply that the Government was prepared 'to admit into Palestine Jewish children, with a proportion of adults, up to the limits of immigration permissible for the five-year immigration period ending 31 March, 1944'.[114] At the same time the Colonial Office resolved to maintain the ban on those refugees who managed to cross into Turkey independently or became stranded there.[115] The Colonial Office also refused to issue general instructions to the relevant immigration and passport officials to override the inevitable procedural delays involved in providing the necessary documentation for those who would be selected to emigrate, preferring to discuss individual points of difficulty 'as they arise'.[116]

Such difficulties arose almost at once. As there had been no further developments on the unofficial Rumanian proposal to ransom Rumanian Jews,[117] all efforts concentrated on the Bulgarian Government's willingness to allow Jews to emigrate. Complicated negotiations followed between the British, Palestine, Turkish and (via the Swiss) Bulgarian governments and the Jewish Agency concerning the selection of the potential immigrants, security screening, the issuing of visas, and transport across Turkey. At the outset the Bulgarians had warned that they were under intense German pressure to commence deportations to the major death camps in Poland. Nevertheless each stage of the negotiations met with lengthy delays.[118] Eventually,

[114]H.C. Debs/5s/386/Cols 864-7/ 3 February 1943.

[115]Protocol of interview between Col. Stanley and a Jewish Agency delegation, 5 February 1943, CO 733/444//75872/26C (1942-3).

[116]Gater to Namier, 6 March 1943, *ibid*.

[117]An account of the Rumanian proposal based on Axis records is given in R. Hillberg, *The Destruction of European Jewry* (New York, 1973), pp. 503-9. The American response to the proposal is examined in H.L. Feingold, *The Politics of Rescue: The Roosevelt Administration and the Holocaust, 1938-1945* (New York, 1972), pp. 180-5.

[118]To the delays caused by the inevitable difficulties of transportation and organisation were added lengthy delays caused by the Palestine Government's insistence that the conventional procedures of indentification and distribution of documents be carried out in full by the Swiss Embassy in Sofia on its behalf. These were to be followed by security checks of the children and accompanying adults in Turkey, even though the Turkish Government was reluctant to have groups of Jews held up on its territory. In addition the Bulgarian Government insisted that it alone select the people who would be allowed to emigrate under the scheme, which both the Palestine Government and the Jewish Agency opposed. All the differences were greatly complicated by the need to communicate between the large number of (British) official bodies concerned, and through the offices of the Swiss Government. Only after the Germans forced the closure of the Bulgarian-Turkish border did anything like a sense of urgency enter into the negotiations, by which time, as the Swiss pointed out, it was really too late. The negotiations which were conducted from June to December 1943 were only an attempt by the Bulgarians to play for time (cf. CO 733/438//75113/57A Parts 1 & 2(1943); CO 733/438//75113/71(1943) and CO 733/439//75113/72(1943), *passim*.)

the scheme came to the attention of the German authorities in Bulgaria and as a result the Bulgarian Government was forced in mid-May 1943 to close the Bulgarian-Turkish border to all Jews. Negotiations with the Bulgarians continued until December 1943, but although individual Bulgarian Jews did succeed in escaping across the Turkish border, no organised groups were brought out under the scheme.

The experience of the negotiations on the scheme to bring out the Bulgarian Jewish children had, by mid-1943, made the relevant authorities in London realise what had in fact been true since late 1941 — that far from intending to expel the Jews and embarrass the Allies thereby, the Germans had resolved to prevent their escape. In any case, the lack of transport, also demonstrated by the experience of the Bulgarian scheme, made any such expulsion unlikely. Once these facts had been recognised in London the fear of 'opening the floodgates' was removed from official deliberations on refugee policy. Instead there were now other causes for concern: public reaction to the failure of the Bulgarian scheme (which was Britain's only significant rescue operation) and the continued availability of large numbers of unused immigration certificates. Between 1 April and 30 June 1943 only 1,227 immigrants, most of whom had not come from enemy-controlled territory, succeeded in reaching Palestine, and MacMichael reported that for the remaining nine months of the White Paper immigration period there were over 32,000 vacancies out of the 75,000 total.[119] Many of the immigration certificates had in fact been set aside for possible future use by the Bulgarian children and for specific individuals within occupied Europe. The issue of certificates to the latter groups was only a life-saving ploy, and their immigration before March 1944 was not seriously anticipated.[120] Thus by mid-1943 it became apparent that as a consequence of the circumstances of war, as a direct result of the campaign against illegal immigration and the rigid administration of the immigration legislation, and in particular as a result of the ban on immigration from enemy-

[119]MacMichael to Battershill (letter, 8 May 1943, CO 733/436//75113(1943)), and HCr to CO No. 1031, 24 August 1943, *ibid.*

[120]The possession of a formal certificate for immigration to Palestine was often sufficient to save families from deportation to extermination centres, and the Jewish Agency succeeded in allocating over 2,700 certificates for this purpose once the Palestine Government approved their allocation to 'veteran Zionists', doctors and rabbis. Although by the end of the war a larger number of certificates was made available for this propose, in 1943 the Palestine Government refused to allocate more than the permitted 5% of the remaining immigration certificates to be used in this way, and the Foreign Office was unwilling to make further use of this method of rescue because it required indirect dealings with the German authorities in order to distribute the certificates (CO 733/439//75113/72(1943) *passim*).

controlled territory, almost half of the potential Jewish immigration promised under the White Paper would not be realised.

Consequently, in June 1943 the Colonial Office decided to abolish the ban on immigration from enemy-controlled territory as well as the policy of allowing into Palestine only those immigrants who arrived there by their own means. According to this latest policy any Jewish refugees who succeeded in reaching Turkey would, after a security check, be permitted entry to Palestine rather than being sent to Cyprus. (Although the ruling applied universally, transport difficulties meant that it applied only to refugees filtering across the Turkish border). The Colonial Office made it clear to the High Commissioner that this final step in dismantling the protective barriers which had been erected around the immigration restrictions of the White Paper was being taken only because the number of outstanding immigration certificates was so large and the numbers of refugees likely to take advantage of the ruling was expected to be small. In any event, MacMichael was informed: 'The numbers to be admitted under these new proposals would *not* entail any increase in the number of immigrants allowed under the White Paper.'[121] Furthermore, as on each previous occasion when the Colonial Office had made concessions, it insisted that no public announcement of the change in policy be made lest it stimulate the flow of Jewish refugees into Turkey.

The Colonial Office circulated these recommendations to the High Commissioner, the Minister of State in Cairo and all the relevant government ministries in London for consultation. MacMichael endorsed them immediately,[122] but before bringing the proposals to the Cabinet, the Colonial Office made two further suggestions — that should there still be unused certificates by the time all Jewish immigration was to end according to the White Paper (31 March 1944), then the time limit would be abandoned, and conversely, should all the certificates be exhausted before the time limit expired, then Jewish immigration should be allowed to continue until the end of the war to a maximum of 15,000 per annum.[123] MacMichael rejected this latter proposal vehemently ('I can conceive of nothing more calculated to cause violent reaction throughout the Middle East. . . . I cannot make my warning too strong. . . . ', but he conceded that the time limit, which had seemed so central to the White Paper as a whole in 1939, could be abandoned with advantage. As he pointed out, any

[121]CO to HCr, Most Secret and Personal, 4 June 1943, CO 733/436//75113(1943).

[122]HCr to CO, Private and Personal, Most Secret, 5 June 1943, *ibid*.

[123]CO to HCr, Secret and Personal (1 & 2), 23 June 1943, *ibid*.

outstanding immigration certificates remaining in 1944 'will serve usefully to tide over critical period at the end of March, and act as a cushion between the past and the future'.[124]

It is not possible to establish with certainty why the Colonial Office raised the possibility of abandoning the overall ceiling of 75,000 stipulated by the White Paper, as it showed no intention of supporting the idea in Cabinet itself.[125] The explanation probably lies in the predictability of MacMichael's response. The Cabinet was scheduled to debate a number of recommendations relating to Palestine on 2 July and the Colonial Office could safely anticipate that the question of abandoning the White Paper ceiling on Jewish immigration would be raised as well. Stanley specifically requested that MacMichael's very negative response to the suggestion be placed amongst the papers which he took with him to the Cabinet meeting.[126]

The Cabinet paper which the Colonial Office had circulated containing its recommendations on immigration policy explained that as a result of German policy there was no longer any possibility of legal immigration (i.e. the children schemes) from enemy territory, and that illegal immigration was also expected to be small. The paper then set out the concessions which had been under discussion since early June: 'In future all Jews, whether adults or children, who may succeed in escaping to Turkey will be eligible (after a preliminary security check. . .) for onward transport to Palestine. . . This policy will also apply to Jews who manage to escape to other neutral countries; but where they have escaped to countries in which they are safe they will normally remain there....'[127] The paper added that these concessions would remain secret, and would apply only until the 75,000 limit had been reached. When the Cabinet debated these proposals on 2 July, Stanley was able to offer a further concession — that the time limit of 31 March 1944 be abandoned as well.

While the Cabinet endorsed the concessions which the Colonial Office had proposed, it added (presumably at Churchill's insistence) that its decision 'is not to be taken as prejudicing later decisions by the War Cabinet on immigration policy when the White Paper figure (of 75,000) had been attained.'[128] As this same Cabinet meeting established

[124]HCr to CO, Secret and Personal (1 & 2), 25 June 1943, *ibid*.

[125]The file containing the minutes relating to the drafting of the telegrams to the High Commissioner (75872 (1943)) remains closed to research.

[126]Thornley minute, 29 June 1943, CO 733/436//75113(1943).

[127]WP(43)277 Cab 66/38.

[128]WM 92(43)2-3, 2 July 1943, Cab 65/35 and Secret Annexe on Cab 65/39.

a Cabinet Committee to examine alternative policies to the White Paper for the future of Palestine, there was no need to deal with the 75,000 limit until the available certificates had been exhausted and Jewish immigration supposed to end — by which time the policy of terminating Jewish immigration may well have been superseded.

The Jewish Agency was informed of the revised immigration regulations one week after the Cabinet debate,[129] but the Government's intention of abandoning the five year deadline was not made public until November 1943.[130] During the last half of 1943 the Agency attempted to have the condition of secrecy on the new concessions lifted, arguing that Britain's desire not to inform even the Turkish authorities of its willingness to accept refugees who crossed into Turkey by land was in fact making it difficult for refugees to cross the Turkish border.[131] However, MacMichael insisted that secrecy be maintained as he feared that otherwise a flood of refugees would follow.[132] Only when it had become apparent in early 1944 that, despite Britain's policy of allowing refugees to proceed to Palestine, very few were escaping, did the Colonial Office overrule the High Commissioner. The Turkish Government was informed orally of the new policy in January 1944 — seven months after it had been adopted.[133]

The concessions of July 1943 did not compensate adequately for the restrictions of the years since the White Paper was introduced in May 1939. By 31 March 1944 — a date which had become of only symbolic significance — over 20,000 vacancies still existed under the White Paper.[134] In fact the limit of 75,000 Jewish immigrants was not reached until December 1945 — the month the immigration provisions of the White Paper were formally suspended. During 1944 a new refugee problem emerged — that of Jews in territories liberated by the Allies who had survived the Holocaust and who wanted to leave Europe. Many of them wanted to go to Palestine, and, whatever other motives they may have had for doing so, the existence of immigration certificates for that country could only provide an additional powerful

[129]Colonial Office-Jewish Agency interview, CO 733/436//75113(1943).

[130]H.C. Debs/5s/393/Cols 1151-1154/10 November 1943.

[131]CO 733/436//75113(1943), *passim*.

[132]HCr to CO No. 1440, 15 November 1943, *ibid*.

[133]Eastwood to Randall, 20 January 1944, *ibid*.

[134]The practice of allocating immigration certificates in order to give some protective documentation to people in occupied Europe who were not in a position to use the certificates meant that the actual number of physical vacancies in the 75,000 total was even larger than the number of outstanding certificates.

incentive. The continued availability of unused immigration certificates thus linked the pre- and post-war refugee problems. Furthermore Britain's record on immigration policy had a profound effect on the Jewish community in Palestine. That record, symbolised by the large numbers of unused certificates was, when the full extent of the Jewish tragedy in Europe became known, the most significant factor alienating the Yishuv from the Mandate and mobilising it into opposition.

6

COLLAPSE OF THE WHITE PAPER

The attempt to find an alternative to the White Paper through Arab federation had been abandoned by the end of 1941. The conclusions of the Middle East (Official) Committee, set out in the Report on Arab Federation of January 1942,[1] clearly stated the belief of the Foreign and Colonial Offices that any proposals concerning the future of Palestine must be based on an internal settlement between Arabs and Jews in Palestine: the imposition by the British government of grand schemes on the lines suggested by Churchill and Amery (reflecting the Weizmann-Philby plan) could not be a substitute for such a settlement.

Between 1939 and 1941 there had been a significant change in the way in which both the Eastern and the Middle East Departments believed that the White Paper would bring this about. As originally conceived, it was to have eased the way to an Arab-Jewish settlement during the steps leading to Palestine's independence. The final stage of the White Paper's constitutional provisions was to have been a constitutional conference (held after the growth of the Jewish National Home had been terminated by the land and immigration provisions of the White Paper) at which the Jews would be able to offer their agreement to the creation of an independent Palestine state with an Arab majority in exchange for guarantees of their minority rights, and perhaps even some limited continuation of Jewish immigration. When it had become apparent that no progress was possible during the war even on the first step of the constitutional provisions (the Heads of Department Scheme), and that a literal interpretation of the White Paper was therefore not possible, official circles adopted a 'functional' approach in its place. Accordingly, it was argued that the specified provisions of the White Paper were not as important as the fact that Britain had adopted a policy which satisfied neither Arab nor Jewish demands, and that the refusal to impose any settlement other than that set out in the White Paper would force the two sides to come together to work out a settlement of their own. In retrospect it is clear that this interpretation of the White Paper was a rationalisation made necessary by the failure of that policy and the lack of any accepted alternative policy for the future of Palestine. This situation continued during 1942, when, as a result of Rommel's advance into Egypt, more time was spent formulating plans for the

[1] ME(0)(42)4, Cab 95/1.

evacuation of Palestine than was devoted to deliberations of future policy.

In July 1941, when Lord Moyne had first raised with the High Commissioner the possibility of attempting a solution through federation, MacMichael had responded with a proposal of his own: that the immigration and land provisions of the White Paper be retained but its constitutional provisions be abandoned; that the Jewish Agency be abolished; and that the Mandate be terminated and Palestine converted into a Crown Colony.[2] In September 1941 he repeated these proposals in a lengthy despatch, arguing that only after prolonged British tutelage unrestricted by the obligations of the Mandate towards the Yishuv, and only by disestablishing the Jewish Agency (which, 'with its palatial offices, its network of Departments, and its powerful international affiliations, tends to overshadow the local Government'), would it be possible to foster the sort of Jewish-Arab cooperation which would permit eventual independence.[3] In subsequent correspondence with the Colonial Secretary, MacMichael gave additional reasons for the measures he proposed:

> If we are not very careful His Majesty's Government will be faced with the dilemma of either having to give way to the exaggerated demands of the Jews and so provoking rebellion in the Middle East. . . or of having to suppress the Jews *vi et armis* (which I do not see them doing). It will be difficult enough, in any case, to avoid bloodshed here at the end of the war and the best way of minimizing the risk is to put the brake on the Jews betimes.[4]

MacMichael's proposals were not well received by the Colonial Office, where it was recognised that Britain was not in a position to change the legal basis of its position in Palestine. Even it if were, MacMichael's proposals would not have resolved any of the causes of tension there.[5] The Eastern Department of the Foreign Office was less negative. Baxter felt that the proposals 'are in theory very sound' but recognised that a step as drastic as changing Palestine's status from Mandate to Crown Colony would have to wait until after the war, when, if all else had failed, the idea could be taken up again.[6] The

[2]HCr to CO No. 1021, Most Secret and Personal, 13 July 1941, CO 733/444(1)/-/75872/115(1941).

[3]MacMichael to Moyne, Despatch, 1 September 1941, CO 733/444//75872/-115(1941).

[4]MacMichael to Moyne, Private and Personal letter, 14 December 1941, *ibid.*

[5]Luke, Boyd, Shuckburgh and Parkinson minutes, 18-23 October 1941, *ibid.*

[6]Baxter minute, 11 November 1941, FO 371/27137 E7150.

150

proposals were discussed at an inter-departmental meeting on 19 December 1941, and as there was no need for any immediate action, the Colonial Office had little difficulty in having further consideration of MacMichael's despatch postponed.[7]

When the High Commissioner returned to London in April 1942 for talks with the Colonial Office, he presented an entirely new version of his proposals. At a meeting on 23 April with the Middle East Department and the Colonial Secretary, and the next day with a Foreign Office delegation, MacMichael repeated his arguments for abolishing the Mandate, disestablishing the Jewish Agency and abandoning the constitutional provisions of the White Paper. This time, however, in place of his proposal to convert the Mandate into a Crown Colony, he put forward a radically different suggestion. MacMichael proposed that a small federation of Palestine, Transjordan, Syria and Lebanon be created under the joint supervision of Britain, France and the United States. Within that federation Palestine was to become a 'bi-national state, probably on a parity basis (between Arab and Jew)'. Such a federation would, he claimed, restore the historic unity which he believed had existed between these four states. At the same time it would allow the Jews some opportunity to expand in an area larger than Palestine, and would reassure the Arabs by preventing Palestine's conversion into a Jewish state. MacMichael argued that his proposals allowed the three supervising powers to ensure their own interests in the Middle East, as well as offering the only prospect for a solution of the Arab-Jewish conflict.[8]

Although nothing was resolved while the High Commissioner was in London, the Colonial Office was even more critical of these new proposals than it had been of the earlier ones.[9] Previously the Colonial Office could point to the difficulties of abolishing the Mandate and the Agency and of overturning the White Paper. Now it objected that any scheme which involved Syria and Lebanon would have to deal with the active opposition of the French. The response of the Foreign Office was similarly negative, and in August (after MacMichael had sent a fuller memorandum defending his proposals from Jerusalem),[10]

[7]Luke minute, 22 December 1941, CO 733/444//75872/115(41).

[8]The full protocols of the talks are on CO 733/438//76155(42). The relevant CO minutes are on CO 732/87(i)//79238(42). In addition to MacMichael's oral presentation of his proposal on 23-4 April, he distributed a memorandum entitled 'Zionism and Arabism is the Near East' (on 76155).

[9]Boyd observed: 'I do not believe that the High Commissioner's plan was carefully worked out in Palestine, and my impression was that he improvised it... in the course of his journey to England.' (Minute, 12 June 1942, CO 732/87(i)//79238(42)).

[10]MacMichael to Cranborne, Despatch, 7 July 1942, *ibid.*

the Colonial Office told him that both it and the Foreign Office considered that his proposals offered no 'reasonable prospects for success'.[11] Although MacMichael continued to defend his proposals during 1942, officials in London felt that nothing was to be gained by any further consideration of policy in the Middle East while Britain's position there was so gravely imperilled by German advances.

In 1941, in his earliest proposals and in all subsequent versions of them, MacMichael had consistently argued that the Jewish Agency must be disestablished if the Jewish community in Palestine was to be prevented from imposing its own solution to the Palestine problem. Even though, officially, his proposals had been dismissed and in any case it was in practical terms impossible to adopt this suggestion, by late 1941 both the Foreign and the Colonial Office had come to share the concern of the British authorities in the Middle East at the growing radicalisation of the Yishuv. The crystallization of a Zionist political programme during 1942, the growth of illegal Jewish military organisations and the opening of a pro-Zionist propaganda campaign in the United States all presented a new challenge to British authority in Palestine at a time of great uncertainty about its own policy there.

As a result of the interviews which Lord Moyne had held separately with Weizmann and Ben Gurion in August 1941, the Colonial Office had realised that authoritative Zionist circles were looking to the creation of a Jewish state in Palestine as a solution to the inevitable post-war problem of Jewish refugees. This prompted the Colonial Office to circulate a Cabinet paper in September 1941 advocating that the government formulate a policy designed to cope with the Jewish refugee problem and at the same time issue a statement of its commitment to the White Paper in order to deflate the Zionists' rising expectations concerning Palestine. However, consideration of the paper was delayed indefinitely and the matter progressed no further at the Cabinet level. Shortly afterwards the question of the post-war Jewish problem came under consideration in the Foreign Office when it learnt that even non-Zionist Jewish circles were beginning to consider that Palestine would have to absorb large numbers of Jewish refugees after the war, contrary to the specific provisions of the White Paper and to the policy it embodied.[12] In December 1941 both the Foreign and the Colonial Offices came into possession of a number of documents which confirmed earlier

[11]Cranborne to MacMichael, Secret and Personal letter, 19 August 1942, *ibid*.

[12]Anthony de Rothschild to Eden, 29 October 1941, FO 371/27129 E7072. De Rothschild was a leading figure in British non-Zionist Jewish circles. His letter was supported by Rabbi Lazaron, a leading American anti-Zionist.

impressions of how both Zionist and non-Zionist Jewish thinking was developing.[13] The most significant of these documents was a lengthy memorandum by Ben Gurion entitled 'Outlines of Zionist Policy', in which the Chairman of the Jewish Agency Executive argued (as he had already done in his interview with Moyne in August) that the Jewish refugee problem could be solved only by large-scale Jewish immigration into Palestine, and that this could only be achieved by a sovereign Jewish government.

The candid comments made by Weizmann and Ben Gurion to Moyne in August 1941, and Ben Gurion's political programme, had not been formally endorsed by any authoritative Zionist body. In fact, during 1941-2 the question of Zionism's final objectives and the means to be employed to attain them, were the subject of considerable controversy in Zionist circles in Palestine and elsewhere. Before Ben Gurion left Palestine in July 1941 for London and subsequently America, he had failed to obtain authority from the Jewish Agency Executive or from the Va'ad HaPoel HaZioni (the Labour Party Executive — effectively the Yishuv's controlling body) to publicly demand a Jewish state.[14] Nevertheless, by late 1941 both the Foreign and the Colonial Offices were convinced that, regardless of whether Ben Gurion's programme had been endorsed or not (a question they did not ask), it did represent the demands which the Zionists would eventually articulate. Subsequent developments in 1942 confirmed the accuracy of their belief. Thus, when Weizmann published an article in January 1942 in the journal *Foreign Affairs,* arguing that: 'The Arabs must. . . be told that the Jews will be encouraged to settle in Palestine, and will control their own immigration; that here Jews who so desire will be able to achieve their freedom and self-government by establishing a state of their own. . . ',[15] there was no

---

[13] The documents had been taken by Censorship from Ben Gurion's luggage when he left the United Kingdom for America in November 1941, and copied. (Boyd to Baxter, 24 December 1941, FO 371/27129 E8556). Amongst them were protocols of a meeting held in September between leading British non-Zionist Jews (including de Rothschild, Lord Bearsted and Sir Robert Waley-Cohen) and Weizmann, Ben Gurion and members of the London offices of the Jewish Agency. The meeting was convened in an attempt to find common ground between the Zionists and the non-Zionists in dealing with post-war Jewish problems. Weizmann put forward his argument that there would be 2½-3,000,000 Jewish refugees who could not be resettled in Europe after the war, and that that fact would require the creation of a Jewish state in Palestine. While the non-Zionists demurred from this conclusion, they supported the argument that Palestine would have to absorb large numbers of refugees after the war. It would not be unreasonable to presume that Ben Gurion wanted these protocols brought to H.M.G.'s attention, and that a good way of ensuring this would be to carry the documents where they would be intercepted by Censorship when he left the U.K.

[14] Bauer, *From Diplomacy to Resistance,* pp. 231-2.

[15] Chaim Weizmann, 'Palestine's Role in the Solution of the Jewish Problem', *Foreign Affairs,* Vol. 20, January 1942, p. 337.

comment from either of the Departments concerned.[16] Similarly, when Ben Gurion succeeded in having the establishment of a Jewish 'Commonwealth' in Palestine after the war adopted as a plank in the formal policy of the Zionist Organisation of America at the 'Biltmore' Conference in May 1942,[17] it was not considered by the British Government to be a particularly significant development.[18]

The Foreign Office considered that Ben Gurion's political programme, which it had discussed six months before the Biltmore Conference, was the definitive indicator of Zionist thinking, and the Eastern, Refugee, American and Central Departments minuted on it at length. The Eastern Department expressed the most obvious British anxiety — that Ben Gurion's programme 'could only be achieved by bloodshed, i.e. not the shedding of Arab and Jewish blood alone, but inevitably of British blood'.[19] However, as Ben Gurion had clearly stated in his memorandum that the creation of a Jewish state could only be accomplished after the war, this was not the Foreign Office's immediate concern. What worried it more was Ben Gurion's strategy for achieving this objective: 'I believe that the centre of gravity of our political work lies, for the moment, in the U.S.A... In America it will be easier to win over public opinion for a radical and maximum solution of the Jewish problem in Palestine than it is in England... American support for a Jewish State is thus the key to our success.'[20]

Since the outbreak of war in 1939, American Jewish opinion had been a source of some concern to officials in London dealing with Palestine. The need to mobilize American support behind the British war effort in the years prior to America's entry into the war had made the Foreign Office sensitive to American Jewry's criticism of British Palestine policy. Between 1939 and 1941 it was gradually recognised that this concern was unnecessary as the Foreign Office came to understand the deep divisions in American Jewish attitudes to Zionism. Even in Zionist circles, despite differences with Britain over

[16]No reference to Weizmann's article has been traced in the files of either the Foreign or the Colonial Offices.

[17]The Conference was formally held under the auspices of the American Emergency Committee for Zionist Affairs, a creation of the Zionist Organisation of America.

[18]Halifax informed the Foreign Office of the Conference's deliberations by Saving (i.e. surface mail) telegram. (Halifax to FO. No. 155 Saving, 21 May 1942, FO 371/31378 E3084). In the Colonial Office the minuted reaction was that 'There is nothing new in this.' (Clark minute, 29 May 1942, CO 733/443//75872/14(1942)).

[19]Caccia minute, 29 December 1941, FO 371/27129 E8556. The reaction of the Colonial Office is on closed files, but it was in any case already familiar with Ben Gurion's views on the political objectives of Zionism.

[20]Ben Gurion memorandum.

Palestine, American Jewish opinion was consistently pro-British in mobilising support for the war against Hitler.[21] However, once America had formally entered the war in December 1941, unquestioning support for Britain was no longer necessary, and American Zionists felt that they could now afford to be more vocal in their criticisms of British policy. Furthermore, by early 1942 the Foreign Office had become concerned that the United States Government would itself anticipate a large post-war Jewish refugee problem, and (like Zionist and non-Zionist Jews) might consider that Palestine must play a larger part in the solution to this problem than the White Paper policy allowed. Consequently, it was feared that the American administration might become increasingly sympathetic to Jewish lobbying.

Within Zionist circles estimates of what could be achieved by mobilising American opinion varied, and neither Weizmann nor Shertok shared Ben Gurion's belief that the focus of Zionist political activity should be shifted from England to America.[22] Nevertheless following America's entry into the war and the failure of the Jewish Army scheme in October 1941, an increasingly vocal Zionist public relations campaign developed in America. During the course of 1942 this campaign was extended to include criticism of Britain's failure to arm the Yishuv adequately against a possible German invasion of Palestine. After the sinking of the *Struma* in February 1942, the immigration restrictions also came under constant attack.

Although this campaign did not become a serious problem until 1942-3, in early 1942 the Foreign Office had already become alarmed at American vulnerability to Jewish pressure about Palestine.[23] In late February 1942 the Ministry of Information and the Foreign and Colonial Offices resolved to launch an information campaign in America designed to counter the effects of Zionist agitation.[24] The campaign was to be directed specifically at leading members of the administration, who were to receive memoranda setting out Britain's case on the Jewish Army and on illegal immigration. More general steps to reach the wider American public had been initiated in 1941,

[21]'The Influence of American Jewry on the Policy of the U.S.A.' CO 733/443/-/75872/14(42).

[22]Bauer, *From Diplomacy to Resistance,* p. 238. Cf. also Shertok's report to the Jewish Agency Executive after his return from the U.K. and the U.S.A. (FO 371/35035 E3689/G).

[23]Baxter minute, no date. FO 371/27129 E8556.

[24]Luke minute, 16 March 1942, CO 733/443//75872/14(42); and Caccia minute, 25 February 1942, FO 371/31378 E1271 & E1928. Ironically this meeting was held on the day the *Struma* sank.

when the British embassy in Washington attempted to encourage American Arab groups to put the Arab case on Palestine more forcefully.[25] This had not proved successful and during 1942 various other measures were taken to try to reach the American public. Lecture tours by British Arabists were discussed (the names of Bertram Thomas and Freya Stark were put forward) and the idea of bringing Indian Moslems to America to speak on Palestine was also suggested (only to be vetoed by the Indian Office).[26] Attempts were made to have pro-British articles on Palestine published in the American press, and to stimulate the anti-Zionist public relations efforts of the Iraqi embassy in Washington.[27] However the efforts to counter Zionist public relations amongst the American public proved ineffective, and the Zionist campaign continued unabated.[28] The initial attempts to forestall the growth of pro-Zionist views in the administration by the discreet dissemination of information also failed to achieve anything noteworthy. In mid-1942 Halifax told the Foreign Office that the central issue which would attract American political support for Zionism was the Jewish refugee problem, and he advised that British efforts to counter such a development should be based on the theme of the unsuitability of Palestine for mass immigration and Britain's attempts to find an alternative refuge.[29] However, as the Colonial Office reminded the Foreign Office, this latter question had been exhaustively examined before the war and during its early years, and the Colonial Office had consistently pointed out that the British Empire offered few opportunities for the re-settlement of Jewish refugees.

An indication that the administration was indeed being influenced in favour of the Zionists came when Lyttelton met Roosevelt in June 1942, and the President talked in terms of luring the Palestinian Arabs away from Palestine by offers of land near Aleppo and by financial inducements.[30] When Richard Law met Sumner Welles, the U.S. Under-Secretary of State, in September 1942, Welles indicated that he held similar views, stating that 'in his view the ultimate solution

[25]N. Butler (Washington) to Baxter, 24 May 1941, on CO 733/443//75872/14(41).

[26]Boyd minute, 19 August 1942, *ibid.*, and minutes FO 371/31379 E4048. Also India Office to Eyres, 23 October 1942, FO 371/31379 E6252.

[27]*Ibid.*

[28]None of the various suggestions could be put into effect, and by November 1942 Peterson had already conceded that the attempts to influence American opinion had been 'a terrible waste of time' (FO 371/31379 E6252).

[29]Halifax to FO, Saving No. 313, 2 July 1942, FO 371/31379 E4048.

[30]Caccia to Boyd, 20 October 1942, CO 733/443//75872/14(42).

could only be a Jewish State with compensation to the Arabs in other parts of the Middle East'.[31] The Foreign Office considered these views 'naive in the extreme', but as it was unable to offer concrete proposals in their place, it recognised that there was no point in having Halifax take the matter up with the administration 'until our own views are clearer about the Palestine question'.[32] The absence of any realistic policy on the future of Palestine which could be advocated by the Foreign Office with any conviction, its inability to offer any territorial solution outside Palestine to the anticipated post-war refugee problem and its failure to counter effectively the publicity campaign of the Zionists, all heightened the Foreign Office's anxiety as to the possible direction that America's emerging policy on Palestine and on the Jewish question might take. Nevertheless, the Foreign Office hoped to prevent the Americans adopting pro-Zionist policies by impressing upon them the danger which it believed that Zionism, in the wake of the radicalisation of the Yishuv, created for Allied interests. Consequently, the Eastern Department sent the embassy the documents which had been removed from Ben Gurion's luggage (including his 'Outlines of Zionist Policy') and a paper which MacMichael had sent from Palestine one year earlier on the growth of illegal Jewish military organisations. The embassy was later able to report that, on the basis of these documents, he had informed Sumner Welles personally that: 'His Majesty's Government possessed very secret information according to which the extreme Jews wished to get possession of arms in order to use them against us.'[33] It was clear from this reply that the embassy had missed, or discounted, the real import of the message which the Foreign Office wanted to impress upon the Americans. Sir Maurice Peterson, Assistant Secretary in the Foreign Office responsible for the Eastern Department, was thus forced to explain that it was not a question of 'extreme' Jews who 'wished to get possession of arms'. The problem, he argued, was that 'some of the leading members of the Jewish Agency. . . already control a fighting organisation of not less than 100,000 men and women, of whom something less than half are at present armed'.[34] These figures, based on information communicated to London by the Palestine Government, were indeed impressive, and were intended to alarm policy-makers in London and Washington. Whether or not they were accurate was a question not discussed.

[31] *Ibid.*

[32] *Ibid.*

[33] Campbell to Peterson, 12 October 1942, FO 371/31379 E6077.

[34] Peterson to Campbell, 23 October 1942, *ibid.*

The problem posed by the illegal Jewish military organisations (primarily the Hagana and the Irgun Zvai Leumi),[35] together with the existence of large number of Jews in the various para-military Police formations, formed to protect Jewish settlement during the Arab revolt, had been raised tentatively shortly before the release of the White Paper.[36] There was concern that despite the Yishuv's record of self-restraint in the inter-communal violence of the Arab revolt, the isolated incidents of Jewish terrorism during the negotiations which had preceded the release of the White Paper and immediately afterwards might presage a more serious attempt by the Yishuv to prevent Britain from imposing the immigration or land sales restrictions of the White Paper, or from implementing its constitutional provisions.[37] Consequently, during 1938, the functional cooperation between the Hagana and the British Army in Palestine, which had developed in the course of the Arab revolt, was terminated.

The outbreak of war saw the cessation of incidents of Jewish terrorism, and in September 1939 over 136,000 Jews registered their willingness to assist the war effort in a campaign organised by the Jewish Agency to demonstrate the size of the Yishuv's potential

[35] The *Hagana* was formed in 1920 in order to defend isolated Jewish settlements from Arab attack. It was controlled by a body representing various sections of the *Yishuv,* but was primarily an organisation of the left-wing *Histadrut* (Trades Union Federation). The *Irgun Zvai Leumi* was formed in 1931 as a breakaway group from the *Hagana,* and pursued a more aggressive military policy. Following a split in its ranks in 1937 it became a purely Revisionist (i.e. right-wing) organisation.

[36] The question was discussed by the 1938-9 Cabinet Committee on Palestine during April 1939 (cf. minutes on FO 371/23234 E2995).

[37] Some circles within the *Hagana* and the official Zionist leadership in Palestine did discuss the possibility of the use of force to prevent the implementation of the new policy. (Slutzky, *Sefer Toldot Hahagana,* pp. 19ff). However as Bauer states, opposition was envisaged 'not in order to deny the British the right to stay in Palestine, but in order to prove that Jewish nuisance value was no less dangerous than the Arab variety and that capitulation to Arab demands contained in the White Paper would not bring peace to Palestine.' (Y. Bauer, 'From Cooperation to Resistance: The Hagana 1938-1946', *Middle Eastern Studies,* Vol. 2 No. 2, 1966, p. 188). Indeed, given the small size of the armed forces which the *Yishuv* had at its disposal (illegal as well as authorized) any opposition to the large number of British troops in the country (and the Arab majority of the population) could only have been of 'nuisance value'. With the outbreak of war only a few months after the release of the White Paper, the Zionist movement as a whole hoped that the strategic worth of Jewish Palestine's industries, and the recruiting potential of the *Yishuv* and of world Jewry, would make Britain realise that much more was to be gained by encouraging the continued growth of the *Yishuv* than by appeasing Arab opinion over Palestine. However H.M.G. had discounted this possibility in the deliberations which led up to the White Paper, and the outbreak of war, rather than re-opening the debate on Palestine only heightened Britain's anxieties about her position in the Middle East and increased her willingness to meet Arab demands. The Jewish world was seen as Britain's 'captive ally', regardless of official policy in Palestine, and the only question which remained was whether the *Yishuv*'s military capabilities presented any sort of threat to Britain's ability to impose the policy which had been adopted.

contribution to the British Imperial war effort.[38] Ironically, the size of the response alarmed the Palestine authorities, who saw it as a measure of the resources which the Agency might be able to mobilise against Britain should it choose to oppose the White Paper by force. In early October, shortly after the registration, forty-three members of the Hagana were arrested during an illegal para-military training exercise, and the G.O.C. in Palestine, LT-General M. Barker took the opportunity to request authority for an energetic campaign designed to reduce the numbers of arms legally available to the Jewish settlements,[39] to reduce the number of Jewish Settlement Police, the best armed and trained of the various Jewish Police formations, and to demand the disbanding of all Jewish illegal organisations and the surrender of illegal arms — to be followed by 'a thorough search for Jewish arms' if the demand was not met.[40]

Commenting on the size of the illegal Jewish arsenal, Barker stated: 'Reports vary widely as to the number of illegal arms held. A fair estimate is 1,500-2,000 rifles and 8,000-10,000 pistols of all types, and a considerable but incalculable stock of hand-grenades.'[41] This was not a particularly large arsenal given the disturbances of the previous three years, when the Palestine authorities had effectively lost control of the countryside to Arab rebel groups. Nevertheless, Barker argued that the continued existence of illegal arms and of the Hagana after the Army had restored law and order, was 'based on the belief that [the Jews] cannot trust the British Empire to produce the necessary forces for the defence of Palestine, and, secondly, a firm determination that sooner or later the Jewish community will occupy

---

[38] For a full discussion of the *Yishuv*'s contribution to Britain's military efforts in the Middle East and elsewhere, cf. Gelber, *Hahitnadvut ve'Mekoma*, chapters 4-8.

[39] G.O.C. Conference, 20 November 1939, WO 169/148.

[40] Barker to WO, 2 November 1939 HP 1589, WO 169/146. The relevant Colonial Office file for 1939 on the disarming of the *Yishuv* (75998(1939)) remains closed to research.

[41] Barker to MacMichael, 10 November 1939, CO 733/398//75156/141(39). In 1939-40 Palestine Military Intelligence estimates of the number of arms held illegally by the Jews were fairly accurate. Furthermore, in 1940 there appears to have been a well-founded degree of scepticism concerning the Jewish illegal arsenal. As the Middle East Department noted: 'The trouble is that we do not know how many Jewish arms there are in Palestine; some estimates are large, while other authorities such as General Haining [Barker's predecessor as G.O.C., Palestine] think that the Jews like us to have the impression that the stocks are much larger than they are in fact.' (Luke minute, 12 June 1940, CO 733/422//75241(1940). According to Bauer (conversation with author), Haining's observation was correct. The Jewish authorities deliberately exaggerated the *Yishuv*'s self-defence capabilities during the Arab revolt as a deterrent against the Arabs. Subsequently, as will be discussed below, it was the British authorities in the Middle East who themselves substantially inflated the estimates of the *Yishuv*'s armed strength.

Palestine by force of arms and hold it against any aggression from any power whomsoever'.[42] However the High Commissioner and Wavell, the Commander-in-Chief, Middle East Forces, were opposed to the policy of active disarmament and wholesale searches for arms which Barker advocated. Instead he proposed that searches be conducted only in cases where there was definite information on the location of hidden arms caches in individual settlements.[43] The Colonial Secretary, Malcolm MacDonald, brought the question to the Cabinet in February 1940, warning in a Cabinet paper which he circulated at the same time that the Jewish illegal military organisations 'though primarily designed for use against the Arabs, might even be used in certain circumstances against the British forces in Palestine'.[44] MacDonald added that the policy advocated by the High Commissioner and the C.-in-C., M.E.F. could only stop the growth of the Hagana and would not force it to disband, but that, nevertheless, the Colonial Office shared their concern that more radical measures of forcible disarmament might cause serious unrest in Palestine. Consequently the Cabinet endorsed the restricted policy of acting only on specific information.[45] It also endorsed an accompanying recommendation that the various Jewish Police formations be reduced 'to the limits compatible with the effective protection of the Jewish settlements'.

Between the trial of the forty-three members of the Hagana who had been arrested in October, and the receipt in Palestine of the instructions on arms search policy there had been further arrests of small groups of Jews engaged in para-military exercises and more arms searches. The last of these, on 22 January 1940, uncovered an arms cache and was followed by a controversial trial (in April 1940), during which the Jewish Agency and other representative institutions issued a public manifesto stating that the arms concerned had been held for purposes of self-defence and claiming that it was the right of Jewish settlements to hold arms for that purpose. As a result of these events, and presumably also of the Cabinet decision not to allow a campaign of active disarmament, the government and the military authorities in Palestine attempted to persuade the Yishuv to surrender its illegal arms voluntarily. In a series of talks between the G.O.C. (Lt. - General G.J. Giffard, Barker's successor), the Jewish Agency

[42]Barker to MacMichael, 10 November 1939, CO 733/398//75156/141(39).

[43]HCr to CO No. 1354, 3 November 1939, FO 371/23251 E7479; and Wavell to WO No. 6077, 4 November 1939, WO 169/146. Wavell argued that Barker's policy was unlikely to produce results, could not be enforced and, as Barker admitted, would cause serious repercussions in Palestine.

[44]WP(G)(40)17, 'Illegal Jewish Military Organisations', Cab 67/4.

[45]WM 39(40)14, Cab 65/5.

160

and other Jewish bodies, the authorities said they would not reduce the number of Jewish Settlement Police and would allow a proportion of the arms surrendered to be registered and returned to the settlements. The alternative, it was stated, was a continuation of the arms searches and the imposition of lengthy prison sentences if arms were found.[46]

Although Giffard's real concern, as he made clear in a report to G.H.Q., M.E.F. in Cairo, was that 'the Jewish leaders may not be able in all circumstances to control their followers',[47] the G.O.C. told the Agency that he was concerned that 'fifth-columnists' might obtain control of the illegal Jewish arms. The Agency replied that the war situation only increased the risk of Arab attacks on Jewish settlements, especially if the front was to approach Palestine, and that any degree of disarmament by the Jews would only encourage such attacks. Giffard then made a compromise proposal: 'Would the Jews be prepared to give him the numbers of arms in their possession, without prejudice to anything else? He would make no promise as to the use he would make of the information, but at least it would tell him where he stood.'[48] This modified proposal was debated at length both by the Jewish Agency and within the Hagana. While there had been a consensus against any voluntary surrender of arms, serious disagreement arose as to whether details of the illegal arms held should be given to the authorities.[49] The Agency finally resolved that it would offer to canvas the settlements as to their holdings of arms on condition that an assurance be given that no arms would be confiscated.[50]

However, when this proposal was put to Giffard, at the third and final meeting in mid-June 1940, he insisted that a proportion of the arms would have to be surrendered ('especially machine guns and bombs') and that he would 'adjust the distribution of arms (as) he saw fit'. The talks were thus deadlocked and Giffard refused to discuss the matter any further, concluding with a threat to greatly intensify the arm searches.[51]

The talks had ended acrimoniously, and the Jewish community anticipated the active resumption of arms searches and a full effort at

[46] Slutzky, *Sefer Toldot Hahagana*, p. 130.

[47] 'Appreciation to Determine the Extent to Which Troops May be Made Available From Palestine For Use Elsewhere.' (7 May 1940, CR/PAL/15956, WO 201/168).

[48] Protocols of meetings, 30 May 1940, CO 733/428//75998 (1940).

[49] Bauer, *From Diplomacy to Resistance,* pp. 104-5.

[50] Protocols of meeting, 14 June, CO 733/428//75998(1940).

[51] *Ibid.*

enforced disarmament. However, Chamberlain's Government had already resolved against such a policy, and a new G.O.C. (Lt.-General Godwin-Austin replaced Giffard shortly after the talks) decided that: 'With regard to hidden Jewish arms, he wanted at the moment to let sleeping dogs lie, and searches for these would not be carried out.'[52] Although the Colonial Office wanted to maintain pressure on the illegal organisations by persisting with the policy of limited arms searches,[53] and Godwin-Austin's successor (Lt.-General P. Neame) did revert to a more active policy,[54] the military crisis in the Middle East of 1941 and 1942, together with Churchill's sympathy with the Yishuv's desire to be able to defend itself,[55] combined to delay any confrontation on the question of Jewish illegal arms until 1943, after the threat of a German invasion of Palestine had passed. Occasional arms searches were conducted in 1941 and 1942, but in view of Churchill's attitude the Colonial Office resolved not to bring them to the Cabinet's attention.[56] The searches were conducted only on the receipt of definite information and care was taken to avoid any unnecessary untoward incident. However, the Colonial Office wanted to pursue the question of disarmament more actively, and resented the constraints that Churchill's attitude placed on it in this matter. In a revealing minute, written in 1941 in response to the Jewish Agency's continued refusal to reveal details of the size of the Jewish illegal arsenal, Shuckburgh expressed something of the frustration the Colonial Office felt on this, and on all other matters relating to Palestine:

[52]G.O.C. Conference, 9 July 1940, WO 169/147.

[53]Lloyd to MacMichael, Despatch, 22 July 1940, CO 733/428//75998(1940).

[54]Neame succeeded Godwin-Austin on 5 August 1940 and new operational instructions were issued shortly afterwards. ('Searches — Illegal Arms Held In Jewish Settlements', 2 September 1940, CR/PAL/16009/G, WO 169/147).

[55]Cf. Churchill to Moyne M524/1, May 10 1940, CO 968/39//13117/15F.

[56]Following an arms search of the Jewish village of Ein Harod in August 1941, the Middle East Department pointed out that the policy of arms searches as a whole had been adopted by the previous Government and had not been endorsed by Churchill's Cabinet, and therefore the matter should be put before the Cabinet once again. (Luke and Boyd minutes, 6 and 8 October 1941, CO 733/445//75998(1941)). However, Shuckburgh wanted to avoid this, and suggested that the Colonial Office resolve that the 'doctrine of continuity' justified them in permitting the Palestine Government to continue with the searches. (Shuckburgh minute, 11 October 1941, ibid.). As Churchill had made clear that on all matters relating to Palestine, and especially on the arms question, he did not endorse the policy of the preceding Government, Shuckburgh's advice was quite unjustified. Nevertheless Lord Moyne endorsed the tactic (Moyne minute, 15 October, ibid.). It was, however, decided to obtain the concurrence of the War and Foreign Offices first. Once this had been received, MacMichael was instructed to continue with the arms searches. (Moyne to MacMichael, 20 November 1941, ibid.).

162

> One cannot help being conscious all the time that [the Zionists]
> consider themselves strong enough owing to their influence in
> high places, to defy the High Commissioner and the C.O. with
> impunity. That is a factor that becomes more and more evident
> as time goes on. No-one can regard such a state of affairs as
> satisfactory; but there it is, and I suppose that we have got to
> make the best of it.[57]

Rommel's successes in North Africa in March–April 1941, and again from March until October 1942, meant that the threat of a German invasion of Palestine had to be taken seriously. On each occasion the Agency and its sympathisers in London demanded that steps be taken to increase the opportunities available to Palestinian Jews to participate in the war effort through enlistment in the British army, and to increase the arms and training available to the Jewish settlements so as to improve the Yishuv's capacity for self-defence in the event of a British withdrawal.[58] These demands clearly conflicted with the desire of the British authorities in the Middle East to prevent the Yishuv from acquiring the sort of military capacity which might eventually allow it to oppose British policy in Palestine by force. During both crises therefore, the military and political authorities in Jerusalem and Cairo successfully opposed almost all the proposals put forward.[59]

Soon after the crisis of 1941, MacMichael delivered his first attack on the Jewish Agency and called for its abolition. Above and beyond the Agency's formal rejection of the White Paper, the increasingly frequent expressions of the demand for a Jewish state, which had so alarmed Moyne in his talks with Weizmann and Ben Gurion in August and September 1941, similarly alarmed the Palestine Government. The British authorities there were well informed of the confidential deliberations of the Agency Executive and also had a generally accurate estimate of the alignment of political opinion in the other institutions of the Yishuv.[60] By September 1941 Military Intelligence observed that: 'The Jews as a whole seem to be working up for a great drive for some form of recognised nationalism,

[57]Shuckburgh minute, 11 October 1941, CO 733/445//75998(1941).

[58]The question has been discussed in detail by Gelber, *Hahitnadvut ve'Mekoma*, *passim*.

[59]Cf. WO 201/2669 and CO 968/39/13117/15F, *passim*. For a full statement of the political objections to meeting the Jewish demands, cf. memo by Luke, 17 March 1942, CO 733/443//75872/14(1942); and Hopkinson (Minister of State's Office, Cairo) to Hoyar Millar (British embassy, Washington), 9 December 1942, *ibid*.

[60]Colonial Office and Minister of State, Cairo, files contain frequent verbatim accounts of the Agency's debates, and it is clear that the political institutions of the *Yishuv* were infiltrated.

and in the present frame of mind of the Agency leaders this might easily lead to trouble in the Zionist ranks.'[61] At the same time, concern at the strength of the illegal Jewish military organisations was revived when, in the wake of the Syrian campaign, the authorities observed an increase in the traffic of illegal arms.[62] The crystallisation of the Zionist political programme around the objective of Jewish statehood, the increase in the Jewish illegal arsenal, and the apparent passing of the threat of an Arab revolt, encouraged MacMichael to take up the question of the military threat which the Yishuv would eventually pose for Britain.

In October 1941 he forwarded to London a lengthy and revealing despatch entitled 'Note on Jewish Illegal Organisations, Their Activities and Finances'. The 'Note' was prepared by the Secretariat of the Palestine Government in collaboration with the C.I.D. and Military Intelligence, and MacMichael considered that it brought 'into the full limelight the fact that the Mandatory is faced potentially with as grave a danger in Palestine from Jewish violence as it has ever faced from Arab violence, a danger infinitely less easy to meet by the methods of repression which have been employed against Arabs'.[63] The 'Note' did indeed present an alarming picture, giving the first official estimate of the size and strength of the Hagana, as some 100,000 members of both sexes, about half of whom could be provided with firearms. In addition, the 'Note' assessed the strength of the right-wing Irgun Zvai Leumi as being between 5,000 and 8,000.

However, the concrete information on the strength of both the Hagana and Irgun was cautiously worded, and occupied only a small part of the sixteen closely-typed pages of the 'Note'. The burden of the despatch was an examination of the close ties between the various institutions of the Yishuv — political, economic, agricultural and military — and the discipline which the leaders of the Zionist movement could command. The despatch itself was intended to reinforce the message which MacMichael was repeating to London on every possible occasion — that the Jewish Agency would have to be disbanded if Britain wished to be able to implement the White Paper or any other policy which did not allow for the creation of a

[61]MilPal Weekly Intelligence Summary No. 15, 22-8 September 1941, WO 169/1040.

[62]MilPal Weekly Intelligence Summary No. 1, 16-22 June 1941, WO 169/1037. In November S.I.M.E. announced: 'A reliable report states that at a recent meeting of the *Hagana* [it was announced that] the buying of arms and ammunition in Syria had been very successful and that their distribution throughout Palestine was practically complete.' (Appendix to Survey No. 655, 10 November 1941, WO 169/1560).

[63]FO 371/31375 E2026.

Jewish state or the continuation of Jewish immigration. In a separate introduction to the 'Note', MacMichael argued that any attempt to disarm the Yishuv and disband the Hagana would be converted into a confrontation with Jewish Palestine as a whole by the Agency, the Histadrut, the Va'ad Leumi and the Labour Party, all of whom were controlled by a closely interlocking leadership which exercised 'almost Nazi control' over the Jewish community. The aim of the leadership, MacMichael argued, was no longer the creation of a 'National Home' but rather the creation of a 'national-socialist state'. He concluded by noting: 'As matters now stand it seems to me inevitable that the Zionist Juggernaut which has been created with such an intensity of zeal for a Jewish national state will be the cause of very serious trouble in the Near East.'[64]

MacMichael anticipated by over a year the formal adoption of the objective of statehood by the Zionist bodies in Palestine. The establishment of a Jewish state which Ben Gurion had set out as his aim in his 'Outlines' in 1941, to which Weizman had committed himself in his article of January 1942, and which had been adopted by the American Zionists in May 1942, was not adopted by the Jewish Agency Executive (and the Inner Zionist Executive, which had an almost identical membership) until November 1942. Nevertheless, like the Foreign and Colonial Offices in London, MacMichael correctly identified the way Zionist thinking was developing. What was distinctive in his despatch was the emphasis on the alleged capabilities of the illegal Jewish military organisations and the intention to employ them in order to achieve statehood.[65]

However, the facts which the High Commissioner wished to impress on London were guesses given the mantle of authority by the ambiguous wording of the 'Note'. Separate reports prepared by Military Intelligence in Palestine and Security Intelligence Middle East in Cairo (S.I.M.E.) made frequent reference to the great difficulties the authorities had in obtaining any accurate information on the military organisations of the Yishuv (as opposed to the political bodies).[66] Estimates of the size of the membership of the Hagana and Irgun were purely conjectural. MacMichael's 'Note' referred to 100,000 members of the Hagana and 5-8,000 members of the Irgun.

[64]MacMichael to Moyne, 16 October 1941, introductory letter to 'Note', *ibid*.

[65]Cf. also HCr to CO Most Secret, Private and Personal, 4 November 1941, CO 968/39//13117/15 Part 2.

[66]Cf. Security Summary Middle East No. 2, S.I.M.E., 5 December 1941, WO 208/1560; and MilPal Weekly Intelligence Summary No. 15, 22-8 September 1941, WO 169/1040.

If one includes the Palestinian Jews serving with the British forces outside Palestine, the total comes suspiciously close to 136,000 — the number of people who had registered with the Agency in September 1939. MacMichael clearly did not want to deprive anyone of the possibility of claiming Hagana or Irgun membership, as the figures he gave (again excluding those serving with the British forces) represented almost the whole male Jewish population between the ages 18-35 and half the female Jewish population of the same age group.

Estimates prepared during 1940, which were, incidentally, fairly accurate, did not justify the alarming figures which MacMichael presented in late 1941.[67] By mid-1942 the sources of information on the Hagana and Irgun available to British Intelligence improved considerably, and more accurate estimates were circulated in Intelligence bulletins. These show that even on the basis of the information available to the authorities, the image of a force over 100,000 strong — half of whom were armed — was a threefold exaggeration.[68] In reality it was an even larger exaggeration.[69]

---

[67] Cf. note 41 above.

[68] In June 1942, S.I.M.E. gave a far more accurate account of the size and arms of the *Hagana*:
> Reports agree in placing the strength of the *Hagana* at 30,000 men, of whom 50-70% are armed. The Jews now serving with the British forces will provide a valuable reinforcement of trained men after the war... The *Irgun Zvai Leumi* may consist of 1,000 active frontline men, of whom half are armed, and possibly 4,000 additional sympathisers and members of Revisionist bodies who would cooperate with the *Irgun* if it were mobilised... The following estimate of Jewish secret arms is stated to come from a reliable source:

	1st class condition	2nd class condition	Total
Machine guns	162	—	162
L.M.G.'s automatic rifles	2,245	2,300	4,545
Rifles	10,000	8,000	18,000
Pistols	12,000	4,000	16,000

(Security Survey, Middle East No. 51, 4 June 1942, WO 208/1561).

[69] According to Bauer (who cites *Hagana* Archives), the actual strength of the *Hagana* in 1944 — i.e. after two years of growth and significant increases in its armoury as a result of arms thefts from British forces, purchases and gleaning from the battlefields of the Western Desert — was: '36,871 members, of whom 1517 were in the Palmach, 4609 in the Field Force, . . a moderately well-trained unit — and the balance in the militia only 4,372 of whose members had received adequate training. The force had 10,338 rifles (or one rifle per three men), 437 sub-machine guns, 132 machine guns and 3933 revolvers. Two-inch and three-inch mortars were being produced, but on a small scale.' (Bauer, 'From Cooperation to Resistance', p. 202). Perhaps the most reliable source of all for the actual strength of the *Hagana* alone in this period is the report of the *Hagana's* own armaments division dated October 1945. According to a

166

However, the question here is the relationship between the information available to the British authorities in the Middle East and the information which the Palestine Government chose to pass on to London. Subsequent reports, prepared after the improvement in access to information, which were despatched to the War Office as well as to the Foreign and Colonial Offices not only failed to revise the impression given by the 'Note' of October 1941, but actually increased the official assessment of the strength of the Yishuv.

Whatever the official reaction to the details given in MacMichael's alarming account,[70] by early 1942 both the Foreign and Colonial Offices had agreed that: 'There seems little doubt that the conclusions to be drawn from the secret material is that the Jews intend to resort to direct action if they fail to secure a post-war settlement compatible with their present aspirations.'[71] The Foreign Office seized upon the 'Note' as a valuable contribution to its public relations efforts in America. However, beyond passing the document on to the embassy in Washington for discreet communication to officials of the administration, no further use could be made of it. While Palestine faced the threat of German invasion in 1942, i.e. in the months which followed the receipt of MacMichael's 'Note', the policy of disarming the Yishuv could not be reassessed, although the policy of February 1940 remained in force and arms searches were occasionally conducted. In March 1942 Cranborne referred generally to the radicalisation of the Yishuv in his Cabinet paper on immigration policy, and he mentioned the inevitability of either a 'showdown' with the Jews, or of meeting their demands and facing a confrontation with the Arabs instead.[72] Although Cranborne did mention to the Cabinet the armed strength which MacMichael attributed to the Yishuv, it was Oliver Lyttelton who examined the question in detail in a draft Cabinet paper on Palestine which he prepared on his return from Cairo in April 1942.[73] However, Churchill dissuaded him from circulating it, and the

published version of this report the *Hagana* was even weaker in October 1945 than Bauer estimated for one year earlier. (Slutzky, *Toldot Hahagana,* p. 290). The discrepancy between the figures given by Slutzky and those given by Bauer might be explained by the impact of British arms searches in the last years of the war.

[70]The immediate reactions of the Colonial Office are on a closed file ('C(10)K'). Apparently the Colonial Office maintained a separate series of highly sensitive files, which remain unrecorded in the holdings of the Public Record Office, Kew.

[71]Luke Memorandum 'The Jewish War Effort', March 1942, CO 733/448/-/76147/A(1942).

[72]WP(42)108, 4 March 1942, Cab 66/22.

[73]Lyttelton's paper was eventually circulated as WP(43)265, Cab 66/38, in June 1943.

question was not discussed by the Cabinet for a further fifteen months.[74]

When the victory at El Alamein had removed the German military threat to Palestine, MacMichael returned to the question of illegal arms, forwarding to the Colonial Office a lengthy document which gave an even more inflated estimate of the total armed strength of the Yishuv.[75] By passing these reports on to London, and by his use of increasingly rhetorical language when referring to the Jewish Agency ('Zionist Juggernaut', 'Todt organisation', pursuing the objective of a 'national socialist state', etc.) MacMichael was attempting to convince the authorities in London that the Agency would have to be suppressed if any policy which embodied the principles of the White Paper was ever to be implemented.

The increasingly strident terms which MacMichael used to describe political Zionism, and the Jewish Agency in particular, were matched only by the efforts of the Minister of State's Office in Cairo. There Bennett minuted on the 'completely totalitarian, militaristic and National Socialist outlook of modern Zionism'[76] and Henry Hopkinson wrote to the embassy in Washington that: 'What we should like reasonable American opinion to realise is that this Jewish Commonwealth (i.e. state) could only be established by force, and that, as a political aim, it is indistinguishable from Hitler's claim for Lebensraum implemented by the subjugation of 'inferior' races'.[77] Such references to Zionism, the Jewish Agency and the Yishuv were no doubt a reflection of their inability to do anything to counter the radicalisation of Palestine Jewry and to defend the White Paper.[78]

[74]Lyttelton sent the draft paper to Churchill with the note: 'I enclose a draft, and would not in any circumstances propose to release it until you say that I may or should.' (Lyttelton to Churchill, 11 April 1942, Prem 4/52/5).

[75]Entitled 'Memorandum on Internal Security in Palestine, December 1942' it covered both Arab and Jewish military capabilities, with the emphasis on the latter (CO 733/439//75156/75(1943)). Whereas his 'Note' of 1941 had mentioned a total Jewish force of 108,000, by late 1942 he argued that the Jews could mobilise 135,000 people in order to oppose British policy and to impose a solution of their own. For a discussion of the origins of this document, cf. R. Zweig, 'British Plans for the Evacuation of Palestine, 1941-42', Studies in Zionism, No. 8, 1983.

[76]Minute, August 1942, FO 921/6.

[77]Hopkinson to Hoyar Miller, 9 December 1942, CO 733/443//75872/14(42).

[78]The strident references to the Jews were matched by increasingly favourable references to the Arabs in an effort to counter the impression created by the record of Anglo-Arab relations during the years of fighting in the Middle East. Thus during 1943 the Foreign Office went to some lengths to encourage the circulation of a lengthy memorandum prepared by a member of its Research Department, entitled 'Arab Nationalism and Great Britain'. When discussing Iraq, the Memorandum argued that the pro-Nazi Raschid Ali revolt should not be seen as a revolt against Britain but rather

Ironically, however, the inflated reports which were received in London had a very different effect from that intended. As all the authorities concerned agreed that nothing could be done during the war to disarm the Yishuv, and as the Colonial Office had dismissed the idea of disbanding the Jewish Agency, the fear that the Jews would attempt to implement their own solution to the Palestine problem, by force if necessary, undermined any residual faith in the White Paper. By the beginning of 1943 both the Colonial and Foreign Offices had accepted that the White Paper would have to be replaced. As the Head of the American Department in the Foreign Office observed: 'White Papers, like Treaties, are sacred but not immortal.'[79] Henceforth their concern was not to defend the White Paper but to uphold its tenets — that the growth of the Jewish National Home should end and Jewish immigration into Palestine cease.

These were essentially departmental deliberations, and disillusionment with the White Paper was expressed only at a departmental level. At the political level the *modus vivendi* on Palestine policy remained in force — that is, the White Paper was considered the definitive statement on Palestine until Churchill's Government was able to reconsider the question, presumably after war. Following the removal of the German threat to the Middle East, it seemed that such an opportunity might have arrived, and Nuri Said in Iraq renewed the call for a declaration by the British Government on its general Arab policy and on the future of the Middle East.[80] Similarly, the Zionists in America intensified their lobbying of the U.S. Government in the hope that the Roosevelt administration might endorse a Jewish state as its contribution to solving the problem of the Jewish refugees. Nevertheless, both Stanley and Eden wished to avoid a Cabinet debate on Middle East policy and on the future of Palestine during 1943. The official acknowledgement in December 1942 of the Nazi extermination of the Jews did not create an atmosphere conducive to a debate which, they hoped, would reaffirm the principles of the White Paper. Furthermore, after El Alamein, it was no longer possible to use the argument that Arab opinion on Palestine had to be appeased. Thus, rather than force the issue, as Lloyd and Halifax (as Foreign

'as a gesture of defiance against the universe' and a release of pent up emotional tension. The Foreign Office ensured that a summary of the memorandum was also published as a feature article in *The Times* (CO 732/87//79031).

[79] Butler minute, 11 April 1943, FO 371/34956 E2039.

[80] In January 1943 Nuri Said approached Casey in Cairo with a series of proposals on the future of the Arab world, including Palestine, calling on both Britain and the United States to make a declaration of their intentions. This demand embarrassed the Foreign Office, and it attempted to dissuade Nuri from raising these questions at that stage. (Minute on FO 371/34955 E1196).

Secretary) had attempted to do in mid-1940, Eden now wished to delay any reconsideration of Palestine until after the war, in the hope that the Peace Conference would resolve the Jewish refugee problem within the borders of Europe.[81] Stanley had no wish to confront the question of future policy during the war either.[82] However, a series of developments in Spring 1943 brought the question to the Cabinet's attention, and the fate of the White Paper had to be squarely faced.

In February 1943 Halifax reported from Washington that the State Department was considering a joint American-British declaration on the Jewish question, designed to dampen the growing Zionist agitation in America.[83] The Eastern Department in the Foreign Office welcomed the willingness of the State Department to make such a declaration, but pointed out that Britain was not able to participate because of the constraints which Churchill had imposed on references to the White Paper.[84] Thus the Foreign Office could only reply that while it could not support the idea of a joint statement, it would welcome any independent efforts by the Americans to counter Zionist lobbying.[85] However, almost immediately afterwards, Halifax informed London that in a series of talks with the State Department, Weizmann had spoken of 'the Prime Minister's plan' to use Ibn Saud to bring about a Zionist solution to the Palestine problem.[86] This alarmed the Foreign Office. If Churchill seemed to favour a Zionist solution in Palestine then the State Department would hardly be able to persuade the administration to issue a declaration rejecting such a solution. Eden wrote to Churchill, pointing out that while he knew the Prime Minister's views on the White Paper, 'there has, I think, been no discussion suggesting that the United States Government should be

---

[81] As Eden minuted on 29 November 1942: 'I had always hoped that we could take a firm line at the Peace Conference that the bulk of the Jews should stay where they were in Europe. One hopes that the post-war Europe will not be a home of recurrent persecution, and there is anyway no room for these people in Palestine, even if every Arab were sent packing.' (FO 371/31380 E6946).

[82] When, in 1943, the Middle East War Council forwarded to London a series of proposals on the future of the Middle East, one of which called for a reaffirmation of the White Paper, Peterson noted: 'Mr. Casey seems to be flying in the face of a hint which, unless I am mistaken, was conveyed to him by the Secretary of State not very long ago, after consultation with Colonel Stanley.' (Minute, 7 June 1943, FO 371/34975 E3234).

[83] Halifax to Foreign Office Despatch No. 77, 8 February 1943, FO 371/35032 E1027.

[84] Eyres minuted: 'We are not allowed to reaffirm the White Paper, which is what we must do if we are to make a statement.' (21 February 1943, ibid).

[85] FO to Halifax No. 1523, 8 March 1943, ibid.

[86] Halifax to FO No. 66, 2 February 1943, FO 371/35031 E826; and No. 52, FO 371/35031 E815.

approached as regards the possibility of modifying it'. And he invited Churchill to refute Weizmann's claim to speak in his name.[87] Churchill did so, but at the same time he added: 'As you know, I am irrevocably opposed to the White Paper which, as I have testified in the House, I regard as a breach of a solemn undertaking to which I was a party'.[88]

The Foreign Office recognised that this reply prevented it from informing the American government that Weizmann had misled it, and from issuing a *dementi* which would have countered the impression created by Weizmann that Britain favoured a Zionist solution in Palestine. As a result, in lieu of any *dementi*, the Eastern Department argued that some sort of statement either reaffirming the White Paper or at least making it clear that Britain did not endorse a Jewish state would now be necessary, even if it meant obtaining Cabinet approval to overcome the ban on references to the White Paper.[89] However, after further deliberation and the intervention of the Colonial Secretary,[90] it was decided that 'it would be injudicious to insist on the (White) Paper in the teeth of a formidable opposition against it in high places'.[91] And a more moderate Cabinet paper was drawn up which made no reference to the White Paper, but simply explained why it was necessary that the U.S. Government should counter Zionist agitation. As was subsequently explained: 'In accordance with an agreement between Mr. Law and the Colonial Secretary, it is intended mainly as a warning note and purposely does not raise the general question of the future of Palestine.'[92]

The draft paper explaining the dangers of Zionist agitation in America took some weeks to prepare, and was further delayed when Stanley was hesitant about giving Colonial Office agreement to its circulation to the Cabinet in case it did, unintentionally, prompt a debate on future policy.[93] However, despite the efforts of the Foreign and Colonial Offices to avoid such a debate, a further minute by Churchill brought the question of future policy to the immediate attention of the Cabinet.

---

[87]Eden to Churchill PM/43/44, 3 March 1943, FO 371/35031 E826.

[88]Churchill to Eden M139/3, 9 March 1943, Prem 4/52/3.

[89]Peterson minute, 17 March 1943, FO 371/35033 E2342.

[90]Grey minute, 2 April 1943, *ibid.*

[91]Butler minute, 19 March 1943, *ibid.*

[92]Caccia minute, 13 April 1943, FO 371/35033 E2341.

[93]Peterson minute, 16 April 1943, *ibid.*

While the Foreign Office Cabinet paper was being considered
Churchill received a letter from Weizmann in which the latter claimed
that both Stanley and his predecessor, Lord Cranborne, had referred
to the White Paper as 'firmly established policy'. Weizmann went on
to argue that: 'Instead of keeping the way open for a revision of policy,
the road to it is being further and further blocked.'[94] In effect
Weizmann was saying that the *modus vivendi* on Palestine policy was
being progressively flaunted by Churchill's Colonial Secretaries, and
this prompted Churchill to send both Cranborne and Stanley a
strongly worded statement of his own views on the White Paper and
on the understanding which governed the continuation of that policy
during the war: 'I have always regarded (the White Paper) as a gross
breach of faith committed by the Chamberlain Government in respect
of obligations to which I was personally a party. . . I am sure the
majority of the present War Cabinet would never agree to any positive
endorsement of the White Paper. It runs until it is superseded.'[95]

Churchill's description of the White Paper as 'a gross breach of
faith' offended Stanley, who had been a member of the Chamberlain
government and in his reply he asked that if Churchill circulated
Weizmann's letter (as Churchill had said he would), then Stanley be
allowed to circulate a paper of his own setting out details of the
'potential dangers' which were developing in Palestine and which
threatened 'a serious outbreak of disorder throughout the Middle
East'.[96] Churchill eventually decided not to circulate Weizmann's
letter, but instead to circulate the Cabinet with his own Commons
speech of May 1939 attacking the White Paper. He prefaced the
Cabinet-paper reprint of his speech with a suggestion that some of the
difficulties inherent in the problem of Jewish immigration into Palestine
might be overcome by the conversion of Eritrea and Tripolitania into
'Jewish colonies, affiliated, if desired, to the National Home in
Palestine'.[97] He concluded with a general attack on the Arab world.[98]
In a separate minute he invited both both Cranborne and Stanley to
submit to the Cabinet papers of their own on the Palestine question.[99]

[94]Weizmann to Churchill, 2 April 1943, Prem 4/52/3.

[95]Churchill to Cranborne and Stanley M291/3, 18 April 1943, *ibid.*

[96]Stanley to Churchill, 19 April 1943, *ibid.*

[97]WP(43)178, 28 April 1943, Cab 66/36.

[98]'With the exception of Ibn Saud and the Emir Abdullah, both of whom have been
good and faithful followers, the Arabs have been virtually of no use to us in the present
war. They have taken no part in the fighting, except in so far as they were involved in the
Iraq rebellion against us. They have created no new claims upon the Allies, should we
be victorious.' (*ibid.*).

[99]Churchill to Stanley and Cranborne M319/3, 27 April 1943, Prem 4/52/1.

Through this series of minutes, and through his decision to circulate his own paper, Churchill had effectively begun the debate on future policy. The fear of doing just that had held the Colonial and Foreign Offices back from seeking Cabinet authority for a statement on Palestine aimed at reassuring the Arabs and countering Zionist agitation in America. Now this constraint had been removed, and a series of Cabinet papers followed.

In a cautiously worded paper prepared by the Colonial Office, Stanley described the growing military strength of the Yishuv and the crystallisation of Zionist policy around the demand for a Jewish state. His paper also pointed out that the Arabs of Palestine, although not as well organised as the Jews, also held 'a considerable number of arms and stocks of ammunition'. Stanley concluded by arguing that while there was no likelihood of a conflict in the immediate future, 'there is obviously much combustible material in Palestine and every effort must be exerted to avoid an explosion. Even if we cannot prevent an ultimate outbreak between the two races in Palestine, I feel we must be extremely careful while the war lasts to avoid any action which is likely to exacerbate either race.'[100] These last comments were intended to discourage the adoption of a new policy on Palestine, and in the Foreign Office paper, circulated shortly afterwards, Eden observed that he too had 'no wish to press my colleagues to take any major decision on our Palestine policy at this moment'. Accordingly, he limited his remarks to a request for Cabinet authorisation to make representations to the United States government appealing to them to take steps to dampen Zionist agitation in America.[101] Despite their clearly-stated desire to avoid a debate on future policy, the papers circulated by Eden and Stanley prompted papers from other Ministers who wished to comment on Palestine. Lyttleton took the opportunity of circulating the paper which he had prepared in April 1942 (and which Churchill had then prevented him from circulating), giving details of the growth of the Hagana and the Irgun and warning of the dangers which the demand for a Jewish State created for British interests in the Middle East.[102] R.G. Casey, Lyttelton's successor as Minister of State Resident in Cairo, who had returned to London, circulated a paper making the same point in more emphatic terms, claiming that Britain faced the risk of a *coup de main* by the Zionists

[100]WP(43)192, 'Palestine: Memorandum by the Secretary of State for the Colonies', 4 May 1943, Cab 66/36.

[101]WP(43)200, 'Palestine: Memorandum by the Secretary of State for Foreign Affairs', 10 May 1943, Cab 66/36.

[102]WP(43)265, 'Palestine: Memorandum by the Minister of Production', 23 June 1943, Cab 66/38: 'I do not think that a Jewish National State can be founded and maintained except by the force of arms, that is by the force of our arms.'

at the end of the war, or even before then.[103] At the same time he circulated the resolutions of the Middle East War Council (on which Casey, MacMichael, the ambassadors in the Arab capitals and the various Commanders-in-Chief in the Middle East theatre all sat) calling for a reaffirmation of the White Paper.[104] Eden had hoped to avoid this demand, and both he and Stanley had eschewed it in their own Cabinet papers.[105] However, once the recommendation had been put forward, it became increasingly clear that the whole question of future Palestine policy would have to be considered.

The various accounts of the growing military capabilities of the Zionists echoed MacMichael's inflated estimates. The risk that the Yishuv would oppose by force any British policy which did not allow for continued Jewish immigration was certainly real and the experience of the early years in dealing with illegal immigration had shown that there was ample scope for confrontation. However, as discussed above, the strength of the Yishuv had been seriously exaggerated. The fear that the Zionists would attempt a coup against the Mandate and the British Army in the Middle East and impose its own solution existed,[106] but it was more a reflection of Britain's vulnerability to

[103] WP(43)246 'Palestine: Memorandum by the Minister of State', 17 June 1943, Cab 66/37.

[104] WP(43)247 'Resolutions of the Middle East War Council on the Political Situation in the Middle East', Cab 66/37.

[105] The Middle East War Council resolution had been adopted despite Moyne's warning (he was then Deputy-Minister of State in Cairo) that to do so would: 'give members of the Cabinet at home the opportunity of re-opening the issue. In short he was against any mentioning of the White Paper at all.' (Lampson Diaries, St. Anthony's College, Oxford, entry for 10 May 1943), Casey repeated the warning two days later: 'Casey said that he had an indication from home (Anthony Eden) that we must exercise great care how we handled this matter or our good Prime Minister would fly off the handle and tear everything up including the White Paper itself (ibid, entry for 12 May 1943). Nevertheless, despite arguments from Casey and Moyne, Lampson and Kinahan Cornwallis (British ambassador to Iraq) insisted that the reaffirmation of the White Paper be one of the recommendations forwarded to London, and they won their point.

[106] In May 1943 Alexander, the Commander-in-Chief, Middle East Forces informed the War Office that 'Internal political situation in Palestine [is] dangerous and there is probability of anti-British revolt by Jews before or immediately after the end of the war. This would inevitably be followed by Arab insurrection. Jews mean business and are now armed and trained.' (C.-i.-C., M.E.F. to WO 0/49079, 12 May 1943, FO 371/35030 E2902). In his paper to the Cabinet Casey warned that 'the explosion is timed to go off as soon as the War ends in Europe, or possibly a few months earlier. Opinions differ as to the form the outbreak will take, whether civil disobedience, revolt civil war, or an attempted coup d'etat, and as to how and by which side the actual shooting will be started.' (WP(43)246, 17 June 1943, Cab 66/37). The resolution of the Middle East War Council, which Casey circulated together with his own paper was more direct in identifying the likely source of trouble: 'The principal danger lies in an endeavour on the part of the Jews, who are rapidly producing a highly organised

pressure from Zionists and their sympathisers than a measure of the real strength of the Yishuv. The officials who participated in the Middle East War Council particularly wanted to challenge Churchill's sympathy for Zionism (the 'influence in high places' which was frequently referred to as the reason why stronger measures could not to be taken against the Jewish Agency and the illegal military organisations) and his support for a Jewish state.[107] At the very least, they hoped to be able to reduce the number of his supporters in the Cabinet. Thus, whereas previously Zionism was seen only as a political embarrassment to Britain's position in the Middle East, by 1943 it was depicted as a potential military threat to Britain.

The Cabinet met on 2 July 1943 to consider the various papers on Palestine, ten in all, which had been circulated in the preceding two months. The question of a joint declaration with the U.S. Government was considered and approved in principle. It was also decided to permit Jewish immigration beyond the 31 March 1944 deadline, to make a number of concessions concerning immigration from enemy controlled territory (discussed in chapter 5) and to continue the policy of acting only on specific information when conducting arms searches. Churchill insisted that there should be no change in this latter policy without specific reference to the Cabinet. The central issue, however, was future policy. All the members of the Cabinet agreed that nothing should be done to re-open public controversy on Palestine at that point in the war, but a majority agreed that, nevertheless, steps should be taken to consider long term policy (i.e. a policy to replace the White Paper) without delay.[108] Amery suggested that partition be reconsidered, and Churchill, contrary to his position in 1937 when partition had been proposed by the Peel Commission, supported him.[109] It was not, however, discussed at any length, and the Cabinet

military machine on Nazi lines, to seize the moment which is most favourable to themselves for the prosecution by force of their policy of establishing an exclusively Jewish state in Palestine.' (WO(43)247, Cab 66/37).

[107]Churchill's last expression of support for Jewish statehood had been in 1941, but while the various Cabinet papers were being circulated in May-June 1943, he confirmed that he still adhered to his earlier views during a talk with Major-General Edward Spears. As Spears subsequently recorded: 'On the previous evening the Prime Minister had laid down his Zionist policy in the most emphatic terms. He said he had formed an opinion which nothing could change. He intended to see to it that there was a Jewish state. He told me not to argue with him as this would merely make him angry and would change nothing. . . There is simply no arguing with him on this subject. He was strongly anti-Arab and would always be turning to the Raschid Ali rebellion as a proof of Arab worthlessness.' (Spears Papers, Box 2 File 7, St. Anthony's College, Oxford).

[108]The Cabinet Conclusions record two separate accounts of the deliberations on 2 July: on WM 92(43)2 (Cab 65/39) and on WM 92(43)3 (Cab 65/35).

[109]Amery had first raised the idea of partition in a letter to Churchill more than a month earlier (Amery to Churchill 29 April 1943, Prem 4/52/1). In his letter Amery

decided instead to appoint a Cabinet Committee 'to consider the long term policy for Palestine' leaving the task of appointing its members to Churchill.[110]

The Cabinet Committee on Palestine commenced its deliberations in August 1943, and in December of that year it was able to submit to the Cabinet detailed proposals for the partition of Palestine.[111] These proposals were adopted by the Cabinet on 25 January 1944,[112] although the White Paper was not formally and publicly abandoned until December 1945. The sudden collapse in mid-1943 of the *modus vivendi* which had governed the Cabinet's position on Palestine since 1940 made it possible for Churchill to revise the policy on Palestine which the Chamberlain Government had adopted in 1939. The Cabinet Committee's recommendations on partition brought British policy full circle, back to the Peel Commission of 1937.

In the course of 1944 the Cabinet Committee on Palestine continued to elaborate on the plan for partition. This gave Eden and the Foreign Office the opportunity to argue against the concept of partition and against the borders which the Committee had first recommended.[113] In the long term both the resurrection of the principle of partition in 1943 and the subsequent deliberations of the Palestine Committee were still-born. The Cabinet was to have debated the Committee's final recommendations in early November, but before it could do so events in the Middle East changed the political atmosphere in London. On 6 November Lord Moyne was assassinated in Cairo by members of the Jewish terrorist group *Lehi* (the 'Stern gang'). Moyne's murder made a great personal impact on Churchill and Amery, the two most important supporters of the Jewish case within the Cabinet.[114] The assassination came only three

pointed out that it would not be possible to go back on the White Paper entirely by resolving that all of Palestine be opened to unlimited Jewish immigration, but that partition was an acceptable compromise. The Cabinet Conclusions do not record who raised the proposal in Cabinet, but Amery, in his diary entry for 2 July 1943, claims that he raised it and that Churchill ('to my delight') supported him (Amery Diaries).

[110]WM 92(43)2, Cab 65/39.

[111]WP(43)563, 'Report of the Committee on Palestine', 20 December 1943, Cab 66/44. The work of this Committee has been considered in detail by M.J. Cohen, 'The British White Paper on Palestine, May 1939, Part 2: The Testing of a Policy, 1942-1945', *The Historical Journal*, 19(3):727-58(1976).

[112]WM 11(44)4, 25 January 1945, Cab 65/45.

[113]For a discussion of the Committee's deliberations during 1944, cf. Cohen, *Retreat From the Mandate*, pp. 171-82.

[114]Amery was a close personal friend of Moyne's, and at the time of the assassination was living in Moyne's home outside of London. The news of the assassination reached London while the Cabinet was in session, and the tension of the moment was reflected

months after *Lehi* had made an unsuccessful attack on the life of Sir Harold MacMichael, and in an atmosphere of growing Jewish terrorism, albeit by a small fringe group, Churchill instructed that the Cabinet debate on the Palestine Committee's final deliberations be delayed. The war ended before Churchill's Government would take up the question again.

Superficially at least the murder of Lord Moyne achieved what officials in the Foreign Office and elsewhere had tried but failed to achieve — preventing Churchill's Government from replacing the White Paper with a policy more favourable to the Jews of Palestine. In fact it made little difference to the course of events. The decision to re-open the debate on Palestine's future and the subsequent suspension of the debate were questions of 'high policy' divorced from the realities of the Middle East. At the more mundane level of colonial administration the White Paper of 1939 had become a hollow shell and was recognised as such by the responsible officials in London and Jerusalem long before the Cabinet took up the question in July 1943.

in a heated argument between Churchill and Amery (on the question of Indian's sterling balances), 'the worst open row with Winston that I have yet had'. As Amery commented in his Diary, Moyne's murder 'inflicted a possibly fatal injury on [Zionism's] cause' (Amery Diaries, 6 November 1944).

CONCLUSION

The adoption of the principle of partition by the British Cabinet naturally meant the abandonment of the White Paper. Although it was not publicly disavowed until the end of 1945 (the decision on partition was officially secret, even though the interested parties had learnt of it well before the end of the war) the detailed provisions of the White Paper became irrelevant. In the course of 1944 the Cabinet Committee on Palestine debated the general outlines of the partition scheme while an official of the Palestine Government was given the task of mapping out the concrete steps to be taken to create two separate states in Palestine, the institutions to be created, and the details of the transfer of power.[1] It was a futile effort. In the course of 1944 the partition scheme was postponed, and although a later version of it was made public by the Labour Government in 1946, it was eventually abandoned when Britain returned the Mandate to the United Nations in 1947.

Since the mid-1930s, when the Foreign Office first intervened in Palestine affairs, Palestine policy had become progressively less and less the exclusive domain of the Colonial Office. The White Paper of 1939 was the last attempt by Britain to find a solution to a colonial problem (albeit a uniquely difficult one) within the framework of general colonial policy. Internal stability was to be guaranteed by the restrictions on the sale of land and on Jewish immigration, thus allowing time for the evolution of participatory institutions and a degree of self-government. In these matters Palestine was a full generation behind the constitutional progress which by the late 1930s was already common in most of Britain's other dependencies. Earlier attempts to bring a greater measure of local Palestinian (Arab and Jewish) participation in the process of government had been blocked: the Jews feared that should the Arab population of Palestine be given any major role in councils of the Mandate they would use their power to block the growth of the Jewish National Home. Only by the late 1930s, under the pressure of strategic considerations, was Britain prepared to ignore Jewish opinion and meet Arab demands by allowing constitutional progress.

Any discussion of Palestine policy during the period 1939 to 1945 must begin with the war and the changing military and political circumstances within which policy was formulated and implemented. Nevertheless, two personalities played a decisive role, and a few

---

[1] Sir Douglas Harris. The record of his labours are on CO 733/461//75872 C-Z.

178

comments on their personal contribution to the course of events are in order. In view of the importance of the constitutional provisions of the White Paper, it is doubtful whether Sir Harold MacMichael was the wisest appointment as High Commissioner. Within the Colonial Office MacMichael had a reputation as a highly capable administrator, but even his closest associates recognised that for all his skills he was not, nor did he consider himself to be, a political innovator.[2] Yet the provisions of the White Paper were very innovative in the context of the Palestine Mandate and they required a determined innovator and improvisor in the role of High Commissioner to make them work and to realise the implicit promise of decolonisation. MacMichael was neither of these things. His obstruction of any progress on constitutional provisions shows how deeply imbued he was with the prevailing Colonial Service thinking on self-government and independence. Although these were in theory the ultimate goals of British colonial policy, in practice the means of bringing colonies to independence was not seriously considered until the 1950s. Until then general colonial policy on constitutional questions consisted of 'piecemeal concessions of varying degrees of participation in Government [which] might be expected somehow to result in the development of political habits which could in the long run be translated into an institutional basis for self-government appropriate to the varying genius of the inhabitants of a given territory'.[3] Such an approach was vague and the pace was very gradual. Self-government would take generations, in some cases even centuries.[4] Although this ethos obviously did not apply to Palestine, it did engender a way of thinking which was incapable of dealing with concrete promises of progress within a very limited time span such as those contained in the White Paper. A later generation of decolonisers in the Colonial Office and the Colonial Service was able to take in their stride problems which seemed insurmountable to Sir Harold MacMichael and his administration in Palestine.

Even more important was the personal influence of Winston Churchill. The close attention he paid to Palestine affairs and his frequent interventions in the formulation of policy delayed implementation of the White Paper until after the war, by which time circumstances had altered so radically that even those who had strongly supported it had to concede that its detailed provisions were a dead letter. Although Churchill was unable to reverse the policy

[2]*The Times,* London 22 September 1969 (obituary).

[3]K. Robinson, *The Dilemmas of Trusteeship* (London, 1965), p. 89.

[4]Cf. speech by Malcolm MacDonald in House of Commons, 7 December 1938, cited in *ibid.*, p. 91.

during the war, he did prevent the implementation of an even more determined campaign against Jewish refugees. Much more significant than his frequent minor victories, however, was his success in avoiding the introduction of irreversible steps towards the termination of the growth of the Jewish National Home, and it was to this goal that he directed his attention. With the fall of his government in 1945 the Zionist movement lost its last great champion within a British Cabinet.

The personal contributions of Churchill and MacMichael to the course of events, and specifically to the lack of progress in implementing the constitutional provisions of the White Paper, were decisive. Other participants played less significant roles. The record of Malcolm MacDonald during the year following the release of the White Paper until his departure from the Colonial Office in May 1940 deserves reconsideration. His father, Ramsay MacDonald, had been sympathetic to the Zionists when he was Prime Minister, and Malcolm was for a long while the favourite son of the Zionist lobby in Britain. Thus his subsequent role in formulating the White Paper was seen as treachery, and everything he did afterwards has been judged in that light. However, his actions in the Colonial Office, often against the strong opposition of his officials, on the difficult immigration question in the period after the release of the White Paper suggest that he was not insensitive to the human issues involved in the Jewish refugee crisis. Although he was careful to remain within the general framework of the immigration restrictions of the White Paper, MacDonald frequently attempted to interpret policy in a generous way. On such specific questions as the issue of supplementary quotas, the duration of the suspension of the legal quotas, deals with the Jewish Agency, the issue of certificates to the Polish children, and the fate of certificate holders in German-controlled territory, MacDonald tried to moderate the rigid interpretation of Colonial Office policy on his own initiative or endorsed the Jewish Agency's appeals to do so. His limited success in this regard is an indication of the power of officials, even relatively junior ones such as Downie and Bennett, to determine the impact of policies adopted by the Cabinet.

Throughout the period under discussion the importance of individual officials in determining aspects of Palestine policy and in implementing policy waxed and waned, as did the degree of consensus amongst officials in different ministries and different parts of the globe. The state of play concerning the interpretation and future of the policy of 1939 looked different in London, Jerusalem, Cairo and the various other capitals of the Arab world where British diplomats were stationed. British military, intelligence, diplomatic and Mandatory

180

officials in the Middle East came under different pressures from those
in London, and consequently they remained committed to the White
Paper, or at the very least to the redirection of Palestine policy which
took place in 1939, long after the consensus in London had dissipated.
In the nature of things it is not possible to document these shifting tides
of official opinion by reference to specific documents. Sometimes a
casual comment can be cited as an accurate reflection of a consistent
view of a given official, but at other times such marginalia, written
either flippantly or in moments of despair and frustration, distort the
complexity and sophistication of the views on the problems under
discussion held by an official over many years. There is, for example,
nothing in the record of Herbert Downie's contribution to Colonial
Office policy during 1939-42 which would suggest that his reputation
in the Refugee Section of the Foreign Office (so anti-semitic that he
could not deal reasonably with Jews)[5] was unjust. On the other hand,
Sir John Shuckburgh once described his own original qualifications
for dealing with the Palestine problem as 'a vague instinct of dislike for
anything with a Jewish label',[6] a flippant comment which certainly
does not do justice to his contribution to the evolution of British policy
on Palestine from 1922 until his retirement in 1942. A description far
closer to the evidence on Shuckburgh's contribution to policy on
Palestine would be 'exasperation'. In this Shuckburgh personifies the
general position of Whitehall. By 1938-9 the Colonial Office had
come to realise that Britain could not afford the Zionist interpretation
of its commitments under the Balfour Declaration, that the Jewish
problem could not to be solved in Palestine (or at least not under the
cover of British arms) and that the Jews were tiresome for not realising
this themselves. The White Paper and its specific provisions
Shuckburgh apparently regarded as a *pis aller* — far from perfect but
necessary in order to win Arab support for Britain and to prevent an
injustice to the Arabs of Palestine. Perhaps even more important,
after the White Paper's release in May 1939 it became the accepted
policy of His Majesty's Government and any second thoughts on it
(such as emanated regularly from Churchill) would only renew the
difficult and heated controversy which had absorbed so much 'official'
energy during the years following the Arab revolt in 1936.

With the changes in personnel which occurred in the Colonial Office
during the war years the firmness of purpose seemed to go out of its
contribution to the formulation of policy. By 1943 the officials of the
Foreign Office were comfortably dominant in Whitehall when the
affairs of Palestine were discussed, and their views were remarkably

[5]Cf. p. 84.
[6]Shuckburgh minute, 9 January 1930, CO 733/182//77050A.

consistent from the mid-1930s on. Only one Foreign Office official, R.T.E. Latham, consistently, and persistently, deviated from the common Foreign Office point of view, and then only on the limited question of immigration policy. Latham's willingness to oppose the general view and to expose the policy of 'firmness' on refugee matters as likely to be counter-productive in the end, invites comment. Why was one official so willing to swim against the tide of official indifference to the human consequences of the policies endorsed and implemented by Whitehall? The answer is simply that Latham was an outsider in the Foreign Office in more ways than one. A Fellow of All Souls, a successful barrister at Lincoln's Inn, an expert on constitutional law, and son of a former Chief Justice of Australia, Latham could not be expected to carry weight with the mandarins of the Foreign Office. He joined the Foreign Office as a contribution to the war effort in 1939 after having been rejected for active service but was accepted by Bomber Command in 1941 and was shortly afterwards killed in action. During the war the views of the Foreign Office were vigorously reinforced by the growing voice of British officials in the Middle East, where the officials of the Political Intelligence Centre, the General Headquarters, Middle East Forces and the advisors of the Minister of State Resident in Cairo supported the by now traditional position of the Chancery of the British embassy in Cairo. That position had always been to favour the general Arab cause in Palestine and to go to any lengths in order to impress on London its opposition to any reappraisal of the policies of the White Paper. British officials in the Middle East were almost unanimously hostile to the Jews in Palestine, and to Churchill's support for them.

The conflict between Churchill and the officials responsible for Palestine affairs had an effect which, although indirect, was to be long lasting. In the course of the war those who had supported the principles of the White Paper attempted to overcome Churchill's obstructionism and the threat that he would reverse British policy once again in favour of the Jews by maligning the Yishuv and presenting it as a danger, not an asset, to Britain's interests. The rhetoric employed and the positions adopted did much to poison Anglo-Zionist relations in the years leading up to Britain's withdrawal from Palestine. Ironically the exaggerated estimates of the threat which Zionism posed to Britain only encouraged the revival of the policy debate in 1943-4 and the re-adoption of partition as the best option remaining to Britain. At the root of this was the recognition that an evolutionary transfer of power in a bi-national Palestine was no longer possible because of radically changed circumstances both in Palestine and in the world generally.

Britain's increased dependence on the United States as a result of the war greatly complicated her problems in Palestine. As the Zionists became more active and more successful in mobilising American Jewish opinion, Britain had increasingly to rely on Washington to counter Jewish pressure, while at the same time preventing American encroachments into Britain's traditional spheres of influence in the Middle East. By the end of the war the American factor was a part of every policy discussion in Whitehall and the growing appeal of the Jewish case to American public opinion became a major asset of the Yishuv. In Palestine itself, the Yishuv's ability to oppose Britain by force of arms should Britain attempt to impose a pro-Arab settlement there also became a factor in any debate on future policy. Initially there was a large element of exaggeration in the estimates of the illegal Jewish military strength. But by 1944 more accurate and more sober information available to the British authorities clearly indicated that Britain's freedom of action in Palestine could only be guaranteed by the costly commitment of significant numbers of troops. In 1942 the Yishuv had articulated the demand for a Jewish state, and whatever the actual strength of the Hagana and the Irgun might have been, it was clear that the Yishuv generally supported this demand and was sufficiently radicalised to attempt to achieve it. In the shadow of the fate of European Jewry during the war, it was the British campaign against illegal immigration which more than anything else alienated the Yishuv from the Mandate and united the Jews of Palestine, America and elsewhere behind the demand for a Jewish state.

At the end of the war a new refugee problem emerged as the remnants of European Jewry concentrated in displaced persons camps and demanded the right to enter Palestine. One of the major objectives of the redirection of Palestine policy in 1939 had been to separate the question of Palestine from the Jewish problem, to make it clear that the Jewish problem could not be solved within the confines of the Mandate. But by the end of the war it was apparent that while Britain could declare such a separation, she was not capable of enforcing it. The failure to implement the White Paper — because of practical difficulties in Palestine as much as for reasons of 'high policy' in London — in effect marked the end of any hope of a British imposed solution. Whitehall had intended to overcome the opposition of Arabs and Jews to the White Paper by its own resolute adherence to that policy. In the course of time, it was reasoned, moderate men would come to see that the policy of 1939 was the most their respective communities could hope to obtain from Britain, and they would therefore come to accept it. However, from the beginning the resolution of British officials was restricted to the campaign against illegal immigration, and even moderates came to believe that they could achieve more without Britain than with her. Having adopted the policy of 1939 when the revolt of the Arab community of Palestine was drawing to a close, Britain could only abandon it as the Jewish revolt began.

BIBLIOGRAPHY

Unpublished Sources

Public Record Office, Kew (P.R.O.)

Air Ministry
Air 23
Air 24
Air 40

Cabinet Office
Cab 21
Cab 23
Cab 27
Cab 65
Cab 66
Cab 67
Cab 79
Cab 80
Cab 95

Colonial Office
CO 111
CO 323
CO 732
CO 733
CO 850
CO 875
CO 935
CO 968

Foreign Office
FO 371
FO 800
FO 921

Prime Minister's Office
Prem 3
Prem 4

War Office
WO 32
WO 169
WO 201
WO 208
WO 216

Australian Archives, Canberra
Department of External Affairs – A.A.CRS A981

Central Zionist Archives, Jerusalem
Protocols of the Executive, London – Z4
Records of the Political Department — S25

Israel State Archives, Jerusalem
Chief Secretary's Papers – Record Group 2

Private Papers

Middle East Centre, St. Anthony's College, Oxford
Lampson Diaries
MacMichael Papers
Philby Papers
Spears Papers
Tegart Papers

Churchill College, Cambridge
Bevin Papers
Hankey Papers
Grigg Papers
Lyttelton Papers
Sinclair Papers

Rhodes House, Oxford
Meinertzhagen Papers
Scott Papers

Cambridge University Library
Smuts Papers

From Private Collections
Amery Papers
Halifax Papers

Published Sources

Official Publications
Government of Palestine: *Department of Migration: Annual Report 1939* (Jerusalem, 1940)
‒‒‒‒‒‒ *Statistics of Migration and Naturalisation* (Jerusalem, 1940)
‒‒‒‒‒‒ *Statistics of Migration and Naturalisation* (Jerusalem, 1941)
‒‒‒‒‒‒ *Statistics of Migration and Naturalisation* (Jerusalem, 1942)
‒‒‒‒‒‒ *Statistics of Migration and Naturalisation* (Jerusalem, 1943)
‒‒‒‒‒‒ *Statistics of Migration and Naturalisation* (Jerusalem, 1944)
‒‒‒‒‒‒ *Survey of Palestine* Vols. 1 & 2 (Jerusalem, 1945-6)
‒‒‒‒‒‒ *Survey of Palestine*, Confidential Volume (Jerusalem, 1946)

186

_____ *Supplement to the Survey of Palestine* (Jerusalem, 1947)

Palestine: A Statement of Policy, Cmd. 6019, London, May 1939

Books and Articles

[All books published in London unless otherwise indicated.]

Abcarius, M.F., *Palestine Through the Fog of Propaganda* (n.d.).

Abu-Ghazaleh, A., *Arab Cultural Nationalism in Palestine* (Beirut, 1973).

Adam, C.F., *The Life of Lord Lloyd* (1948).

Addison, P., *The Road to 1945* (1975).

Aliav, R. (with P. Mann), *The Last Escape* (1975).

Amery, L.S., *My Political Life. Vol. 3: The Unforgiving Years, 1929-1940* (1953).

Antonius, G., *The Arab Awakening* (1938).

Arendt, H., *Eichmann in Jerusalem* (1963).

Avriel, E., *Open the Gates!* (New York, 1975).

Bauer, Y., *From Diplomacy to Resistance. A History of Jewish Palestine 1939-1945* (Philadelphia, 1973).

_____ *My Brother's Keeper. A History of the American Jewish Joint Distribution Committee, 1929-1939* (New York, 1974).

_____ 'From Cooperation to Resistance: The Haganah 1938-1946', *Middle Eastern Studies,* Vol. 2(3):182-210, 1966.

_____ 'Illegal Immigration', *Encyclopedia of Zionism and Israel,* Vol. 1 (New York, 1971).

Ben Gurion, D., *Letters to Paula* (1971).

Berlin, I., *Zionist Politics in Wartime Washington* (Lecture, Jerusalem, 1972).

Birkenhead, Lord, *Walter Monckton* (1969).

Bowden, T., 'The Politics of Arab Rebellion in Palestine, 1936-1939', *Middle Eastern Studies,* Vol. 11(2), 1975.

Boyle, A., *Poor Dear Brendan: The Quest for Brendan Bracken* (1974).

Brodetsky, S., *Memoirs* (1960).

Brodrick, A.H., *Near to Greatness: A Life of Earl Winterton* (1965).

Bullock, A., *The Life and Times of Ernest Bevin Vol. 2: Minister of Labour 1940-1945* (1976).

Burridge, T.D., *British Labour and Hitler's War* (1976).

Butler, J.R.M., *Grand Strategy. Vol. 2: September 1939 - June 1941. History of the Second World War, U.K. Military Series* (1957).

_____ & Gwyer, J.M.A. *Grand Strategy. Vol. 3: June 1941 –*

187

October 1942. History of the Second World War, U.K. Military Series (1964).
Butler, R.A., *The Art of the Possible* (1973).
Casey, R.G., *Personal Experience, 1939-1946* (1962).
Chandos, Lord, *Memoirs of Lord Chandos* (1962).
Chary, F.B., *The Bulgarian Jews and the Final Solution, 1940-1944* (Pittsburgh, 1972).
Churchill, W.S., *The Second World War,* Vols. 1-6 (1949-54).
Cohen, G., 'Harold MacMichael ve'She'elat Eretz Yisrael', *Hamizrach Hahadash,* Vol. 25 (1-2):52-68 (1975).
_____ *Churchill ve'She'elat Eretz Yisrael, 1939-1942* (Churchill and the Palestine Question, 1939-1942) (Jerusalem, 1976).
_____ *HaCabinet HaBrit ve'She'elat Ha'atid Eretz Yisrael, April-Yuli 1943* (The British Cabinet and the Palestine Question, April-July 1943) (Jerusalem, 1977).
Cohen, H.J., 'The Anti-Jewish Farhud in Baghdad, 1941', *Middle Eastern Studies,* Vol. 3 (1):2-17 (1966).
Cohen, M.J., *Palestine: Retreat From the Mandate. The Making of British Policy, 1936-1945* (1978).
_____ 'Appeasement in the Middle East: The British White Paper on Palestine, May 1939', *The Historical Journal,* Vol. 16 (3):571-96 (1973).
_____ 'The British White Paper on Palestine, May 1939, Part 2: The Testing of a Policy, 1942-45', *The Historical Journal,* Vol.19(3):727-58 (1976).
_____ 'The Moyne Assassination, November 1944: A Political Analysis', *Middle Eastern Studies,* Vol. 15 (3):358-73 (1979).
Colville, J. 'The Centenary of Churchill — A Personal Appreciation of Sir Winston's Work and Character', *History Today,* Vol. 25 (1) 1975.
Connell, J., *Wavell, Soldier and Scholar,* Vol. 1 (1964).
Conway, J., 'Between Apprehension and Indifference — Allied Attitudes to the Destruction of Hungarian Jewry', *The Wiener Library Bulletin,* Vol. 27 (New Series 30-1):37-48 (1973-4).
Cosgrave, P., *Churchill at War.* Volume 1: 1939-1940 (1974).
Dilks, D. (ed.), *Sir Alexander Cadogan. Diaries 1938-1945* (1971).
Eden, A., *The Reckoning* (1972).
ESCO Foundation for Palestine, *Palestine. A Study of Jewish, Arab and British Policies,* Vol. 2 (New Haven, 1947).
Evans, T.E. (ed.), *The Killearn Diaries, 1934-1946* (1972).
Feingold, H.L., *The Politics of Rescue: The Roosevelt Administration and the Holocaust, 1938-1945* (New York, 1972).
Furlonge, G., *Palestine is My Country: The Story of Musa Alami* (1968).

Gelber, Y., *Hahitnadvut ve'Mekoma be'Mediniut HaZionit ve'Hayishuvit, 1939-1942* (Jewish Palestinian Volunteering in the British Army During the Second World War) (Jerusalem, 1979).

Gilbert, M., *Auschwitz and the Allies* (1981).

—— *Churchill and Zionism* (lecture, 1973).

—— *Exile and Return. The Emergence of Jewish Statehood* (1978).

—— *Winston Churchill, Volume 4, 1917-1922* (1975).

—— *Winston Churchill, Volume 5, 1923-1939* (1976).

—— *Winston Churchill, Volume 6, 1939-1941* (1983).

Gomaa, A., *The Foundation of the League of Arab States* (1977).

Harvey, O., *Diplomatic Diaries, 1937-1940* (1970).

Hearst, O., 'The British and the Slaughter of the Jews', *Wiener Library Bulletin,* Part 1: Vol. 21(1):32-5 (1966-7); Part 2: Vol. 21(2):30-40 (1967).

Hillberg, R., *The Destruction of European Jewry* (New York, 1973).

Hollis, L.C., *War at the Top* (1959).

Hourani, A., *Great Britain and the Arab World* (1945).

Hurewitz, J.C., *The Struggle for Palestine* (New York, 1968).

—— *Middle East Dilemmas: The Background for U.S. Policy* (New York, 1973).

Hyamson, A.M., *Palestine Under the Mandate, 1920-1948* (1950).

Ilan, A., *America, Britania ve'Eretz Yisrael* (America, Britain and Palestine) (Jerusalem, 1979).

Ironside, E., *Ironside Diaries 1937-1940* (1962).

Ismay, H.L., *The Memoirs of Lord Ismay* (1960).

Katzburg, N., *Mediniut be'Mavuch: 1940-1945* (Policy in the Labyrinth, 1940-1945) (Jerusalem, 1977).

Kedourie, E., *The Chatham House Version* (1970).

—— *Arab Political Memoirs and Other Studies* (1974).

—— *In the Anglo-Arab Labyrinth* (1976).

Khadduri, M., *Independent Iraq from 1932 to 1958* (1960).

Kimche, J. & D., *The Secret Roads. The 'Illegal' Migration of a People, 1938-1948* (1954).

Kirk, G., *The Middle East in the War* (1954).

Laqueur, W., *A History of Zionism* (1972).

—— *The Terrible Secret* (1980).

Loewenheim, F.L., Langley, H.D., & Jonas, M., *Roosevelt and Churchill: Their Secret Wartime Correspondence* (1975).

MacDonald, M. *Titans and Others* (1972).

Macmillan, H., *The Blast of War, 1939-1945* (1967).

Marder, A., *Winston is Back: Churchill at the Admiralty, 1939-1940* (1972).

Mardor, M., *Strictly Illegal* (1964).

Marlowe, J., *Rebellion in Palestine* (1946).

_____ *The Seat of Pilate. An Account of the Palestine Mandate* (1959).

_____ *Arab Nationalism and British Imperialism* (1961).

Maugham, R., *Approach to Palestine* (1946).

Monroe, E., *Britain's Moment in the Middle East* (1963).

_____ *Philby of Arabia* (1973).

Morse, W., *While Six Million Died* (1968).

Namier, J., *Lewis Namier: A Biography* (1971).

Neame, P., *Playing With Strife* (1947).

Ofer, D., 'The Activities of the Jewish Agency Delegation in Istanbul in 1943' in Y. Gutman, & E Zuroff, (eds.), *Rescue Attempts During the Holocaust* (Jerusalem, 1977).

Parkinson, A.C.C., *The Colonial Office From Within, 1905-1945* (1947).

Payton-Smith, D.J., *Oil. A Study in Wartime Policy and Administration, History of the Second World War. Civil Series* (1971).

Pelling, H., *Winston Churchill* (1974).

Peterson, M., *Both Sides of the Curtain* (1950).

Philby, H. St. J., *Arabian Jubilee* (1952).

Playfair, I.S.O., *The Mediterranean and the Middle East, Vols. 1-3. History of the Second World War. U.K. Military Series* (1954, 1956, 1960).

Porath, Y., *The Palestine Arab National Movement, 1929-1939* (1977).

Prinz, A., 'The Role of the Gestapo in Obstructing and Promoting Jewish Immigration', *Yad Vashem Studies*, Vol. 2:205-18 (1958).

Reitlinger, G., *The Final Solution* (New York, 1969).

Robinson, K., *The Dilemmas of Trusteeship* (1965).

Rose, N., *Gentile Zionists. A Study in Anglo-Zionist Diplomacy, 1929-1939* (1973).

_____ (ed.) *Baffy: The Diaries of Baffy Dugdale* (1973).

_____ *Lewis Namier: A Political Biography* (1981).

Roskill, S., *Hankey, Man of Secrets*, Vol. 3 (1974).

Sachar, H.M., *Europe Leaves the Middle East, 1936-1954* (1974).

Sharett (Shertok), M., *Yoman Medini* (Political Diary), Vol. 4 (Jerusalem, 1974).

Sherman, A.J., *Island Refuge: Britain and the Refugees from the Third Reich, 1933-39* (1973).

Slutzky, Y., *Sefer Toldot Hahagana* (History of the Hagana) (Tel Aviv, 1976), Vol. 3 Pt. 1.

Stein, L., *Weizmann and England* (1964).

Sweet-Escott, B.A.C., *Baker Street Irregular* (1965).

Sykes, C., *Crossroads to Israel* (1967).

Thomas, C., & Morgan-Witts, M., *The Voyage of the Damned* (1974).

Trevor, D., *Under the White Paper* (Jerusalem, 1949).

Urofsky, M., *American Zionism from Herzl to the Holocaust* (New York, 1975).

Wasserstein, B., *Britain and the Jews of Europe, 1939-1945* (1979).

Weisgal, M., and Carmichael, J, (eds.), *Chaim Weizmann: A Biography by Several Hands* (1963).

Weizmann, C., *Trial and Error* (New York, 1966).

————— *Letters and Papers of Chaim Weizmann* Series A. Vol. xx July 1940-January 1943 (Jerusalem, 1979).

————— 'Palestine's Role in the Solution of the Jewish Problem', *Foreign Affairs,* Vol. 20:324-38 (1941-2).

Wheeler-Bennett, J. (ed.), *Action This Day: Working With Churchill* (1968).

Wilson, Lord, *Eight Years Overseas, 1939-1947* (1949).

Wischnitzer, M., *To Dwell in Safety* (Philadelphia, 1948).

Woodward, L., *British Foreign Policy During the Second World War,* History of the Second World War, Civil Series (1962), Vols. 1, 2 & 4.

Wyman, D., *Paper Walls. America and the Refugee Crisis, 1938-1941* (Massachusetts, 1968).

Yahil, L., 'Selected British Documents on Illegal Immigration into Palestine, 1939-40', *Yad Vashem Studies,* Vol. 10 (1974).

Zweig, R.W., 'British Plans for the Evacuation of Palestine, 1941-1942', *Studies in Zionism,* No. 8, October 1983.

————— 'Britania, HaHagana ve'Goral HaSefer HaLavan' (Britain, the Hagana and the Fate of the White Paper), *Cathedra,* No. 29, October 1983.

INDEX

Advisory Council, Arab-Jewish, 37-9, 41-2
Aghios Nicholaos, 48 n.19
Aghios Zoni, 47 n.17
Aguda Yisrael, 55
Alamein, El, 167-8
Alami, Musa, 32-3
American Jewish Joint Distribution Committee, 63
Amery, Leopold S: opposes White Paper, 4, 21; Middle East policy, 29; proposes Arab Federation, 102-7, 111, 148; proposes partition, 174-5
Amnesty, 12-15, 19, 33
Anglo American Declaration, 169, 174
Antonius, George, 11
Arab Federation, ch. 4 *passim,* 148, 150
Arab Higher Committee, 3, 9-11, 15, 31-6, 49
Arab Revolt (1936-9), 1, 2, 157, 183
Assimi, 48 n.19
Astir, 48 n.19
Athlit, 52, 75, 77, 117
Atlantic, 70-1, 73, 75, 77
Attlee, Clement, 26, 139
Auchinleck, Major General Sir Claude, 111 n.83
Australia, 75
Austria, 45, 50, 57

Baggallay, Lacy, 27, 79, 94-5
Balfour Declaration, the (1917), 1, 2, 113
Balkans, 48, 50-1, 67-8, 81, 116, 131
Barker, Lt.-General Michael G., 12, 158
Battershill, Sir William, 133
Baxter, Charles W., 149
Ben Gurion, David, 109-10, 151-2
Bennett, John S., 51, 55, 63, 132, 167
Bevin, Ernest, 106
Biltmore Conference (1942), 153
Boyd, Edmund B., 133, 135
Bracken, Brendan, 4, 106
British Council, 32
British Guiana, 45-6, 50, 79, 81, 87
British Guiana Refugee Commission, 45-6
Bruce, Stanley M., 75 n.163